DECISIONS BY THE BOOK
(First Revised Edition)

Cover Design © 2004 Rebecca D. Long
Layout and Type-Setting © Rebecca D. Long

Unless otherwise indicated, all scripture references quoted in this work are taken from the King James Version of the Holy Bible.

Where indicated in this work as "NIV", scripture taken from the Holy Bible, New International Version. Copyright 1973, 1978, 1984 International Bible Society. Used by permission of Zondervan Bible Publishers.

Written by: John F. Deal

Balanced by: Donna K. Deal

Published by Insight To Freedom, Inc.
4510 South Laburnum Avenue
Richmond, Virginia 23231
USA

"Insight To Freedom" is the Registered Service Mark of Insight To Freedom, Inc.

ISBN 0-9649860-1-9

Library of Congress Catalog Card Number
#2003101810

Printed in the United States of America

www.info@insighttofreedom.com

To Donna

My wife and best friend
the mother of our daughters
my faithful partner in adversity and in joy
never complaining and always supportive
and a rope of caution around my neck
when I get ahead of God.

A special Thank You To

Pat, Marcia and Debbie who, using ancient typing machines, typed out innumerable drafts of the outlines and study guides that led to this book.

Winifred, who using somewhat better equipment, typed countless drafts of this book.

And Particularly to

Our youngest daughter Becky, the graphic artist who, using state of the art equipment, designed the cover and the layout to make this book look like a book. What a joy it was for Donna and me to work with Becky in spreading the Gospel of Jesus Christ.

Introduction

To

Decisions By The Book

Anyone who lives on milk, still being an infant, is not acquainted with the teaching about righteousness. But solid food is for the mature, who by constant use have trained themselves to distinguish good from evil. Therefore let us leave the elementary teachings about Christ and go on to maturity . . .
(Hebrews 5:13-6:1 NIV).

The purpose of this book is to demonstrate that the Bible is the ultimate practical source of wisdom for making all of our decisions in life.

Regretfully, we are too often content to make decisions based only upon a milk-level knowledge of the Word. When we are not willing to pay the required cost of diligence needed to seek spiritual maturity through Christ, we will not have the spiritual maturity necessary to make decisions in a righteous manner.

We must learn the vast difference that exists between our being made righteous by Christ versus our walking in the righteousness of Christ. There is certainly no intent here to belittle our being made righteous by Christ, but we must understand that Jesus never meant for us to stop there. He means for us to mature beyond the elementary principle of salvation and proceed on into a daily walk of righteousness with Him.

And I heard another voice from heaven, saying, Come out of her

(Babylon)*, my people, that ye be not partakers of her sins, and that*

ye receive not of her plagues (Rev. 18:4 emphasis added).

I

The practical effect of our milk-level existence as Christians is that we make decisions just like non-Christians (the Babylonians). Living proof of our milk-level existence is the divorce rate, adultery, church bickering and financial problems encountered in Christian families today.

These conditions confirm the statement in Revelation 18:4 that many of today's Christians are partaking of Babylon's sins and receiving her plagues. No wonder the world often sees Christians a being hypocritical – we say we are Christians but, at the same time, we make decisions and live just like the non-Christians (Babylonians). It is easy to understand why so many in the world do not care to know our God!

God is not a respecter of persons, He and His principles are righteousness. He desires that we make decisions according to righteousness, and not in the ways of the world. That is why God is continually calling Christians *(". . . my people . . .")* out of the Babylonian ways of this world (Revelation 18:4). The way out is to seek the solid food of the Word of God, and constantly use that Word in our everyday life to distinguish good from evil. Then we will know how to live and make decisions in a righteous manner.

God's principles apply equally to the corporate giant and the corner market, the famous and the unknown, the rich and the poor, large churches and small, governments of nations and city councils, and to all other levels of society and government.

God did not write the Bible because He did not have anything else to do; He wrote it for us to live by in our home, church, government and work place. Now let us put the Bible to the use that God intended, and make all of our decisions based on God's wisdom as contained therein. Then we will *". . . go on to maturity . . ."* in Christ (Hebrews 6:1 NIV).

In His Service,

John and Donna Deal

THE PURPOSE OF
INSIGHT TO FREEDOM

Insight to Freedom, founded in 1983 by John and Donna Deal, is a ministry born out of their struggle to walk out of a $6,500,000 indebtedness from 1974-1986.

The irony is that John and Donna incurred this debt to make investments from which some of the anticipated profits would be committed to ministry. Looking back, they see the gross error of that so-called good intention. It is quite easy to promise to give away what we do not yet have.

It did not take long for the Deals to realize that they and their fellow investors could not free themselves from such an enormous debt. Choosing to turn to God, the Deals began to seek Him first in their life. All they did was to pray, study God's Word and walk out what they learned from that prayer and Bible study. Then God began revealing to them His Ways for them to walk out of their bondage.

As John and Donna began to walk in God's Ways, even though they were millions in debt, suffering foreclosures, being sued and pressured by creditors, their marriage became stronger and not weaker. They began to understand from the Bible that matters such as debt, divorce, church strife, con-tention, and the like, were only symptoms of a greater problem. They discovered that their problem was spiritual deficiency, their lack of a mature walk with God.

While Donna and John were still deep in debt, people began to come to them for counseling on debt, business and family matters. The people who were serious with God over-came their problems, while those who were not serious did not.

So, the purpose of Insight To Freedom is to teach people how to gain the Biblical insight necessary to identify their spiritual deficiencies, and how to set themselves free from those deficiencies. Then the people must decide if they are content to continue living with these deficiencies or do they want to learn diligence from God's Word and eliminate the deficiencies.

How To Use This Book

The purpose of Decisions by the Book is to demonstrate that the Bible is the ultimate practical source of wisdom for making decisions in our everyday life. Of course, every issue we will ever face in life is not addressed in this book, but every issue is addressed in the Bible.

If you are at the point of having to make a decision, think of a key word or phrase that identifies the issue to be decided. Then look in the "Cross Index" for that or a similar word or phrase.

Turn to the page and study the scripture set out at the top of the page in the context of the decision you have to make. The text below the scripture is designed to illustrate why that scripture is applicable to the decision you are about to make. As you are studying the scripture and the illustration, it is important that you also read the portion of the Bible from which the scripture was quoted. This will afford to you the balance of reading the scripture in the context in which it was written in the Bible.

As you are searching the "Cross Index", please remember that every principle in the Bible applies to every area of our lives. For instance, you may be looking in **"Marriage"** for an answer that in your particular situation is contained in **"Priorities"**; or, you may be looking in **"Debt"** for an answer that is contained in **"The Importance of Our Wife's Counsel."** Therefore, it may be well for you to read this book in its entirety.

May God bless you as you use Decisions by the Book to access the Bible, and allow Him to impart His wisdom to you in all of your decision making.

CROSS INDEX

XI

ADULTERY

But whoso committeth adultery with a woman
lacketh understanding:
he that doeth it destroyeth his own soul
(Proverbs 6:32).

The Sin and the Wound

We are one with God through Christ, and one with our spouse through marriage. That is why intimacy in marriage is to the physical realm as worshiping God is to the spiritual realm. Spiritual adultery against God and physical adultery against our spouse have the same effect, they both violate the intimacy of God's creation, marriage. What man commits against God and his spouse, he commits against himself, and that is how he destroys his own soul. When sin crouches at our door, we must master it *(Genesis 4:7)*.

Adultery is a dual attack against our spouse, it is a sin against and a wounding of our marriage partner. While we may repent for our sin, and allow the blood of Christ to wash the sin away, the wound is still there and must be treated with loving care for a long period of time; but, God will, if we let Him, use that extended treatment period to build patience in us - and patience always leads to Godliness which restores our marriage.

Adultery - Guaranteed to Lead to Reckless Decision Making

. . . Set ye Uriah in the forefront of the hottest
battle, and retire ye from him,
that he may be smitten, and die
(II Samuel 11:15).

The soul is the collective interplay of the mind, will and emotion. Thus, when we destroy our own soul, we destroy our mind, will and emotion; and this destruction impairs our ability to reason and make decisions. This is why David, after committing adultery with Bathsheba, made the reckless decision to have her husband murdered. This reckless decision to commit murder came out of David's mind, will and emotion as they were being destroyed by the sin of adultery.

Of course, this destruction can be stopped by repentance, and the mind, will and emotion restored. Repentance is not just feeling sorry because we were caught; rather, it is a definite and sustained change in the course of our lives towards righteousness and away from sin. Repentance bears fruit, sorrow does not.

Adultery Is Evidence that an Employee Cannot be Trusted

Making women available to customers and looking for female companions when our wives are not around are two of the oldest practices in commerce. If we commit adultery, or encourage others to do so, we must ask ourselves these questions:

Is sexual pleasure for a moment worth the destruction of our soul and the soul of our customer? and

Will our employee or customer who is unfaithful to his wife be faithful to our business?

Unfaithfulness is a character deficiency that pervades all areas of the lives of the unfaithful, including marriage and business. An employee who is unfaithful to his wife cannot be trusted with his employer's business or the intimacy of marriage. The same needs to be said for the person providing the female companion to a favored customer.

Illicit relationships foster a weird sense of trust and confidentiality between those in the relationship. This weird behavior is evidence that our soul is in the process of being destroyed.

OVERCOMING ADVERSITY

... Their strength is to sit still
(Isaiah 30:7).

Once the initial shock of an adverse situation has passed, the adversity is seldom as severe as it first appeared. The question then is, how do we overcome the adversity remaining after the shock has subsided?

When we are faced with adversity, our natural tendency is for us to launch into a frenzy of activity. We somehow believe that this frenzy of activity will produce positive results. Too often this frenzy obscures the problem causing the adversity, and the frenzy makes the situation worse.

As always, the Bible tells us what to do in the midst of adversity *... sit still ...* and assess the situation. Faith in God's Word will give to us the strength to sit still, even in the face of great adversity. Out of the strength of sitting still will come the Godly insight for us to properly assess the cause and effect of the adversity, and overcome both.

The Value Of Adversity

It is good for me that I have been afflicted;
that I might learn thy statutes
(Psalm 119:71).

The Psalmist knew the value of adversity, for it was in such times that he learned the Word. Adversity is an inexpensive tuition, provided we remember and apply the lessons learned in those hard times.

3

How to Face Adversity

Fearfulness and trembling are come upon me, and horror hath overwhelmed me. And I said, Oh that I had wings like a dove! For then I would fly away, and be at rest. Lo, then would I wander far off, and remain in the wilderness. Selah
(Psalm 55:5-7).

. . . David ran quickly toward the battle line to meet him
(Goliath)
(I Samuel 17:48 NIV emphasis added).

Psalm 55:5-7 was written by David, and I Samuel 17:8 was written about David. All of us have a lot of David in us. When adversity comes we, as David, are tempted to escape, especially when fear of the future seems to overwhelm us. In such times we wish we were as doves and could just fly away and leave the hard times behind. But the truth is, escape does not erase the issues at hand, it only delays our meeting them.

Let each of us have the courage of David to run quickly toward our Goliaths, for if we will, what seemed at one time to be insurmountable will now fall before us. We can then leave the field of battle with the reputation of being servants of The Most High God, and not servants of fear.

ALCOHOLISM AND GLUTTONY

For the drunkard and the glutton
shall come to poverty...
(Proverbs 23:21).

The Word of God places the alcoholic and the glutton in the same category, and declares they both shall come to poverty. Both the alcoholic and the glutton are where they are because of a lack of discipline in their lives.

ANGER

He that is slow to anger is better than the mighty; and
he that ruleth his spirit than he that taketh a city
(Proverbs 16:32).

The Bible does not say we are not to get angry, it says be slow to anger *(Exodus 4:14)*. God made us in His image and He gets angry. We, too, can get angry, we are just not to get angry quickly.

To anger quickly is to lose control of ourselves. It is better to rule ourselves than to conquer a city, for what good is the city to us if we cannot control ourselves.

How To Find The Answer
To Every Question In Life

But seek ye first the kingdom of God, and his
righteousness;
and all these things shall be added unto you
(Matthew 6:33).

How many millions of dollars and man hours do we spend seeking what appears to be elusive answers to critical questions about our home, church, government, business and employment? We ask friends, call in expensive consultants, hire accountants and attorneys, seek assistance from governmental agencies – and still the questions remain unanswered.

Well, how do we get the answer? By seeking God first, and He will then add unto us all the things (the answers to our questions) we need. We may be an expert in our particular field, but He started the world and He is The Expert. He has the answers to all of our questions.

How do we consult with Him? By seeking first His kingdom and His righteousness through repenting for our sins, accepting His Son Jesus as our Savior and doing what He wants us to do rather than what we want to do. Jesus never had an unanswered question because He knew how to seek God first.

The Word of God affords to us the answer to every question we will ever have, and it does so through the Holy Spirit. God speaks to us with an ever so gentle voice. When we are frantically running around demanding answers, we cannot hear Him. The question is, will we seek Him first for the answer, or will we continue on "our own way?" To seek first the kingdom of God and His righteousness is the way to find the answer to every question in life.

What Do I Do
Until The Answer Comes?

*... **The effectual fervent prayer of a righteous man
availeth much***
(James 5:16 emphasis added).

***But let patience have her perfect work, that ye
may be perfect and entire, wanting nothing***
(James 1:4 emphasis added).

All of the great men and women of God in the Bible, except for Jesus, were faced with situations where they just did not know what to do. So, what did they do? They took their eyes off of the problem, focused on God and patiently prayed in earnest. God always answered. He cannot wait to do the same for us if we, too, will only take our eyes off of the problem and patiently focus on Him in earnest prayer.

One of our greatest temptations is that God's timing for His answer generally does not coincide with our time for the answer. He is never late, we are impatient. He is looking out for our eternal good, and we are looking at the pressure of the moment. If we will only be patient and let patience have her perfect work in us, God will always release the answer in His time.

Patience and diligence are the same. They are one way we show God we know that He is in control and that we are leaving the next step to Him.

ARGUING

Vs.

REASONING

Come now, and let us reason together,
saith the LORD . . .
(Isaiah 1:18).

The nature of God does not permit us to argue with anyone about anything. Why? Because to argue is to prove our point and be in contention with another, while to reason is to explain in love.

Let us not be so prideful as to believe that through the contention of arguing we can lead another to see the love of God. In truth, when we start arguing about anything, even the Bible, we are more interested in proving our point than in communicating the love of God to another. That is why God offered to His contentious people . . . ***Come now, and let us reason together, saith the LORD . . .***

Basic Authority Principles For The Family, Church, Government & Employment

Let every soul be subject unto the higher powers. For there is no power but of God: the powers that be are ordained of God. Whosoever therefore resisteth the power, resisteth the ordinance of God: and they that resist shall receive to themselves damnation (Romans 13:1-2).

God Is the Source of All Authority

Let every soul be subject unto the higher powers. For there is no power but of God . . . (Romans 13:1).

Jesus answered, Thou couldest have no power at all against me, except it were given thee from above... (John 19:11).

What Keeps Us from Submitting to Authority?

Pride. *Only by pride cometh contention . . . (Proverbs 13:10).* Pride keeps us from hearing the Word of God *(Jeremiah 13:8-10).*

What Does God's Word State About Willing Obedience to His Word?

If ye be willing and obedient, ye shall eat the good of the land: but if ye refuse and rebel, ye shall be devoured with the sword: for the mouth of the Lord hath spoken it (Isaiah 1:19-20).

How Should We Conduct Ourselves When Our Authority Gives to Us A Directive That Violates Our Conviction About God's Word?

Through diligent prayer, fasting and study of God's Word, confirm that our conviction is in accordance with the Word;

If our conviction is in accordance with the Word, we should prevail upon our authority to change its directive;

If the appeal is unsuccessful, we must conduct ourselves in accordance with our conviction; and

Should the authority continue to attempt to suppress our conduct, we are free to act in accordance with our conviction; however, all the while we must be willing to accept the consequences of our actions.
(Jesus, Esther, Daniel, Peter and John)

Comment

God never violated the authority structure He established in the Bible; He did not violate it even to save His own Son from the cross. Certainly, God will not violate His authority structure for us. Our strength as believers in Jesus Christ rests upon our obedience to the authority established by God. All authority is ordained by God *(Romans 13:1)*.

THE FOUR AREAS OF

	Family	Church
Establishment of Authority:	*...the husband is the head of the wife...* (Eph. 5:23 NIV). *Wives should submit to their husbands in everything* (Eph. 5:24 NIV). *Children, obey your parents in the Lord, for this is right* (Eph. 6:1 NIV).	*...Thou art the Christ, the son of the Living God...and upon this rock I will build my church...* (Matt.16:16-18).
Illustrated in Scripture:	Moses and Zipporah (Ex. 4:21-26).	*...In the name of Jesus Christ of Nazareth rise up and walk* (Acts 3:6 NIV).
Duty of Those in Authority:	*Husbands, love your wives...* (Eph. 5:25 NIV). Fathers teach your children (Deut, 4:9). *A wife looketh well to the ways of her household* (Prov. 31:27).	*...to seek the law of the Lord, and to do it, and to teach in Israel statutes and judgements* (Ezra 7:10).
Duty of those under Authority:	*Wives should submit to their husbands in everything* (Eph. 5:24 NIV). *Children, obey your parents in the Lord, for this is right* (Eph 6:1 NIV).	Submit to the authority. There is no scriptural authority for majority rule in the church concerning spiritual matters *(see the entire Bible)*. However, the Pastor should seek counsel from his elders, deacons and five-fold ministry relationships prior to making decisions (Prov. 11:14).

AUTHORITY IN OUR LIFE

Government	Employment
... For there is no power but of God: the powers that be are ordained of God (*Rom. 13:1*).	*Servants be subject to your masters with all fear; not only to the good and gentle, but also to the froward. For this is thankworthy, if a man for conscience toward God endure grief and suffering wrongfully* (*I Pet. 2:18-19*).
... Render to Caesar the things that are Caesar's, and God the things that are God's (*Mk. 12:17*).	Joseph in Potiphar's house and in prison. (*Gen. 39*)
Leaders are to seek the wisdom of God, for it is through wisdom that *... princes rule* (*Prov. 8:16*).	*Masters give unto your servants that which is just and equal; knowing that ye also have a Master in Heaven* (*Col, 4:1*).
We are to pray, intercede and give thanks for kings, *... and for all that are in authority* (*I Tim. 2:1-2*).	*Servants, obey in all things your masters according to the flesh; not with eye service, as men pleasers; but in singleness of heart, fearing God; And whatsoever ye do, do it heartily, as unto the Lord, and not unto men; ...* (*Col. 3:22-23*).

Authority and Responsibility Must Always Remain Equal

Then he called his twelve disciples together, and gave them power and authority over all devils, and to cure diseases. And he sent them to preach the kingdom of God, and to heal the sick
(Luke 9:1-2).

God gave the disciples authority over all devils and to cure diseases. At the same time, He gave them the commensurate responsibility to preach the kingdom of God and to heal the sick. God always delegates authority commensurate with responsibility. For us to do otherwise is to frustrate those under our authority and invite their poor performance.

BANKRUPTCY

(See the complete books of Isaiah and Jeremiah)

Introduction

Bankruptcy is not something new to the 21st century or our culture. The nation of Israel became well acquainted with bankruptcy 2,500 years ago during the time of the Prophets Isaiah and Jeremiah. The "B" word was just as dreaded then as it is now, and its cause and effect were the same then as they are today.

The True Cause of Bankruptcy

In most cases, the true cause of bankruptcy is not high interest rates, recessions, depressions, oil crises, government regulations, etc.; rather, the true cause is that we have turned our backs on God as our supply and toward the world's system as our master. But then there are those cases where medical bills, natural disaster, etc. where others are forced into filing bankruptcy. This section of this book is not focused on those unfortunate people, but on those who are filing bankruptcy because of their undisciplined use of credit.

Through Isaiah and Jeremiah, God told the Israelites many times and in many ways, "You have left me and refuse to return, so I am turning my back on you." God then appointed the heathen King Nebuchadnezzar as His servant to take the Israelites captive to Babylon and disburse their wealth to the nations. The Israelites then had no time to, nor were they in the position to, serve God. They and all they had were at the whim of King Nebuchadnezzar and his army. They had forfeited the privilege of serving God for the pleasures of the world, and now they were paying the price. This was bankruptcy in its true and cruel form.

15

God knew that if He allowed the adversity of bankruptcy to come against His people, they would call upon Him and He would deliver them from captivity. How often do we, in the midst of bankruptcy, weep in repentance and call upon God to deliver us. If we are truly repentant, and walk in repentance, He will deliver us just as He delivered Israel from Babylon. His delivery comes in His time and in His way, so we must patiently endure until His time comes.

What Is Bankruptcy?

Think of King Nebuchadnezzar as the bankruptcy judge, his army as our creditors and the Israelites as ourselves in bankruptcy. We are before the judge because we have moved away from God and made the world system our master. The army of creditors is moving in under the direction of the judge to take all that we have, even down to our home and the clothes on our back. Bankruptcy is the consequence of our sin of having moved away from God, and the judge and the creditors are His chosen instruments to bring those consequences upon us. In the midst of bankruptcy we must remember that all the judge and our creditors are doing is what we have, in the midst of our moving away from God, allowed them to do.

Should We File Bankruptcy?

This is not a proper question. The proper question is "where are we with God?" If we just make the decision to file bankruptcy, and do not understand the scriptural reasons of why we are where we are, we will most probably return to bankruptcy again.

But, if we will seek to find where we are with God in the midst of our financial dilemma, God will show us why we are in financial trouble. At that point God may well decide, just as He did with Israel, that we must suffer the consequences of bankruptcy; or, in His grace, He may deliver us from filing bankruptcy. Rest assured that He loves us and will bring into our lives the circumstances that are best for us and His purposes at the time.

How each man interprets his circumstances at the time, relative to filing bankruptcy, is between him and God. So, we really do not make the decision to file or not to file; rather, we should recognize and repent for our sins that caused us to be where we are. Then we allow the combination of the circumstances and the peace of God in our lives at the time to guide us in the making of the decision to file or not to file.

How Do We Come Out of Bankruptcy?

. . . and when you and your children return to the Lord your God and obey him with all your heart and with all your soul according to everything I command you today, then the Lord your God will restore your fortunes . . .
(Deuteronomy 30:2 NIV).

Bearing Another's Burdens
vs.
Becoming Entangled In Their Burdens

Bear ye one another's burdens and so fulfill the law of
Christ
(Galatians 6:2).

No man that warreth entangleth himself
with the affairs of this life . . .
(II Timothy 2:4).

Galatians 6:2 directs us to bear another's burdens, but *II Timothy 2:4* warns us to not become entangled in those burdens. As always, Jesus set the example of how we are to bear one another's burdens. He sacrificially bore the burden of our sins so we could be restored to God, but did not become entangled in our sins.

Unlike Christ, in the process of helping others, we often fail to see any difference in bearing another's burdens and becoming entangled in their burdens. We just assume that to bear a burden requires a certain amount of entanglement with that burden. Too often, the result is that we start out to help others, but wind up just as entangled as they – and then the burden becomes even heavier for them and for us.

Bearing Another's Burdens Out of Emotion Leads to Entanglement.

. . . So then with the mind I myself serve the law (Spirit)
of God; but with the flesh the law of sin
(Romans 7:25 emphasis added).

The word "entangleth" comes from the Greek word "impleko" which means to braid or to entwine. This braiding or entwinement begins to occur the very moment we start to bear another's burden out of emotion, rather than help them in accordance with the Word. Remember that although Jesus, like us, experienced the emotions of love, compassion and anger, He always acted in the Spirit and never out of emotion. He did only what the Father said to do, otherwise, He would not have remained above our sins, He would have become entangled in our sins.

So, why does entanglement occur? Hosea 4:6 answers this question, *My people are destroyed for a lack of knowledge...* As humans, our natural tendency is to act out of emotion rather than in the Spirit, especially when we see another suffering under the load of a burden. We do not realize that if we bear another's burdens out of emotion, we are likely to become entangled in those burdens. This lack of knowledge can result in our being destroyed by another's burden we sought to bear. Why?

Emotions, being out of the flesh, do not concern themselves with the spiritual causes of another's burdens, they only create a desire to relieve burdens and give little or no regard to why the burdens exist. They obscure the fact that burdens are only symptoms, and that spiritual deficiencies are the root cause of those burdens.

Unilateral Commitments - The Ultimate in Entanglement

(See Joshua and the Gibeonites - Joshua Chapter 9)

Bearing another's burdens out of emotion causes us to make commitments to others without requiring a corresponding commitment from them. Our justification for making these unilateral commitments is that the others are burdened, and we do not want to burden them further with a commitment to us. Our emotions blind us from realizing that their burdens most often arise out of their inability to commit to Godly discipline in everyday life.

Therefore, Shortly after making the commitment, we often find ourselves bearing their burdens, and those persons doing nothing toward relieving their burdens. In the end, we become entangled with them in their burdens and they become upset at us because the burdens are still there.

Summary

Bear ye one another's burdens, and so fulfill the law of Christ *(Galatians 6:2)*, but do so in that manner which keeps us free of entanglement with those burdens. Otherwise, the time and effort we waste in those entanglements will greatly limit our ability and opportunity to fulfill the law of Christ to bear another's burdens.

Entanglement occurs when we start performing for others what <u>they can and should be</u> performing for themselves.

BEING CALLED VS. BEING CHOSEN
AS A BUSINESS & PROFESSIONAL PERSON

(See the lives of Moses and David)

Placing Our Occupations in Their Proper Perspective

Occupations are not gods, they are simply tools to be used by us to establish the kingdom of God on this earth (Deuteronomy 8:18). As the owners of businesses and professions we must ask ourselves this question, Do we want to learn the ways of God so our business and professions we can be used of God, or do we want to use them only to make a profit and gather acclaim for our worldly pursuits?

The Call

...for many be called... (Matthew 20:16).

God calls us into business and professional occupations just as He called Moses and David to lead Israel. The purpose of the call is God telling us that He desires to use us in a particular business or profession to bring forth fruit in His kingdom. This call may take the form of an idea, a word from another person, the influence of a teacher or however else God may ordain that the call be communicated. These forms of communicating a call are just as real to business and professional people as the angel was to Gideon and the burning bush to Moses.

Why Many Are Called
But Few Chosen

...but few chosen (Matthew 20:16).

Many are called into occupations, but only a few will become eligible to be chosen by God to use those occupations

21

to bring forth fruit in His kingdom. The period of years that normally pass between the time of the call and the time of being chosen is packed solid with God-given opportunities for us to learn His wisdom, understanding and knowledge. Not all who are called want to pay the severe price of that learning period. Therefore, many who are called render themselves ineligible to be chosen. God chooses only those who are of a mind to pay the price required to learn His ways and walk in them.

Now, this does not mean that those called and not chosen are cast down or away. Many who are called and not chosen may become very profitable and well known but, in the midst of all that profit and acclaim, they have rendered themselves ineligible to be chosen by God. Of what value is profit and acclaim if it is earned at the expense of not being chosen by God to serve Him?

THE FIRST RESPONSIBILITY
OF A CHRISTIAN BUSINESS &
PROFESSIONAL PERSON

... Fear God, and keep his commandments:
for this is the whole duty of man
(Ecclesiastes 12:13).

The pressure to be profitable can be enormous. But we must remember that making a profit is not our first responsibility; rather, our first responsibility is to fear God and keep His commandments. It is in our fulfilling this responsibility that God will cause our business to accomplish His will, whatever that may be.

The issue for us to decide is, are we going to obey God's commandments, or are we going to sacrifice His commandments for the price of a profit? God well knows if we do not make a profit, we will not be around long to carry out His will.

God's will is larger than the universe, and making a profit is not even the size of a peanut. If we will meet our first responsibility of obeying Him, He will cause our business to be profitable in His time, not ours.

WHO IS A CHRISTIAN BUSINESS & PROFESSIONAL PERSON?

Therefore if any man be in Christ, he is a new creature: old things are passed away; behold, all things are become new
(II Corinthians 5:17).

He is a person who has met Christ, accepted Him as Savior and walks in His ways. He is a new creature in Christ, his old business and professional ways are no more. Behold, he is a new person.

His standard is Christ, and he is true to that standard.

He is a person who keeps both feet in the Word. He does not keep one foot in the world and the other in the Word.

He is a person who knows that being a Christian may well cost him the association and esteem of his peers, and he is willing and eager to pay that price.

He is a person who does not have to boast about being a Christian. He does not use the cross and the name of Christ as an advertising tool to increase his business. He does not display the "right plaques and medallions in his office" in the hope that they will promote his business; rather, he is a man who allows the fruit in his life to evidence his relationship with Christ.

He is a person who puts righteousness first, even at the expense of profit.

He is a person who sees his business or profession as a tool in the hands of God, not as a money making machine.

He is a person who completes his work on time, in a God like manner and for a fair price.

He is a person who knows that all he has and is comes from the person of Christ, his Lord and Savior.

He is truly a Christian business and professional person.

THE DIFFERENCE IN A BABYLONIAN BUSINESSMAN & A CHRISTIAN BUSINESSMAN

Is not the whole land before thee? Separate thyself,
I pray thee, from me: if thou wilt take the left hand,
then I will go to the right; or if thou depart to the
right hand, then I will go to the left
(Genesis 13:9).

In *Genesis 13:9,* Abraham found himself having to terminate his contentious business partnership with Lot. In this termination process Abraham had his eye on ending a wrong relationship, even if it cost him dearly to do so. On the other hand, Lot had his eye on making a profit out of a bad situation - so Lot took Abraham's offer of that half of the land with the most apparent value, and left Abraham with the apparent less valuable half.

The Christian businessman, like Abraham, preserves Godly standards - even to his hurt; but the Babylonian businessman keeps his eye on making a profit even when he knows to do so will hurt others. That is the difference in a babylonian businessman and a Christian businessman.

The irony of the Abraham and Lot story is that Abraham eventually regained ownership of all that Lot took from him, and much more. Such is the power of God in the lives of those who put serving Him above making a profit.

WHY A BUSINESSMAN OF THE WORLD ("BABYLONIAN") ACTS AS HE DOES

And he cried mightily with a strong voice, saying, Babylon the great is fallen, is fallen, and is become the habitation of devils, and the hold of every foul spirit, and a cage of every unclean and hateful bird. For all nations have drunk of the wine of the wrath of her fornication, and the kings of the earth have committed fornication with her, and the merchants of the earth are waxed rich through the abundance of her delicacies (Revelation 18:2-3).

Babylon's Foundation
Is Self Gratification

The "Babylon," spoken of in the Book of Revelation, is not a city - it is today's modern worldwide political, social and economic order. And its current spiritual condition is described quite vividly in *Revelation 18:2-3.*

God calls our modern day society "Babylon" because its ways, and the ways of ancient Babylon, are the same. All that separates our society from ancient Babylon is about 2,600 years. While science and technology have advanced by leaps and bounds during those years, the desire of man's flesh to gratify himself, rather than please God, has remained constant.

The modern Babylonian system exists, not because of concentrations of wealth or political control, but because of man's sinful desire to gratify himself rather than honor God. The irony is that true fulfillment, which sinful man thinks self gratification will provide to him, comes only through a constant walk in the meat of God's Word. Without this walk, even Christians will not know the difference between good and evil *(Hebrews 5:13-6:3).* So the very foundation of the Babylonian system is the sinful illusion that fulfillment will come from self gratification.

Babylon is not evil because it has great concentrations of money and power. It is evil because its citizens use that money and power for self gratification rather than to honor God. There is nothing wrong with money or power; by themselves they are no more than tools lying on a work bench. We all need money to purchase our basic needs of food, clothing and shelter; and, there has to be duly constituted authority with power to enforce the law or anarchy will reign. So Babylon does not exist because of the money or power that it controls, it exists because of the sinful condition of the hearts of those who use that money and power for selfish purposes.

Just how sinful has our modern Babylonian society become? It is:

> *... the habitation of devils ...*
> *the hold of every foul spirit ...*
> *a cage of every unclean and hateful bird.*
> *... kings of the earth have committed*
> *fornication with her, and*
> *the merchants of the earth are waxed rich*
> *through the abundance of her delicacies*
> *(Revelation 18:2-3).*

Out of this sinful condition comes wars, bankruptcies, famine, poverty, perverted legal systems, no regard for the truth, instability in all areas, spiritual blindness, haughtiness and everything else that is not of God. Such is the condition of a society that seeks self gratification, and does not honor God. Self has become so important to these people that they have no need of God.

The Portrait of A True Babylonian Businessman

The portrait of a true Babylonian is best set out in *Revelation 3:17:*

Because thou sayest, I am rich, and increased with goods, and have need of nothing; and knowest not that thou are wretched, and miserable, and poor, and blind, and naked.

The portrait of a true Babylonian is the picture of a person refusing the love of God and denying the sovereignty of God. The Book of Revelation sets forth in detail his motivation, lifestyle, spiritual condition and his ignominious end. As Esau sold his birthright for a bowl of porridge, so does the true Babylonian sell his entitlement to the righteousness of God for a buck and a little bit of temporary rule over those of whom he takes advantage – all in pursuit of an illusion.

Why Does Wealth and Power Seem to Concentrate in the Hand of the Babylonians?

Two of our most critical assets are (time) and (the power to create). God gives us both of these assets, and He lets us determine how we will use them.

(Time)

To every thing there is a season, and a time to every purpose under the heaven: A time to be born, and a time to die...
(Ecclesiastes 3:1&2).

God gives to each of us a time to be born and a time to die, and we determine what we will do with our lives during the period between those two events. We must decide to either honor God or to gratify ourselves. If our choice is to gratify ourselves, we shall spend our time accumulating assets and/or acquiring power - and generally by means, if necessary, that are not pleasing to God. We shall then be more likely to gather for ourselves more assets and power than will mature Christians who spend their time concentrating on those things that honor God.

Yet, that is not at all to say that to be a mature Christian is to ask to be poor. To the contrary, there are many mature Christians who by Godly means accumulate wealth and are placed in positions of power. The difference is that these Christians chose to spend their time doing that which pleased God. Their goal was not wealth and power, rather, it was to honor God.

Out of that heart after Him, God chose, for reasons known only to Him, to bestow upon them wealth and positions of power. And He is still in that business - when it will serve His purposes. If we are one such recipient, that is fine - if we are not, that is fine too. However, a Babylonian cannot comprehend this mindset because wealth and power are his gods.

(The Power to Create Wealth)

...it is He that giveth thee the power to get wealth...
(Deuteronomy 8:18).

God has bestowed creative power on everyone. All we have to do to receive that creative power is to be born. Why? Because we are created in His image, and He is the master creator and the ultimate Delegator of power.

In the Hebrew, the words **"to get"** as used in Deuteronomy 8:18 mean **"to create"**, and the word **"power"** means **"from giant lizards to good fruit."** (See *Strongs Exhaustive Concordance,* published by Baker Book House, Grand Rapids, Michigan (1985).) So when each of us is born we receive the power to create things from giant lizards to good fruit. Obviously, to create giant lizards is to spend time in life doing that which is not of God, and to create good fruit is to spend time in life doing that which furthers the kingdom of God.

If we determine to use our creative power for self gratification, our time will be spent creating things that are short of good fruit and on the way to becoming giant lizards. That use of our creative power does not honor God; rather it lends itself to entering those types of transactions that financially reward us at the expense of, and to the detriment of, others. Some of our most famous museums, foundations and endowments bear the name of those who made their fortunes in this manner. Babylon does not judge its heroes by commitment to Godliness, but by the number of dollars and amount of power possessed.

With this mindset, sacrificial giving and serving other are not in the vocabulary of a Babylonian. If a Babylonian gives or serves others at all, he does so only when convenient and preferably when public acclaim accompanies the giving. What do we want for our labors on this earth, the gratification of seeing our names engraved on museums, dormitories, church foyers and college "big givers" roles, or do we desire the fulfillment of having our names written in the Lamb's Book of Life?

But when thou does alms, let not thy left hand know what thy right hand doeth: That thine alms may be in secret: and thy Father which seeth in secret himself shall reward thee openly (Matthew 6:3&4). Good fruit honors God, but public honorariums are likened to lizard eggs. It is quite ironic how a Babylonian will give a large amount of money to a cause. Then he will pose for a photograph to be placed in a publication with a circulation of several hundred thousand as part of an article extolling his modesty relative to the gift he just gave. When Christ was in the temple, He observed the heart of the giver toward Him, not the amount the giver gave.

Babylonian Christians

And I heard another voice from heaven, saying, Come out of her (Babylon), *my people, that ye be not partakers of her sins, and that ye receive not of her plagues* (Revelation 18:4).

There are spirit-filled, born again Christians living Babylonian lifestyles. If that were not true, God would not be calling them to out of Babylon in *Revelation 18:4*. He decrees that if these Babylonian Christians do not come out of Babylon, they will commit her sins and receive her plagues. Many of these Babylonian Christians will remain in church leadership all the while. They will be just as blind to the causes of their problems as are the nonbelievers. As goes the Babylonian, so goes the Babylonian Christian, for instance:

When the Babylonians are forced to file bankruptcy, so are the Babylonian Christians;

When the Babylonians file for divorce, so do the Babylonian Christians;

When the children of the Babylonians are in trouble with the law, so are the children of the Babylonian Christians;

As the Babylonians fight, manipulate and play politics to gain and retain positions of control in business and politics, so do the Babylonian Christians for positions of control in their business, politics and churches;

As the Babylonians will reject a loser, so will the Babylonian Christians reject a Christian who has fallen;

As the Babylonian shareholder feels he must have a right to vote to protect his investment, so do the Babylonian Christians believe they must vote in the church to protect what they have already given to the Lord;

As the Babylonians give much recognition to large givers, so do the Babylonian Christians;

As the Babylonians give much attention and expense to promote their public image, so do the Babylonian Christians; and the list goes on in adnausem.

Such is Modern Day Babylon. So let us answer God's call and come out of this Modern Day Babylon and enter into the kingdom of God and His righteousness *(Matthew 6:33)*.

The Balance in Acquiring Wealth and Power

God is not against people acquiring wealth and power. If He is, He made a mistake with Joseph, Abraham, Job, David, Solomon, Job, Cornelius and many others. What He is concerned about is how we acquire and use that wealth and power. Was it acquired and used in the illusory quest for self gratification, or was it bestowed on us by Him to accomplish His purposes in our lives?

WHEN DOES A BUSINESS & PROFESSIONAL PERSON BECOME A WHORE?

For true and righteous are his judgments:
for he hath judged
the great whore, which did corrupt the earth
with her fornication,
and hath avenged the blood of his servants at her hand
(Revelation 19:2 emphasis added).

The intimacy of worship between man and God is paralleled only by the intimacy of husband and wife. As a woman is called a whore when she sleeps with a man other than her husband, so is man a spiritual whore in the eyes of God when he worships anything or anyone other than God.

Thus, the servants of the great whore in *Revelation 19:2* include the collective body of business and professional people who worship the world's social and economic order, rather than Jesus Christ. These individuals are whores in that they give intimate worshipful attention and respect to money and class rather than to Christ; hence, they are having an illicit business relationship with Babylon. Would to God that the Christians would give the same intimate attention to the Bible that the Babylonians give to their contractual agreements. Some everyday examples of this illicit business relationship are:

Sacrificing integrity to increase profits;

Making a camel out of a gnat portion of a contract;

Not caring about the truth of an issue, but only about winning on the issue;

Taking advantage of another because that person is in a vulnerable position;

Using our assets to over-power another even though their position reflects more of the truth than does ours;

Making false statements;

Breaking previous commitments because new commitments "seem to offer" more profit;

Hiding behind the law rather than honoring God in the matter;

Accountability for the truth is often ignored in the name of, "It is our company policy to not comment on such matters;"

The company's interest is "expected" to take priority over all else including worship and family;

Paying bribes to obtain favors;

Belittling another for his faith in Christ;

Putting another down to raise ourselves up;

Throw a few pennies at a "worthy social project" in an attempt to reap huge advertising benefits; and

On in ad nauseam.

God loves us all, whether we be a whore or righteous, but He cannot use a whore to do the work of a righteous man. So, even though our Heavenly Father loves us beyond our wildest dreams, He cannot use us as long as we go "a whoring after the dollar and self gratification" rather than seeking first His kingdom and His righteousness. *(Matthew 6:33)*

COLLECTION OF ACCOUNTS RECEIVABLE

He becometh poor that dealeth with a slack
hand: but the hand of the diligent maketh rich.
(Proverbs 10:4).

It is no fun to sell a product or perform a service and not get paid. There are generally two reasons we do not get paid: (1) we were slack in granting credit in the first place, and/or (2) we were slack in collecting the receivable. Either way we become poor; but if we will be diligent in extending credit and collecting the receivable, we will become rich. The slack hand is the cause of our going broke, but the state of the economy is generally used as the excuse.

To be slack in the granting and collecting of accounts receivable will surely lead us into becoming entangled in the affairs of our debtor, and before we know it, our debtor will be "calling the shots." While we are required to bear one another's burdens, we are never to become entangled in those burdens *(Galatians 6:2);* but, when the receivable becomes large enough, we inevitably become entangled in the debtor's burdens. (See also *Bearing Another's Burdens vs. Becoming Entangled In Their Burdens* at page 18)

THE MOST EFFECTIVE ADVERTISING

Let another man praise thee, and not thine own mouth;
a stranger, and not thine own lips.
(Proverbs 27:2).

The most effective advertising is word-of-mouth praise by satisfied customers. When we praise ourself or our product, the potential customer approaches us with reticence. But, when we let another praise us or our product, the potential customer approaches us with confidence.

We must be careful to do our work correctly, on time and for a fair price. Such diligence causes our customers to praise us to others, and that is the most effective advertising.

The Fallacy of Hype

It is better to trust in the Lord than to put
confidence in man
(Psalm 118:8).

The purpose of hype is to build up a person's confidence in some thing or person, rather than in God. Therein lies the fallacy of hype. Since hype is built upon emotion, tomorrow's hype must be better than today's hype; otherwise, tomorrow will be a time of disillusionment that will discredit the emotion of today.

Just as some churches draw constitutions and bylaws without consulting the Bible because they think the Bible is not practical for church government, so do some businessmen distrust the Bible to be a potential source of counsel in the operation of their business. Therefore, they put their trust in programs, sales rallies, slogans and other forms of hype rather than in the Lord.

The Lord roams the face of the earth looking for the man who seeks Him. Imagine what God will do for the man who puts his trust in Him rather than in hype!

Who Needs an Image?

And thou shalt not make unto
thee any graven image . . .
(Exodus 20:4).

What was the image of Jesus at the whipping post and on the cross, Isaiah being sawn in half, John the Baptist eating locust and wild honey, Peter being crucified upside down or Jonah in the whale's belly? Men and women of God do not focus on their image, rather, they focus on obedience to Him whom they serve. It is impossible to serve an image and God at the same time.

So the next time (and it will probably be before this day is out) we just need that car, boat, house, membership or certain clothes to help us project what we are not, let us cast those thoughts away as Moses did the golden calf. Maintaining an image is frustrating and unfulfilling, while being content is most fulfilling. Who needs an image?

Telling vs. Selling

And, behold, one came and said unto him, Good Master,
what good thing shall I do, that I may have eternal life?
. . . Jesus said unto him, If thou wilt be perfect, go and
sell that thou hast, and give to the poor, and thou shalt
have treasure in heaven: and come and follow me. But
when the young man heard that saying, he went away
sorrowful: for he had great possessions
(Matthew 19:16, 21 & 22).

When does telling become selling? Answer - when we begin the attempt to control (manipulate) the mind of another. That is why we feel "taken" when we have been sold something. The Word addresses this issue head-on.

The story of the rich young ruler *(Matthew 19:16 - 26)* tells us a great deal about manipulation in our "high pressure sales economy." Jesus did not try to "sell" the young man on believing Him, even though the young man's soul was at stake. Jesus was not about to manipulate the young ruler into "believing the Word;" rather, He simply told the young man the Word and let him make up his own mind in the matter. Jesus had a good product that did not need to be sold. When the young man walked away from Jesus, Jesus did not chase him down the street to make a sale, He let him go.

So, why do we attempt to control the minds of our customers with a "sales pitch" to manipulate them into buying our product? Why don't we just "tell" our customers about the product, stop short of manipulation and let them make up their own minds in the matter. After all, if the Lord wants our customers to purchase our product, He is well able to cause that to happen without our "selling." But, if God does not want them to purchase the product, we should not thwart His purpose in their lives and ours by "selling." Is our product so inferior that it needs to be "sold," or, are we so distrustful of God that we do not trust Him to move upon our customers to make the correct decision?

Puffing in Marketing

. . . Go ye into all the world, and
preach the gospel to every creature
(Mark 16:15).

In the Greek, the language of the New Testament, "to preach" means to herald the divine truth. Truth does not need to be puffed, it only needs to be told. When the truth is told it will go as far as God desires.

Likewise, in marketing our products, we need only to tell the truth about them. It is not necessary for us to puff our products and services. If the truth about the product will not sell the product, then we best take it off the shelf. Otherwise, we endanger our witness to the buyer when he discovers the truth, and he will.

HIDDEN AGENDAS

*... we faint not; But have renounced the
hidden things of dishonesty, not walking
in craftiness, nor handling the word of God
deceitfully; but by manifestation of the
truth commending ourselves to every man's
conscience in the sight of God
(II Corinthians 4:1-2).*

Hidden agendas are born out of the fear that if we tell the truth we will not get our way in the matter. Hidden agendas hide the truth behind the mask of a lie to achieve a desired result.

When we entertain hidden agendas, our pride has caused us to believe two lies: (1) that no one sees the hidden agenda, and (2) that hidden agendas are not deceitful. No agenda is hidden from God, and any agenda whispered in secret will eventually be shouted from the housetop *(Luke 12:3)*. A man with a hidden agenda is a man who cannot be trusted and who has just fooled himself.

Examples of hidden agendas are:

Asking someone to play golf when we really intend to sell them insurance;

Telling someone that we want to tell them about our ministry, when what we really intend to do is to ask them for money; and

Attending a funeral to "be seen", rather than out of respect for the decedent and his family.

THE ASSETS WE HAVE IN OUR HAND TODAY ARE ALL WE NEED TODAY

*. . . for I have learned, in whatsoever
state I am, therewith to be content*
(Philippians 4:11).

As entrepreneurs we quite often give much thought to wishing we had more of certain assets than we have, for we believe that if we had more we could do so much more. This mind-set is sinful because it evidences that we are not content with what we have. If God, the Creator of the Universe, wanted us to have more today than we have, He is well able to so provide. We should not continue on in discontentment, rather, we should spend our time asking God for His mind in the matter and thanking Him for the assets we do have.

A few assets in the hand of a man seeking God's Ways are of inestimable and eternal value. Remember Gideon and his 300 men with clay pots and torches against over 135,000 of the enemy; the widow who gave two pieces of copper that Christ, because of her heart, saw to be of more value than all of the gold and silver given by others; Moses, who used his rod as a symbol of authority over the entire Egyptian empire and the Israelites; the widow who used her meal cake to feed the prophet, and never went hungry; Esther who used her faith, and saved the Israelites; and, David who, without sword and shield, used a sling and a stone to kill Goliath.

We do not need more assets today than we have in our hand today; rather, we should learn to be content with what we have. God is well able to use our current assets to accomplish His purposes in our lives. If we need more, He will provide what we need when we need it.

How Are We to Use Our Assets?

*But thou shalt remember the Lord thy God:
for it is he that giveth thee the power to get wealth,
that he may establish his covenant which
he swore unto our fathers ... (Deuteronomy 8:18).*

The next time we look at our balance sheet let us ask ourselves the question, how am I to use the assets shown on this balance sheet? The answer is, God wants us to use our assets in a way that will establish His Covenant on this earth.

This does not mean we must give all of our assets to a church or ministry, although we should certainly use a portion of them for that purpose. The way that we use our assets in causing our business to grow, reinvesting assets to create more jobs, or bringing a higher yield may well be a witness that will bring others closer to God - and that contributes toward establishing His Covenant on this earth. We are to always use our assets unto the glory of God *(I Corinthians 10:31).*

The Real Value of Our Assets

*And the Lord said unto him, What is that
in thine hand? And he said, A rod (Exodus 4:2).*

*And thou shall take this rod in thine hand wherewith
thou shall do signs (Exodus 4:17).*

How often do we look at a machine, vehicle, building or tool, and all we see are assets. That is just what Moses did. He looked at his shepherd's staff and all he saw was a rod. To Moses, that rod was simply an asset needed by him for use in controlling and protecting sheep.

But, when the power of God entered into Moses' life, that rod became valued as a symbol of authority over Pharaoh, the Red Sea and God's people. Likewise, when we allow the power of God to come into our lives, the real value of our machines, vehicles, buildings and tools become all that God wants them to become.

So, if we are to realize the real value of our assets, we must allow God to enter into our lives and use our assets as He wills. Moses always held the rod, but he used it as directed by God. Likewise, God will let us hold our assets, but He wants us to use them at His direction - then, we will realize their real value.

THE HINDRANCE OF
SHARED AUTHORITY

Abraham and Lot *(Genesis 13:9-18)*

God never directed two men to share authority over a mission; rather, He always placed one man in authority and surrounded him with other men who were of a mind to serve the man He had placed in authority. God chose Abraham to establish the promised land. On his own, Abraham shared his God-given authority with Lot as his fellow voting shareholder/partner. Look what happened; Abraham wound up giving half of all he had to Lot.

For instance, the primary reason we form general partnerships and stock corporations is to secure capital and talent. There is nothing wrong with partnerships and corporations having many partners/shareholders, but capital and talent should never be secured in a manner that causes God's anointed leader of the enterprise to lose control of the enterprise. That is why limited partnerships, non-voting corporate stock, voting agreements, etc. should be considered if capital and talent are needed and thereby made available.

Look what happened to Abraham once he severed his general partner/voting shareholder relationship with Lot, God could then give him the promised land *(Genesis 13:9-18)*. God could not give Abraham the promised land as long as Lot was his partner, because God knew Abraham would give half of the land to Lot.

If it becomes necessary to form a partnership or issue stock, then do so in a manner that leaves God's anointed authority in control over the enterprise. Otherwise, if we share our God given authority with others we, too, may render ourselves unable to receive our promised land as did Abraham for a time. To share our God given authority with another is to place ourselves under a hinderance that precludes God from providing for us and others as He wills.

Let's not confuse sharing authority with seeking wisdom, for in the multitude of counselors is wisdom and the establishment of

God's purposes. God's man in authority can often benefit from the wisdom of others, but he should not share his God given authority to secure their wisdom or their investment capital.

In Corporate and Partnership Forms of Business, The Authority Should Rest on the Anointed and Not Necessarily on the Investor

And as Peter was coming in, Cornelius met him, and fell down at his feet . . . .
(Acts 10:25).

Cornelius was a Roman Centurion (commander of 100 troops). He was *"A devout man, and one that feared God with all his house, which gave much alms to the people, and prayed to God alway"* (Acts 10:2). He fell at Peter's feet because he saw God's anointing on Peter. Even though he could have easily attempted to do so through his position, Cornelius did not try to exercise control over Peter. He desired to serve Peter since he knew that Peter was God's anointed.

God anoints individuals to become business and professional people just as surely as He anointed Peter to become an apostle. With that God given anointing to be a business or professional person comes the God given responsibility and authority to fulfill that calling. The investor should never be given authority over God's anointed for the venture, just because the investor is the man with the money. The inevitable tendency of a Babylonian investor is to place more value on his investment than he does on God's anointed for the venture.

With the anointing always comes the power of God to fulfill the responsibility of the anointing. The issue for the person under God's anointing is, will he exercise the faith and patience to wait for God's supply; or, will he take the investor's funds in exchange for control to receive his supply NOW?

In summary, the investor may be anointed of God to lead an enterprise, and if he is so called, he definitely should take the lead. But, the investor should never make the mistake of attempting to lever his investment into a position of control over God's anointing on another person, regardless of the amount of his investment. If God trusts a man with the power of His anointing, the investor should certainly trust the man with his investment. Otherwise, if the man with the anointing bows to the demands of the investor for control, the anointing will leave and the enterprise will be frustrated.

> ***Without counsel purposes are disappointed: but in the multitude of counsellors they are established***
> *(Proverbs 15:22).*

Yet, at the same time, the visionary should see the need for him to solicit and meditate upon the wisdom of his partner/ shareholders. Often times investors have disciplines that are sorely needed by visionaries. It is through the wisdom of the counsel of many that God's purposes are established. (See also *Godly Capital* at page 53)

SELECTING BOARD MEMBERS
FOR OUR BUSINESS

Then the Lord said to Moses, "See I have chosen
Bezaleel ... and I have filled him with the Spirit of
God, with skill, ability and knowledge ..."
(Exodus 31:2 NIV).

God filled Bezaleel with the Spirit of God, skill, ability and knowledge for the purpose of assisting Moses in building the Tabernacle. He was brought by God into Moses's life when Moses needed him, and not before.

If we, as Moses, are in the will of God in our business or profession, God will bring to us Bezaleels who will give to us Godly counsel which is proven by their skill, ability and knowledge. It is these men that we should select as members of our board of directors.

Notice Bezaleel's first qualification, he was filled with the Spirit of God. It is the Spirit of God that focuses and hones our skills, ability and knowledge. Therefore, we should select as board members for our business only those men who have humbly allowed the Spirit of God to focus and hone their skill, ability and knowledge. They will give Godly counsel to us; men of less statue will lead us and our business off course and away from God.

BOASTING - THE POISON IN PLANNING

Boast not thyself of to morrow; for thou
knowest what a day may bring forth
(Proverbs 27:1).

As business and professional people, we must diligently plan for the future, but we must be careful not to allow boasting to enter into that planning process. This is so because diligence comes from a heart toward God, and boasting from a heart that ignores God. The first person that a boasting person deceives is himself, because in his ignoring God he has come to believe his own boasting.

Diligent planning is based upon sound historical data, a careful survey of the current status of our assets and liabilities, reasonable expectations for the foreseeable future and a plan "B" to cut losses in the event that plan "A" does not work. On the other hand, boasting ignores historical data, puffs up our assets, down plays our liabilities, depends upon presumptuous expectations and makes no provision for plan "B" because the one boasting does not believe plan "A" will ever fail. It only takes a little boasting to poison an otherwise diligent plan.

The diligent always leave room for the hand of God in a matter, but those who boast ignore God's hand in the matter.

BRIBES

The king by judgment established the land:
but he that receiveth gifts overthroweth it
(Proverbs 29:4).

It is quite tempting to place a few dollars in "the right hands" to insure we will receive what we want. However, to pay a bribe is to cause the overthrow of the authority to whom it is paid.

Thus, while bribery seems joyous for the moment, its net effect is to bring down the payor and the one bribed. In a bribery situation, when both the bribe and the favor are gone, the payor becomes a two-time looser and society is eroded. Bribery it also known as T-H-I-R-T-Y P-I-E-C-E-S O-F S-I-L-V-E-R!

Chasing The "Big" Business Deal
That Will Solve
All Of My Problems

He who works his land will have abundant food, but he
who chases fantasies lacks judgment
(Proverbs 12:11 NIV).

Chasing the "big" business deal that will solve all of my problems is like chasing fantasies. Why? Because we have put our trust for deliverance in the deal rather than the hand of God, and to do that is to chase a fantasy.

As fantasies are ever elusive, so are the closing dates for these "big" deals. The closing date is always just around the corner, but as fantasies never come, neither does the closing date for the "big" deal.

If we work our jobs diligently, we will have food; but if we chase fantasies such as "big deals", we will show everyone that we lack judgment, and we will go hungry in the process.

THE COST OF FALLING IN LOVE WITH A BUSINESS DEAL

And it came to pass afterward,
that he loved a woman in the
valley of Sorek, whose name was Delilah
(Judges 16:4).

Samson represents the man of God, and Delilah represents the world. When Samson focused his love on the world, He lost his objectivity, his walk with God and his calling from God. The same happens to any man who falls in love with a business deal; he, too, loses his objectivity, his walk with God and his calling from God.

We serve what we love, be it God or a business. As Samson lost his hair, objectivity and life when he loved Delilah, whom he should not have loved, so will we when we fall into the pit of loving a business deal.

Praying For The Outcome
Of Business Deals

... O My father, if it be possible, let this cup pass
from Me: nevertheless not as I will, but as thou wilt
(Matthew 26:39).

How many of us have said, "Man, I know this deal is of the Lord," only to later have it rammed down our throat sideways. Then, at other times, when our back is to the wall we pray, "God, I've just got to have this deal go through, so make it come together." Later the deal goes through and becomes a noose around our neck.

We should pray about the outcome of business deals like Jesus prayed in Gethsemane when his life was on the line, "If it be possible, let the deal go through, but if You do not want it to go through, that is fine with me, too."

In short, the real issue is, do we want the deal more than we want God's will? To put the decision into God's hands is to want His will; otherwise, we do not want His will. Let us learn to pray about the outcome of deals as Christ prayed for His own life - put the outcome in God's hands, not ours.

Yet, at the same time, we have to be diligent in our affairs. We are not to let prayer serve as an excuse for our being sloppy in the way we manage that which God has given to us.

So, work diligently on the matter, bathe it in prayer, refrain from manipulation and let God perform His way with your deal in His time.

Securing Capital

***But my God shall supply all your need according
to his riches in glory by Christ Jesus***
(Philippians 4:19).

In *Philippians 4:19,* God promises He will supply all of our
need through Jesus Christ, and His supply will never put us in
bondage *(See the entire Bible).* Jesus came to set us free, and did
so. The question is, are we willing to believe that God's principles
of supply and freedom apply to securing capital in our everyday
business and profession?

Borrowing

With that question in mind, let us consider borrowed
capital. According to *Romans 13:8,* we are to, **Owe no man
anything but to love one another . . . ;** *Proverbs 22:7,* the lender
is the master and the borrower is the servant; and *Matthew
6:24 . . . ye cannot serve God and mammon.* How then can
borrowed capital be Godly if it causes us to owe a man something
other than to love him, and causes the lender to be our master?
(Please balance the above by reading *Not Borrowing, Rule Or
Relationship* at page 129.)

Also, let us consider the Babylonian practice of giving the
investor control of our business in return for his investment of
capital. If God entrusted us with the idea for the business, then
He also entrusted us with the authority over that business and
does not want us to give control to another just to get his capital.
The investor should trust us as much with his money as God
does with the idea to carry on the business. If the investor does
not have that degree of trust in us, then his capital is not Godly
capital and we should not accept his money. It is Godly that we
be accountable to those who invest money with us, but to be
accountable does not mean to give up control.

Godly Capital

Godly capital is that capital which can be secured free of the bondage of another's control. If such capital is not available at present, we should have the faith and patience to wait until it does become available. If the enterprise is of God, He will supply capital for the enterprise. If capital is not supplied, that may well be God telling us not to proceed with the venture at this time, or perhaps not at all. Are we willing to obey God's "wait" or "no", or are we stubbornly going to proceed in spite of God's will to the contrary?

The Cost of Impatience in Securing Capital

Abraham and Sarah having Ishmael
(Genesis 16:1-6).

Abraham and Sarah became impatient while waiting upon God to give them the son He had promised. So they decided "to help God out" by calling in Hagar to conceive by Abraham and give birth to their son. Hence, Ishmael was born of Hagar and Isaac was later born of Sarah. Ishmael was Abraham's supply to himself, while Isaac was God's supply to Abraham. It is Ishmael and his descendants who have constantly plagued Isaac and his descendants, the Israelites.

Likewise, every time we secure capital for our business out of impatience we, too, will create an Ishmael who will plague us for a long time to come. As God was trying to let patience have her perfect work in Abraham and Sarah while they were waiting for their son of promise, Isaac, so is He trying to *. . . let patience have her perfect work . . .* in us while we are waiting on the capital for our business *(James 1:4).*

Abraham was close to 100 years of age and Sarah 80 when Isaac was born, well beyond child bearing age. Sometimes our ability to secure capital looks just about as bleak, but remember that we have the same God as did Abraham and Sarah.

When we allow *. . . patience to have her perfect work . . .* in us, in His time and if it is His will, we will have our capital. But consider this, perhaps it is not His will for us to secure the capital for a particular venture. Are we willing to accept "no" for an answer, or are we going to act out of impatience and secure the capital on our own? If we act out of impatience, we will most certainly create an Ishmael.

WHY OUR CASH FLOW IS CUT OFF

The silver is mine, and the gold is mine,
saith the LORD of hosts
(Haggai 2:8).

Interruption of cash flow is never just a fluke or a happenstance. Since all of the gold and silver belong to the Lord, we need to seek Him first to learn why our cash flow has been cut off. Following are a few insights from scripture that may explain why our cash flow has been cut off.

God's Way of Telling Us that A Change Is Coming in Our Lives

Now when Jacob saw there was corn in Egypt,
Jacob said unto his sons, why do you look
one upon another?
. . . get ye down thither, and buy for us from thence . . .
(Genesis 42:1-2).

Cash flow cut off can be a devastating event. Too often, our tendency at such times is to remain dormant in the hope that things will soon change. Jacob saw the fallacy in such tendency and told his sons, "Don't sit dormant looking at each other in the hope that things will change, go to where you can get some supply, even if it is in Egypt."

Jacob did not realize at the time, and most often we do not either, that God was using this cut off of supply to move Jacob and his family to Egypt. The cut off of Jacob's food supply was an integral part of God's plan for the entire nation of Israel. While Jacob saw only an empty plate, God saw the making of a new nation in Egypt that would return in power to the promised land.

So, when our cash flow is cut off, God may well be speaking to us that it is time for a change in our lives. Remember, just as Jacob did not realize what God was doing at the time, we probably will not either. But Jacob did have the courage and diligence to move to Egypt where he could get the supply he needed. An added benefit of this move was that he found his son, Joseph, whom he thought was dead.

Improperly Spending the Cash We Have

Is it time for you, O ye, to dwell in your ceiled houses, and this house lie waste? Now therefore thus saith the LORD of hosts; consider your ways. Ye have sown much, and bring in little . . . (Haggai 1:4-6).

The Israelites were spending their cash flow on building large houses for themselves, and the Lord's house lay waste. So God cut off their cash flow while waiting for them to consider their ways. He promised that if they would build His house first, their cash flow would be restored.

Do we tithe, give to the poor, spend our cash flow to establish His covenant with His people, or do we spend it on ourselves? We must consider our ways.

Chastisement

*Until the time that his word came:
the word of the LORD tried him
(Psalm 105:19).*

Sometimes God, in His wisdom, allows His Word to try us until the time comes for His Word to deliver us. Anyone who has ever experienced a cut off of cash flow knows what a trial it can be. Why does God chasten us in this manner? Because it is through the adversity of chastisement that He prepares us to be partakers of His Holiness *(Hebrews 12:10)*.

God wants to know if He or our cash is going to be our supply. What better way to find out than cutting off our cash flow.

Not Treating Our Wives with Respect

Likewise, ye husbands, dwell with them according to knowledge, giving honour unto the wife, as unto the weaker vessel, and as being heirs together of the grace of life; that your prayers be not hindered
(1 Peter 3:7).

If we do not treat our wives with respect, our prayers will be hindered - they will not even reach God. So let us respect our wives in obedience to His Word. Then He will hear and answer our prayer for cash flow.

How can a man respect God if he does not respect his wife with whom he is also one? We do not have any better relationship with God than we have with our wives.

Summary

When our cash flow is cut off, let us be obedient to *Matthew 6:33* and seek God first to find out why. If we will, and change our ways to be in accordance with His Word, He will restore our cash flow regardless of the condition of the economy at the time. God is not bound even by time, much less the world's economy.

THE WISE UNDERDOG'S

COMPETITIVE ADVANTAGE

A wise man scaleth the city of the mighty, and
casteth down the strength of the confidence thereof
(Proverbs 21:22).

If the underdog will seek the wisdom of God, God will give him wisdom liberally *(James 1:5)*. With this God given wisdom, the underdog can map out his plans to compete with his mighty competitors and undermine their strength.

This same wisdom is also available for the asking to the underdog's mighty competitors. The issue is, will the mighty competitors trust in their wealth as their strength, or will they place their trust in the wisdom of God? If the mighty will seek the wisdom of God, both they and the underdog will prosper. This is true because the wisdom of God will show them how to work together rather than against each other.

WRITTEN CONTRACTS

(See the entire Old and New Testaments)

How often do we say, "We don't need to put our agreement in writing because . . ." To the contrary, God, knowing the nature of man, put His old and new agreements (Testaments) with us in writing. Are the people with whom we are contracting more reliable than God? Then we had better reduce our agreements to writing.

Interpreting Contracts

Ye blind guides, which strain at a gnat, and swallow a camel (Matthew 23:24).

We have all signed lengthy contracts only to have the other party take a gnat portion thereof and attempt to blow it up to the size of a camel. Well, Jesus saw this happening in His time too. It happened then and it happens now because the sin of pride has not changed since Jesus' time. In Jesus' time the scribes and pharisees were distorting God's Word just as many lawyers and their clients of today are distorting the interests of the parties to contracts.

As God's Word must be studied in balance, so must a contract be interpreted in balance. When our eyes are on Christ we will review the contract in balance. But, when our eyes become jealous about "our rights in the contract," we will pervert the entire contract by straining at gnats and swallowing camels.

It is a sad note that Christians do not study the Word of God as diligently as the Babylonians study their contracts. (See also *The Difference in a Babylonian Businessman and a Christian Businessman* at page 26)

COST CONSCIOUSNESS VS. GREED

Woe unto him that buildeth his house by
unrighteousness,
and his chambers by wrong; that useth his neighbor's
service without wages . . .
(Jeremiah 22:13).

The difference in cost consciousness and greed is the condition of our heart. Are we cost conscious out of a desire to achieve maximum profitability, or are we cost conscious because we want more for ourselves at the expense of others? The former is good business, the latter is greed.

God blesses those who cut costs out of a proper motive, but . . . ***woe*** . . . unto them who cut costs to hoard up for themselves.

WHAT CONTROL CAN WE HAVE OVER OUR CREDITORS?

Thus saith Cyrus king of Persia, The LORD God of heaven hath given me all the kingdoms of the earth . . .
(Ezra 1:2).

Cyrus, king of Persia, was the heathen king of the Medo-Persian Empire that conquered the Babylonians. He was not a nice man. He was a false god worshiping heathen who could have anyone killed, tortured or enslaved at his whim. Even so, by virtue of the Godly lifestyle and prayers of men such as David, Shadrach, Meshach, Abednego, Ezra and others, God moved upon Cyrus' heart and caused him to proclaim in writing throughout his entire empire:

Thus saith Cyrus king of Persia, The LORD God of heaven hath given me all the kingdoms of the earth; and he hath charged me to build him an house at Jerusalem, which is in Judah. Who is there among you of all his people? his God be with him, and let him go up to Jerusalem, which is in Judah, and build the house of the Lord God of Israel, (he is the God,) which is in Jerusalem. And whosoever remaineth in any place where he sojourneth, let the men of his place help him with silver, and with gold, and with goods, and with beasts, beside the freewill-offering for the house of God that is in Jerusalem (Ezra 1:2-4).

If God moved upon the heart of a false-god-worshiping-heathen-king to set the Israelites free, restore the temple of God and help pay for that restoration, guess what kind of control our Godly walk and prayers can provide to us over our creditors? God can even cause our creditors to serve us just as He caused king Cyrus to serve Ezra. If we will only return to God, He will return to us and move upon our creditors for our benefit in His time.

How Does A Businessman Compute His Tithe?

Thou shalt truly tithe all the increase of they seed, that the field bringeth forth year by year
(Deuteronomy 14:22).

Honour the LORD with they substance, and with the first fruits of all thine increase: ... (Proverbs 3:9)

The key word is "increase." God is the consummate businessman. He knows that a businessman's increase is his profit, and that the businessman had to incure costs to produce that profit. God does not expect a tithe on that portion of a businessman's income that represents the return of his costs, but only on that portion of income that represents his pretax profit-for that is his increase.

How Does A Businessman Compute His Pretax Profit on A Weekly Basis?

When a person is touched by God, he wants to tithe on his income but he often does not know how to compute his profit on a weekly basis. Why a weekly basis? Because he loves God, and wants to tithe each week when he goes to church. But for many businessmen, that can often present a problem.

Some businessmen have sophisticated accounting equipment and can compute their profit on a daily basis, but most do not have this equipment. So what do they do?

One suggestion is to establish a separate checking account as a tithe account. Then, each time the businessman takes money out of his business for personal reasons, he could deposit at least 10% of that amount into the tithe account.

What If A Businessman Is Taking Money Out of His Business To Pay A Tithe, but the Business Is Not Making A Profit?

That is called "eating your capital", and the business will not last but so long if this trend continues. In any event, if there is no profit there is no increase, and if there is no increase there is no income upon which to pay a tithe.

The Balance

And she said, as the lord thy God liveth, I have not a cake, but an handful of meal in a barrel, and a little oil in a cruse: and, behold I am gathering two sticks, that I may go in and dress it for me and my son, that we may eat it, and die (I Kings 17:12).

When the widow was asked by Elijah to give him a portion of her last meal cake, she did not stop to see if she had made a profit. She unquestionably responded with the last she had, even the food out of her and her son's mouths. May we all have that kind of respect for the Lord. If we will, He will honor us as He honored her and the countless millions of others who have followed her example. (See also *Giving* at page 181)

CHARACTER - THE BASIC CRITERIA IN HIRING EMPLOYEES

And his name through faith in his name
hath made this man strong . . .
(Acts 3:16).

Businessmen are constantly in search of competent people to staff their businesses. Should the criteria for hiring center on talent or on character, the foundation of talent?

God gave us our talents, but our character determines how our talents will be used. If we exercise a strong faith in Christ, that faith will make our character strong; and strong character will maximize the use of our talents.

Just Compensation for Employees

Masters give unto your servants that which is just and
equal; knowing that ye also have a master in Heaven
(Colossians 4:1).

Just compensation for employees is, and always has unnecessarily been, a touchy issue. The sensitivity of this issue is caused by employers believing, "The more I pay my employees the less I will have for myself."

If we concentrate more on being just with our employees, and not on how much we can keep more for ourselves, our Master in Heaven will bless us accordingly. A true employer is a servant to his employees in that he finds their needs, supplies those needs and rewards his employees according to their efforts.

If employers think such an attitude is setting themselves up to be taken advantage of, they do not know much about being a leader. A righteous employer knows he is a servant to his Master in Heaven, so he treats his employees as he wants God to treat him.

PROPER STAFFING OF EMPLOYEES

Where no oxen are, the crib is clean: but
much increase is by the strength of the ox
(Proverbs 14:4).

Achieving the proper level of personnel is a never-ending task. Ever shifting supply and demand makes that level a moving target. If we are consistently over or understaffed, our crib (the checkbook balance) will be clean. But, if we want to get the job done, we must hire people sufficient to do the job.

It is the staff who produces the cash in the checkbook. The boss may own the field, but the employees pull the plow.

One Aspect Of Disloyalty

Be not deceived; God is not mocked: for whatsoever
a man soweth, that shall he also reap
(Galatians 6:7).

If we have a problem with employee loyalty, we should first review our past, for we may be reaping the seeds of disloyalty that we sowed when we were under authority. It is interesting to note that David never experienced a problem with disloyalty in his family or army until he was disloyal to God in his affair with Bathsheba. As a result, following that incident of disloyalty, he suffered disloyalty at the hands of his own children, the general of his army and others.

Let us go back to the employees to whom we have been disloyal, ask their forgiveness and observe the impact of our asking for their forgiveness. Even better, let us not tell our employees of our confession and repentance, and watch God change their attitudes without their even knowing what we have done.

The Rebellious/Complaining Employee

An evil man seeketh only rebellion: therefore a cruel messenger shall be sent against him
(*Proverbs 17:11*).

A rebellious employee will always cause trouble. The question is how long do we keep him? The answer is in two questions:

1. How long do we want seeds of rebellion to remain in our organization; and

2. Do we want to suffer with him when God sends an evil messenger against him, for He surely will?

The rebellious employee is most often identified as the complaining employee. Complaining is sin because it is not being content with what we have (*Hebrews 13:5*), and sin is rebellion first against God and then against the employer. Why should we ever want someone in our employ who is rebellious to the God of this Universe?

Quite often an employer will attempt to reason with or placate the rebellious/complaining employee. However, seldom if ever are these attempts successful because it is futile to try and reason with or placate sin. Sin sees such attempts as signs of weakness in the employer. The rebellious/complaining employee must be dealt with according to the sin for which they have not repented; otherwise, the employer will ultimately pay the price for not dealing with that employee.

The Foolish Employee

***As a dog returneth to his vomit,
so a fool returneth to his folly***
(Proverbs 26:11).

All employees make mistakes, but only a foolish employee makes foolish mistakes. The question then arises, "How long do we keep the employee who makes foolish mistakes?"

The answer is, how long can we afford to wait before he makes another foolish mistake? For just as surely as a dog returns to his vomit so will the foolish employee continue to make foolish mistakes. The foolish employee does not care even for his own well being, so how can we expect him to care for our business?

Deal with the foolish employee now, or pay for his mistakes later. The choice is ours. To retain him is to bring upon ourselves the disrespect of our other employees.

The Sluggardly Employee

***The sluggard is wiser in his own conceit
than seven men that can render a reason***
(Proverbs 26:16).

Each of us has experienced the sluggardly employee who can render endless excuses telling why the task assigned to him has not and/or cannot be completed. The question then arises, "How long can we keep this sluggardly employee?"

The answer is, how long can we afford to listen to his excuses, and the task remain uncompleted? For just as surely as the sluggardly employee will continue to render excuses, so will the task remain uncompleted. The sluggard cares not that he constantly walks on the ragged edge of keeping his job, so what kind of care will he take with our business?

To retain the sluggardly employee is to bring upon ourselves the disrespect of our other employees.

The Talebearing Employee

Where no wood is, there the fire goeth out:
so where there
is no talebearer, the strife ceaseth
(Proverbs 26:20).

Given enough time and circumstance, a talebearing employee will become the nerve center of our business and generate more strife than we can imagine; but, when he is removed, the strife will cease. To retain the talebearing employee is to bring upon ourselves the disrespect of our other employees. (See also *Adultery Is Evidence That An Employee Cannot Be Trusted* at page 2)

THE COST OF EXPANDING TOO FAR TOO FAST

. . . he (Moses) ***went out unto his brethren, and looked on
their burdens: and he spied an Egyptian smiting a
Hebrew . . . And . . . he slew the Egyptian . . . .***
(Exodus 2:11-12 emphasis added).

Moses and many businessmen have one thing in common,
they move too far too fast. Just as God called Moses to deliver
the Israelites, so does He call people to be in business and
professions. But, just as Moses moved too far too fast when he
killed the Egyptian soldier and was chased out of Egypt, so do
we get chased out of business when we expand too fast.

It takes more discipline to expand at a slow rate than at
a fast rate. Why grow too fast to "take advantage of an
opportunity," when that very "opportunity" may undermine our
whole company? While Moses was moving too fast he could
see only one Israelite who needed freedom, but God saw
3,000,000 Israelites who needed freedom. When Moses learned
to move at a Godly pace, he freed all 3,000,000 Israelites and
did not have to slay any Egyptian soldiers in the process.

Do we have an Egyptian soldier opportunity before us
today? Are we going to take the "opportunity" to slay him, or
are we going to move forward at a Godly pace and reap greater
rewards later?

FATHERS AND SONS WORKING TOGETHER

For God so loved the world that
he gave his only begotten son . . . .
(John 3:16).

. . . Father, into thy hands I
commend my spirit . . . .
(Luke 23:46).

God the Father and Jesus the Son worked very well together. Why? They had a Godly Plan and disciplined themselves to follow the Plan, even at great sacrifice.

The basis for the Plan was the love that the Father and the Son had for each other. The execution of the Plan required the Father to trust the Son to conduct the Father's business; and, the Son had to step down from His seat next to the Father and follow the Plan.

The Father was not set in His ways, and the Son was not brash toward the Father. Their hearts were set on serving others, and not on pleasing themselves. The Father was willing to release the Son, and the Son was willing to be released.

Fathers and sons should be able to work together in peace, but this will not happen unless the father has the heart of the Father and the son has the heart of the Son.

THE CAUSE OF AND CURE FOR
FINANCIAL DIFFICULTIES

(See the entire Bible)

Whenever the Israelites were in right relationship with God, they prospered. But, whenever that relationship became deficient, they suffered a multitude of problems including financial difficulties; the same holds true for us today.

The circumstances that we call financial problems are not problems at all; rather, they are just symptoms of underlying spiritual deficiencies in our lives. If we will only come into a right relationship with God, the financial difficulties in our lives will disappear as a by-product of that right relationship.

This was proven true in the life of Jesus. He was responsible for the support of His mother, the 12 disciples and their families; He lived in enemy occupied territory and had no visible means of support; yet, He never had a financial difficulty because He never had a problem with His Father. The same will hold true in our lives too if we will honor God as He did.

Financial difficulties will not go away by our acquiring more money; rather, they are resolved only by our repenting for our wrong relationship with God and then living in accordance with the repentance. When we are broke, the last thing we need is money. What we really need is to turn from our ways and towards God. It is then that God will supply all of our needs through Christ Jesus *(Philippians 4:19)*.

If we will come into right standing with God, He will satisfy us even in days of famine *(Psalms 37:19)*. We must blend into the above what Jesus taught us to pray, ***Give us <u>this day</u> our daily bread.*** (Matthew 6:11) Let us always remember to measure "prosperity" in terms of what we have in our hands for today. (Also read "Chastisement" beginning at page 101)

"ACCEPTABLE" FRAUD

Divers weights, and divers measures, both of
them are alike abomination to the LORD
(Proverbs 20:10).

How easy it is for a mechanic, lawyer, plumber, etc. to say, "I worked ten hours" when he only worked six, or for the repairman to say, "the repair took four parts" when it only took two parts. All such fraudulent practices are abominations to the Lord.

Those committing such fraudulent practices attempt to make their actions acceptable by using the excuse, "Everyone does it," but that is simply not true. Everyone does not do it. Which is the most important, monetary gain or righteousness? If we will concentrate on righteousness, God will create the monetary gain for us *(Joshua 1:7-8).*

Fraud Prevention

When wisdom enters into thine heart, and knowledge
is pleasant with thy soul; Discretion shall preserve thee,
understanding shall keep thee: To deliver thee from the
way of the evil man, from the man that
speaketh froward things . . .
(Proverbs 2:10-12).

Who bears the greater guilt, the fraudulent or the defrauded? The fraudulent is certainly guilty; but, is the defrauded any less guilty since he did not diligently seek the wisdom and knowledge of God to prevent the fraud?

If we focus on what was taken, we will convict the fraudulent. But, if we focus on God we must convict ourselves for not having sought God's wisdom and knowledge to prevent the fraud. Fraud is preventable, but only if we will slow down and seek the wisdom and knowledge of God in all of our affairs.

The Necessity Of Dying
To Our Goals

*. . . Except a corn of wheat <u>fall into the ground and die,</u>
it abideth alone: but if it die it bringeth forth much fruit*
(John 12:24 emphasis added).

It is good to set goals, but we should not let our goals become our god. Our goals have become our god when we act ungodly if they are not met.

While we may set a goal, for whatever reason God may not want us to meet that goal. To accept that fact is to *. . . fall into the ground and die.* Then God can bring forth much fruit in our lives, and our goals may be met, or perhaps not. It is not that God does not want us to meet our goals; rather, He desires that we concentrate on honoring Him rather than meeting our goals.

The world says that growth must always be constant, but the Word of God says growth comes only after we let our goals *. . . fall into the ground and die . . .* Again, we see the truth of Isaiah 55:8 fulfilled *. . . neither are your ways my ways, saith the LORD.*

How To Make A Business Grow

Without

Impatience And Discontentment

...for I have learned, in whatsoever
state I am, therewith to be content
(Philippians 4:11).

There is nothing wrong with wanting to make our business or profession grow, but there is something wrong in not being content with its current size. The wrong is that it is a sin to be discontent and impatient.

The way to make our business or profession grow is to first learn to be content with what we now have. The discipline of contentment affords to us the inner strength to wait and allow God, in His time and way, to show us how to bring about the increase. This discipline of contentment is born out of our trust in God to bring about the growth in His time, not ours.

So, we have a choice. Do we **make** our business grow ahead of God's timing by the sinful fuel of discontentment, or do we **allow** it to grow in God's time through the discipline of contentment?

WHEN TO BUILD A HOUSE

Prepare thy work without, and make it fit for thyself
in the field; and afterwards build thine house
(Proverbs 24:27).

As a human needs blood to live, so does a business need capital to survive and grow. If we drain our business of needed capital in favor of building our personal house, our field will not be fit nor prepared. When the field is neither fit nor prepared, the field, the capital and the house will soon be lost.

THE COST OF EXCESSIVE INVENTORY

. . . but some of them left of it (manna) *until the morning,
and it bred worms and stank: . . . and when the sun
waxed hot, it melted*
(Exodus 16:20-21 emphasis added).

Manna and inventory have much in common. When the Israelites gathered more manna than they needed, the excess manna turned into worms, melted and stank.

So does excessive inventory turn into worms that eats up capital, space and profits and, thereby makes the business stink. Then, by the time those who supplied the inventory turn up the heat to collect their accounts, the value of our excessive (and now outdated) inventory has melted and cannot be returned for credit on account or sold for payment on account.

This is the cost of excessive inventory.

SELECTING SOUND INVESTMENTS

But thou shalt remember the LORD thy God:
for it is he that giveth thee power to get wealth . . .
(Deuteronomy 8:18).

The obvious reason that we make investments is to acquire wealth. Well, since it is the Lord that *. . . giveth thee the power to get wealth . . .,* if we want to select sound investments we must first develop a relationship with the Lord. The wisdom flowing from that relationship will direct us in the selection of our investments according to His plan. Otherwise, we are totally at the mercy of the fickled world monetary system in our selection of investments.

God has the ultimate investment plan and it is very simple, yet excruciatingly painful to our flesh. His plan is that if we will seek first the kingdom of God and His righteousness, He will add unto us the wisdom to acquire all of the things we need to serve Him as He wills *(Matthew 6:33).* That is the most sound investment plan anyone can ever hope to have.

Laboring For Self

Is Laboring To Be Empty

There is that maketh himself rich, yet hath nothing: there is that maketh himself poor, yet hath great riches
(Proverbs 13:7).

We were created by God in the image of God, and not by the world in the image of the world. So, we will find fulfillment only in the Ways of God, and only emptiness in the ways of the world. Witness today's divorce and crime rate.

The world's reward for our worldly labors is that we are never satisfied, and the harder we labor the more empty we become. Fulfillment comes not in laboring for self, but in laboring for others. To labor to acquire wealth for self is to labor to be empty, but to labor for others in the Ways of God is to be rich.

LEASES

(For scripture references See Debt at page 127)

The nature of a lease is debt i.e., the lessee is promising to pay to the lessor money in the future that the lessee does not have in hand today. That is debt. Therefore, the scriptural insights applicable to debt also apply to leases.

LEVERAGE - BABYLON'S KEY TO SUCCESS

Vs.

FREEDOM & SERVANTHOOD -

GOD'S KEY TO SUCCESS

. . . neither are your ways my ways, saith the LORD
(Isaiah 55:8).

Babylon's key to success is for us to place ourselves
above other people by leveraging them into a position where
they have to serve us.

Conversely, God's key to success is for us to set other
people free to perform according to the talents and abilities that
God has given to them. Then we are to serve them in their
calling. Truly, *. . . neither are your ways my ways, saith*
the Lord.

FILING LITIGATION

Moreover, if thy brother shall trespass against thee, go and tell him his fault between thee and him alone; if he shall hear thee, thou hast gained thy brother. But, if he will not hear thee, then take with thee one or two more, that in the mouth of two or three witnesses every word may be established. And if he shall neglect to hear them, tell it unto the church: but if he neglect to hear the church, let him be unto thee as an heathen man and a publican
(*Matthew 18:15-17*).

Should we file suit to collect money, enforce contracts, preserve rights, etc.? We can certainly consider doing so, but only after we have first sought to resolve the matter according to Matthew 18, i.e., the parties submit the issues to their church leaders for resolution and agree to be bound by the decisions of their church leaders.

Obviously, not all of the people with whom we deal are going to want to submit matters to the Church for resolution. According to Matthew 18, their refusal automatically requires that they be treated as heathens. Likewise, when Christians submit matters to the Church for a decision, and will not abide by such decision, then they, too, are to be treated as heathens.

How then are we to resolve matters with those regarded as heathens? The answer is found in *I Timothy 1:9*, ***Knowing this, that the law is not made for a righteous man, but for the lawless and disobedient, for the ungodly and for sinners, for unholy and profane, for murders of fathers and murderers of mothers, for manslayers.*** The heathen, by not submitting to the discipline of the Church, has proven his lawlessness and has thereby subjected himself to the law of the land; and, we know from *Romans 13:1-2* that all authority is ordained of God which, of course, includes the court system of our land.

However, consider the following. Even though we are permitted by scripture to file suit against an individual it may be that, for whatever reason, the Holy Spirit will not allow us to proceed with suit. Who knows the work of the Spirit at any given time. Although we may be free to file suit, we need to be sensitive to the leading to the Spirit and allow Him to control our actions. Jesus had the legal right to defend himself, but his obedience to the Spirit caused Him not to exercise that right.

On the other hand, it may be that the Spirit desires that we bring the heathen to judgment through the court system of the land; for which of us knows what the Spirit may be doing in another's life by having him subjected to the law of the land?

The decision is yours, after prayer.

FINDING ADDITIONAL
BUSINESS LOCATIONS

. . . and ye shall be witnesses unto me both in
Jerusalem, and in all Judea, and in Samaria,
and unto the uttermost part of the earth
(Acts 1:8).

Jesus Christ was the most efficient man who ever lived. He was charged by God to establish a pattern through which every living human in the world could learn of the Gospel. In His characteristic simple manner, Jesus told His disciples to tell the Gospel first in Jerusalem where they were, then in the adjacent area of Judea, then in the next adjacent area of Samaria and so on in the same manner unto the uttermost parts of the earth.

That is the same efficient way we should find additional business locations, i.e. in the geographic location next to where our business is already located. Why should we hop, skip and jump over adjacent market areas and locate businesses in areas long distances from our current locations? Management, communication and efficiency decrease by the mile, and thus does our ability to efficiently tell our story to our customers.

KNOWING WHEN TO CUT LOSSES

. . . Arise, and let us flee;
for we shall not else escape from Absalom:
make speed to depart, lest he overtake us suddenly,
and bring evil upon us,
and smite the city with the edge of the sword
(II Samuel 15:14).

One of the most difficult decisions to make in business is knowing when to cut our losses by closing down and moving on to something else. David was faced with the same decision, he made it, moved on and thereby saved his kingdom.

The optimist in us tends to make us believe if we hold on just a bit longer things will turn around, but they seldom do. The ostrich in us tends to make us believe if we ignore the problem it will go away, but it does not. The time to cut losses is different in any given situation; but when losses continue to occur, there comes a time for the ostrich and optimist to leave and the realist to take control.

Optimists and ostriches file bankruptcy, but realists like David know when to cut their losses and work out of a bad situation. David was already in a bad situation, but saw a worse situation coming and acted before it could occur. He made the decision to cut his losses and move in another direction, and so should we.

Timely Appointment Of
Succession In Management

But charge Joshua, and encourage him,
and strengthen him:
for he shall go over before his people,
and he shall cause
them to inherit the land which thou shalt see
(Deuteronomy 3:28).

Appointment of A Successor

Scripture requires that we appoint our successor in management, and it directs that we are to charge our successor with his duties and strengthen and encourage him. Our reluctance to appoint a successor is a reflection of our ungodly mismanagement.

Whey We Do Not Appoint A Successor

Generally, we do not appoint a successor because we do not want to give up control. This possessive attitude leaves no room for strengthening and encouraging others, and has a penalty that is quite severe for us and for others.

So, let us give up our possessiveness, and encourage and strengthen others to step into our shoes. Then the Godly principles which we have established will serve as the foundation for others to build upon.

The Penalty for Untimely Appointment
of Succession in Management

My lord the king, the eyes of all Israel are on you, to learn from you who will sit on the throne of my lord the king after him. Otherwise, as soon as my lord the king is laid to rest with his father, I and my son Solomon will be treated as criminals
(I Kings 1:20-21 NIV).

David failed to timely appoint Solomon as his successor to the throne in Israel. This failure encouraged one of David's son's, Adonijah, to proclaim himself king and David's chief general, Joab, to support Adonijah as king rather than Solomon. Thus, one of Solomon's first acts as king was to have Adonijah and Joab executed for their rebellion against David and Solomon. David's failure to timely appoint Solomon as successor to him placed the entire Nation of Israel in peril.

Failure to timely appoint our successor is a failure in leadership. This failure causes uncertainty, division and strife among those under our leadership, and thereby jeopardizes the continued existence of the enterprise we have worked so hard to build.

Summary

Let us surrender our possessiveness and train, encourage and strengthen others to take up our position when we leave. Then, the Godly principles which we have established will serve as the foundation for them to build upon.

A Ministry Is Not
A Profit Making Business,
And A Profit Making Business
Is Not A Ministry

(See Joseph as a businessman in Egypt
vs. the life of Paul the Servant and Apostle)

Both Joseph and Paul were called by God to serve His purpose for their lives. Both were disciplined, obeyed the Word and accomplished the tasks assigned to them by God. Yet, in performing their respective tasks, one justly accumulated all he could for the benefit of his Master; and, the other gave all he had to the people in obedience to his Master. The difference was that Joseph was operating a business, and Paul a ministry.

The objective of a business is to accumulate, while a ministry's objective is to give away what it has. That is why a ministry cannot be operated like a business, nor a business like a ministry. Yet, at the same time, both the businessman and the ministry head are required by God to be good stewards, exercise discipline and seek Him first in all things.

Those of us who confuse business and ministry are often the ones who go broke. Why? Because we are confused about "God's call" on our life. We do not know if we are "called" to accumulate or to give away, and to try and accomplish both is double mindedness. *"... give diligence to make your calling and election sure: for if you do these things, ye shall never fall..."* (2 Peter 1:10).

Now this does not mean that we cannot minister in business; but it does mean that we cannot conduct our business as if it is a ministry, nor can we conduct our ministry as if it is a business.

NEGOTIATIONS -

AN EXERCISE IN PATIENCE

A fool uttereth all his mind: but a wise
man keepeth it in till afterwards
(Proverbs 29:11).

The wise negotiator will cause his opponent to reveal his plan before he reveals his own, but the foolish negotiator just cannot wait to reveal his own plan to his opponent.

A good negotiator allows patience to have her perfect work in the transaction *(James 1:4)*. He knows that his exercise of patience will cause him to inherit what God desires for him to have from the negotiations *(Hebrews 6:12)*.

OWNERSHIP CAN BECOME A GOD

... I will keep the passover at thy house ...
(Matthew 26:18).

In our society it has become so all important that we own our home, church, office building, etc., and we strive for that ownership even though it may mean years of bondage. We look upon those who rent as if they were second class citizens. The goal of ownership has truly become like a god, and we often make it the prime focus of our lives.

Let us not allow the god of ownership to delude us. If ownership is acquired by debt, then during the period of indebtedness, the lender is the controlling party and we hold ownership subject to the lender's dictates. If we do not think this is true, then just miss a few payments. The truth is, we own only that which is free of debt.

Jesus kept things in a much better perspective than we do. He deemed His mission more important than what He owned. Even when it came to performing the first communion service at Passover, Jesus did not care that it was held in a rented facility. He saw the upper room as God's supply for His need, and He cared not that the upper room was not His own.

There is nothing wrong with owning of property but, let us put ownership in its proper place behind meeting the call of God on our lives. Otherwise, ownership will become a god and hinder our service to Him.

THE COST OF DISHONEST PARTNERS

Whoso is partner with a thief hateth his own
soul: he heareth cursing, and bewrayeth it not
(Proverbs 29:24).

Sometimes we may find ourselves partner with a thief, but because the relationship is profitable we justify its continuance. When others begin to question us about our partner's ethics, we respond with sayings such as, "What my partner does on his own time is his business, not mine." For us to conduct ourselves in this manner is for us to hate our own soul.

If we are partners with a thief, his wrong will ultimately wind up on our doorstep. So to continue in partnership with a thief (not all thieves have guns and knives, some use only pens and pencils) is to ask to be thought of and become a thief. To permit that to happen is for us to hate our own soul.

(For more information on Partners and Partnerships, See also *Unequally Yoked,* at page 322; *The Hindrance Of Shared Authority,* at page 44; and, *In Corporate And Partnership Forms of Business, Authority Should Rest On the Anointed And Not Necessarily On The Investor* at page 45)

PRESSURE, AND OVERCOMING IT

God never puts us under pressure,
but He does place us in trials
(See the entire Bible).

Pressure is a distorted state of mind induced by our sinful, negligent, over-worked and over-committed flesh. God never over-worked or over-committed anyone; rather, these are situations in which we place ourselves through the exercise of improper priorities in our lives.

Pressure is present today because we live in a society that is truly Babylonian. The god of the Babylonian Society is the dollar, and the dollar god demands that we sacrifice God and family for the dollar. Unlike God, who offers fulfillment, Babylon does not know the meaning of fulfillment. Babylon is never satisfied. Hence, we are constantly subjected to the pressure of trying to satisfy a god, who by its own nature, can never be satisfied. The spirit of Babylon is truly the prince of pressure.

Pressure is easily overcome if we are willing to step from the flesh and over into the Word of God. It is from the Word that we can secure the faith and insight to eliminate the pressure. Once we have taken this step, we will produce more, have peace and be fulfilled by the love of Jesus Christ, the Prince of Peace. Furthermore, we will then have the wisdom and insight of God which will cause us to excel, even by Babylon's own monetary standards

(God does place us in trials, and that issue is dealt with in the section of this book entitled *Chastisement* at page 101.)

PROFIT

... Ask him to sell it to me for the
full price as a burial site among you
(Genesis 23:9 NIV).

Abraham's wife Sarah died, and he needed to purchase a burial place for her. He was willing to pay full price, which we can well assume included a profit to the seller. The story of Joseph in *Genesis Chapters 37-50* is replete with accounts of Joseph making a profit for Pharaoh at the direction of God. Peter, James and John were fishermen; Elisha was a farmer; Moses, Jacob and David were sheep herders; and Paul made tents - all presumably for a profit. God honors profit, but only as long as the profit is earned in a manner that honors Him.

God knows that if a business does not make a profit, that business will not be around for long. He wants us to profit, for to do so is to increase - and that honors Him; it is a fulfillment of His promises. The word "increase" is used 88 times in the King James Version of the Bible.

However, the Bible has much to say about how profits can be detrimental.

Fast Profits and Their Fallout

... but he that maketh haste to be rich
shall not be innocent
(Proverbs 28:20).

He that hasteth to be rich hath an evil eye, and
considereth not that poverty shall come upon him
(Proverbs 28:22).

Ethics In A Time Of Shrinking Profit

There is a generation that are pure in their own eyes,
and yet is not washed from their filthiness
(Proverbs 30:12).

We humans have a way of attempting to "purify our motives" by justifying our actions. This is especially true when profits begin to shrink and losses begin to appear. The pressure of that moment, if we are not careful, will cause us to substitute our own value system for God's Word. As we attempt to make that substitution, we are pure in our own eyes, but yet not washed from our filthiness before God.

The Penalty Of Placing Profit As A Priority Over Family

He that is greedy of gain troubleth his own house . . .
(Proverbs 15:27).

When profit becomes a priority over our family, greed has set in and the penalty will be a troubled family. At that point, we feebly attempt to justify the priority of our profit by spending a portion of those profits on our family.

Our family does not want our money - they need our time. When we give our families part of our profit and little of our time, we penalize our families with trouble.

Keeping Integrity and
Profit in Proper Perspective

A good name is rather to be chosen
than great riches, and loving favour
rather than silver and gold
(Proverbs 22:1).

Every day we are faced with choosing between "the bottom line" or our good name, and we will make the choice that is most important to us. Eventually, we will place the profit and loss statement in storage, and the amount of the bottom line will be forgotten; but our name follows us wherever we go, even to the grave.

Profit seems ever so important at the moment of decision, but when profit is divided by the number of years in eternity, it comes to much less than one cent per year regardless of the size of the enterprise. Let us keep profit and integrity in proper perspective.

FINANCIAL PROJECTIONS

Boast not thyself of to morrow; for thou
knowest not what a day may bring forth
(Proverbs 27:1).

There are two basic types of financial projections: (1) those used to <u>sell</u> deals, and (2) those used to provide us with information based on established past history, current events and "reasonable" expectations in the future.

Financial projections used to <u>sell</u> deals are most often boastful in nature because they are given to sell a venture that is not yet even in existence. So who can say, without boasting about tomorrow, what this untried venture will cost or make in profits? These kinds of projections are tools of manipulation.

On the other hand, financial projections that are used as a tool to provide us with information based on established past history, current events and reasonable expectations in the future are not boasting about tomorrow. These kinds of projections are planning tools for the future.

The difference in these two types of projections is the difference in selling and telling; and, the difference between the two is equal to the degree of manipulation in the selling.

(See *From Diligence To Manipulation To Burnout* at page 152; and, *Telling vs. Selling,* at page 38)

THE TRUE VALUE OF REAL PROPERTY

The lambs are for thy clothing, and the goats are the price
of the field. And thou shalt have goats' milk enough for
thy food, for the food of thy household, and for the
maintenance for thy maidens
(Proverbs 27:26-27 emphasis added).

It is easy for us to become so in love with a piece of real property that we pay too much for it. But, if we will remember that real property is worth no more than the number of goats it will support (in the Twentieth Century we call it "return on investment"), we will pay the correct price. Otherwise, we will pay too much for the property and run short of milk (cash).

IF WE ARE NOT CAREFUL, SUCCESS WILL BREED INTOXICATION

***And the men took of their victuals, and
asked not counsel at the mouth of the LORD
(Joshua 9:14).***

Because the Israelites had taken counsel from God, they enjoyed complete success in their battle against Jericho and the second battle of Ai. The Israelites victories in those battles caused the Gibeonites to ask the Israelites for protection. The Israelites, being intoxicated by their victory thought, "Why should we ask God about the simple matter of making an agreement to protect the Gibeonites, let's just agree to protect them."

This intoxication led the Israelites to believe that they no longer needed the counsel of God in making minor decisions. This decision, made without the counsel of God, caused the Israelites to have to fight five nations at one time. What the Israelites did not know was that the Gibeonites were defrauding them. If they had sought God's counsel, He would have revealed the fraud to them.

Success can be intoxicating and thereby cause us to forget the source of our success, seeking counsel at the mouth of God. Thus, if we do not keep our mind on God, it will be difficult for us to tell the difference between intoxication brought on by success on the one hand, and alcohol on the other.

(1) Tax Planning & Tax Paying

(2) Excessive Taxes Are Symptoms Of Our Rebellion Toward God

... Then saith he unto them, Render therefore unto Caesar the things which are Caesar's; and unto God the things that are God's
(*Matthew 22:21*).

When Jesus spoke these words, Caesar was on the throne in Rome and operating a tax collection system that would make the United States Internal Revenue Service look like a lamb. Jesus' words simply state that tax planning and tax paying are scriptural, regardless of who is collecting the taxes and how the taxes are being used by the government.

Now this does not at all mean that God always approves of how a certain government taxes its citizens and spends its dollars, but it does mean that we are to obey the taxing authority in the exercise of their authority over us.

The above scripture must be remembered in the context that God never intended for Rome to rule Israel. When the Israelites continually disobeyed God, He placed hard task masters (the Romans and others) over them in the hope that this chastising leadership would cause the Israelites to return to Him. But, when the Israelites did not return to God, they continued to live in slavery.

Harsh and inequitable taxes always grow out of rebellion to God by the people being taxed. So Jesus was really saying, "Do not concentrate on the tax because that is just the symptom; the problem is that we are in rebellion to Him by rebelling against the authority He has placed over us."

If we want to see our taxes reduced, we need to repent and return to God. He will then restore Godly government that will properly govern its affairs and tax us in a just manner.

TAX EVASION

*An unjust man is an abomination to the
just: and he that is upright in the
way is abomination to the wicked*
(Proverbs 29:27).

The man who does not report all of his income, and the man who does report all of his income, are each an abomination to the other. The tax evader attempts to justify his tax evasion by saying how stupid (abominable) the righteous man is if he does not steal from the government. On the other hand, the righteous man views the acts of the tax evader as an abomination because he is stealing from the government. *. . . render therefore unto Caesar the things which are Caesar's . . . (Matthew 22:21).*

The essence of tax evasion is rebellion to authority and all rebellion is ultimately directed at God. So the tax evader first has a problem with submitting to God's authority, and that problem manifests itself in the natural through tax evasion against the authority of the government. The spirit of evasion is eliminated only by a truly repentant heart toward God. One fruit of a repentant heart is willing submission to authority, including the filing of amended tax returns for the rebellious years.

PROPER TIMING

To every thing there is a season, and a time
to every purpose under the heaven: ...
(Ecclesiastes 3:1).

Timing is of utmost importance in all areas of our lives. Millions of dollars are spent annually in an attempt to "guess when" products and services should be brought on the market, etc. The search for proper timing probably causes as much anxiety in our lives as does any other single factor.

God tells us there is a season and a time to every purpose under the heaven. How often do we seek Him in our quest for proper timing? After all, He made the world so He knows the proper timing for everything. He promises that if we seek Him first, proper timing will be added unto us *(Matthew 6:33)*. The question is, do we have the patience to seek Him and wait for His time which is our proper timing?

CHASTISEMENT

Until the time that his word came;
the word of the Lord tried him
(Psalm 105:19).

Introduction

Chastisement is the Word of God trying us until the time comes for the Word of God to deliver us. It is God allowing us the opportunity to die to our ways and come alive in the Way of Christ.

Chastisement is probably the least known and most misunderstood of all of God's ways. This ignorance and misunderstanding stems from unscriptural views of God that are prevalent in christianity such as:

> God is available at my beckoned call to give me what I want when I want it, so all I have to do is ask and believe and I will receive;

> God must be causing these awful circumstances in my life and I am left by myself to suffer through; and

> God cannot be interested in my needs, why should He care for me.

These, and other unscriptural views of God cause us to focus on ourselves and what we think is the hand of God. We so often just do not understand the heart of God. His heart is expressed in His Word, and through His Word:

> He tells us His love and desires for us *(John 3:16);*

> He reaches out to us wherever we are *(John 3:16);*

He creates and allows circumstances into our lives that are designed by Him to humble us, prove us, find what is in our heart and find whether or not we will keep His commandments *(Deuteronomy 8:2);*

He delivers us *(Psalms 105:19);*

He judges us *(Isaiah and Jeremiah);* and

He accomplishes whatever else He desires to accomplish in our lives and in the lives of others.

As we begin to submit to His chastisement, we will become partakers of His Holiness *(Hebrews 12:10).* It is then that the same Word that is trying us, will begin to deliver us.

When Does Chastisement Occur?

And thou shalt remember all the way which the LORD thy God led thee these forty years in the wilderness, to humble thee, and to prove thee, to know what was in thine heart, whether thou wouldest keep his commandments or no. And he humbled thee, and suffered thee to hunger . . . (Deuteronomy 8:2-3).

Chastisement occurs when the Lord creates and allows circumstances into our lives that are designed by Him to humble us, prove us, find what is in our heart and find whether or not we will keep His commandments.

Why Does God Chasten Us?

Our fathers disciplined us for a little while as they thought best; but God disciplines us for our good, that we may share in his holiness (Hebrews 12:10 NIV).

He chastens us so we will have the opportunity to die to our self, come alive in Christ and share in His Holiness.

Are Sickness And Divorce Forms Of Chastisement?

No, Absolutely Not!

Which of you, if his son asks for bread, will give him a stone? Or if he asks for a fish, will give him a snake?
(Matthew 7:9&10 NIV).

God gets no glory from divorce and illness. He is not the author or cause of divorce or illness, He is The Restorer and The Great Healer.

How Are We to Act During Periods of Chastisement?

Chastisement affords to us the choice to praise God, become paranoid or wallow in self-pity. *(See Joseph in the well, as a slave and in prison, Genesis Chapters 37-40).*

Even though chastisement seems grievous for the moment, we are not to despise it, faint or become weary; we are to endure chastisement *(Hebrews Chapter12).*

We should pray to learn the lesson of chastisement, not pray that it be lifted *(Psalm 105:19).*

We are not to murmur. When we murmur in chastisement, we are really murmuring against God *(Numbers 14:9).* Murmuring is as rebellion and rebellion is as witchcraft *(I Samuel 15:23).*

Joseph was faithful in chastisement and was delivered out of chastisement *(Psalm 105:19).* The generation of Israel that came out of Egypt was unfaithful in chastisement and, therefore, died in judgment *(Numbers 14:23).*

We are to say to God as Jesus did in Gethsemane,...
nevertheless ... not as I will, but as thou wilt (Matthew 26:39).

What Is the Greatest Danger We Face When We Are Suffering Chastisement?

That we will allow the **pride** of our heart to prevent us from recognizing and enduring God's chastisement (*Jeremiah 49:16*).

Comment

We must learn that it is not a sin for us to feel pride, anxiety, pity and fear as they come against us in a time of chastisement. However, when we feel them coming we must, through our knowledge of and faith in the Word of God, resist and suppress those feelings and not allow them to be manifested in our lives. We must have the same resolution to obey the Word of God as did Jesus in Gethsemane... *nevertheless not as I will, but as thou wilt* (Matthew 26:39).

When we want to faint or become weary in the midst of the chastisement, we should remember that Jesus will never leave us or forsake us (*Hebrews 13:5*). He simply wants us to die to our way, and come alive in His Way. Then, and only then, can we truly serve Him.

The Three Sources of Pain in Our Lives

There are three sources of pain in our lives:

Chastisement, which is from God to prepare us to be partakers of His Holiness;

The consequences of our having acted outside of God's Word, which are the result of our sin; and

Tribulation, which is from Satan to kill steal and destroy us so we will not enter into the kingdom of God and His righteousness.

It is important that we be able to identify the source(s) of pain in our lives; for if we cannot, how will we know how to pray in the midst of the pain? Too often we blame Satan for chastisement, God for tribulation and give no thought that our sins of the past may be causing us pain today.

On the following page is a Chart that illustrates from Scripture the source, effect and purpose of each of the three sources of pain in our lives. The Chart also illustrates from Scripture how we are to handle the pain in each case.

THE THREE SOURCES OF PAIN

IN OUR LIVES

1 Chastisement	2 The Consequences of Our Having Acted Outside of God's Word	3 Tribulation
Source: Brought directly into lives by God to give us the opportunity to die to our self and come alive in Christ *(Hebrews 12:6)*.	**Source:** We bring adverse consequences on ourselves when we live outside of God's Word *(Jeremiah 2:19)*.	**Source:** Brought directly against us by Satan *(John 10:10)*.
Effect: Positive	**Effect:** Negative	**Effect:** Negative
Purpose: To prepare us to be partakers of God's Holiness *(Hebrews 12:10)*.	**Purpose:** The penalty for sin; i.e., the result of our living outside of God's Word *(Numbers 14:16)*.	**Purpose:** To kill and destroy us so we will not enter into the kingdom of God and His righteousness *(John 10:10)*.
Illustration: Joseph in the well, a slave in Potiphar's house and a prisoner *(Psalm 105:19)*.	**Illustration:** Israelites in the wilderness for 40 years *(Exodus, Leviticus, Numbers, Deuteronomy through Joshua 3)*.	**Illustration:** Satan entered into Judas to bring about the betrayal of Jesus *(John 13:27)*.
How To Handle the Pain: It is to be endured by us that we may partake of God's Holiness *(Hebrews 12:7 & 10)*. To rebuke Satan here is to blame him for what God is doing for us. We must patiently endure that God's Word can work Its purpose in us.	**How to handle the Pain:** Overcome by repenting, accepting God's forgiveness and obeying God's Word *(Acts 26:20)*. No need to rebuke Satan. Here, we suffer from our own disobedience of God's Word. Repent & proceed on into the righteousness of Jesus Christ.	**How to Handle the Pain:** Overcome by standing in the armor of God *(Ephesians 6:13-18)*. We need to rebuke Satan; and, if we tithe, God will rebuke him for us *(Malachi 3:12)*.

Any given painful situation in our life may be caused by 1, 2 and / or 3 above. God will not bring 2 and 3 into our lives to teach us; but He can, if we let Him, use them for our good. Joseph said to his brothers *. . . ye thought evil against me; but God meant it unto good. . .* *(Genesis 50:20)*.

A Short Treatise On Godly Church Governmental Structure, And Its Purpose

The Church is the Bride of Jesus Christ; therefore, all the more reason that the Church should embrace the governmental structure that Christ gave to men for all time as He ascended into Heaven:

The Five Fold Ministry

Wherefore he saith, When he ascended up on high,
he led captivity captive, and gave gifts unto men . . .
And he gave some, <u>apostles;</u> and some, <u>prophets;</u>
and some, <u>evangelists;</u> and some, <u>pastors</u>
and <u>teachers</u> ("the five fold ministry");
For the perfecting of the saints, for the work of
the ministry, for the edifying of the body of Christ:
Till we all come in the unity of the faith,
and of the knowledge of the Son of God,
unto a perfect man, unto the measure of the stature
of the fulness of Christ:
That we henceforth be no more children,
tossed to and fro, and carried about with every
wind of doctrine, by the sleight of men, and cunning
craftiness, whereby they lie in wait to deceive;
But speaking the truth in love, may grow up into him in
all things, which is the head, even Christ:
From whom the whole body fitly joined together
and compacted by that which every joint supplieth,
according to the effectual working in the measure
of every part, maketh increase of the body unto the
edifying of itself in love
(Ephesians 4:8 & 11-16 emphasis added).

The above 8 verses:

> Set in place apostles, prophets, evangelists, pastors and teachers as the government of the church, with that grouping commonly being referred to as "the five-fold ministry;"
>
> Define the purpose of the five-fold ministry to be that of perfecting the saints for the work of the ministry, and to edify the body of Christ;
>
> State the promise that through the government of the five-fold ministry, we will all come into the unity of faith, and the knowledge of the Son of God trained towards perfection unto the measure of the stature of the fullness of Christ;
>
> State the promise that the result of being trained by the five-fold ministry is to no longer be children anymore, tossed about by the wind of false and fraudulent doctrine; and
>
> As a result, we will become mature in Christ, and take our God given part in the Body of Christ.

A Bit Of Church History
(How democratic government crept into the Church)

If we are to set a course for the future of the Church, we must first understand why the Church is where it is on the issue of Church constitutions and by-laws.

Ephesians 4 sets forth God's will for Church government. And, please notice that all of the above promises in Ephesians 4 are accomplished without a vote of the Church membership, or action by its Church board. Why? Because God has ordained that the Church be governed as a theocracy from Heaven down and not as a democracy from the pew up. We must remember that the Church is the bride of the Righteous Groom, therefore, we should all the more be eager to submit to God's theocracy than to man's democracy.

God intended that the Church be to us as Heaven will be when we arrive there. The Church is no more ours than is Heaven, the Church belongs to God. We have no ownership in the Church by virtue of our membership or contributions, for our contributions were supposed to be free-will offerings to God - not entitlement to ownership or a position in management. Only the will of God prevails in Heaven, and the case should be likewise in Church. What we will be all about in Heaven is praising God, and that is the way it should be in Church.

However, somewhere in the last 2000 years much of the Church has gone astray. What happened? Over the centuries many in the Church decided to worship God on their terms, and not in accordance with the Bible. <u>As that decision was made time and again, it continually became necessary in each generation for man to devise a religious order of his own that met his desires for what he wanted God to be in his life.</u> Thus, man in his restructuring of the Church over the centuries, drew himself further and further away from God. Man desired to more be acceptable to man than he did to honor God, and the majority of Church government today reflects that to be the case.

The primary motivation for this change was to lower the worship of God to man's standard rather than to meet God's standard of the Bible; for man did not know, and did not want to know, the Bible because it too constricted his lusts to have his own selfish way in his church life. <u>Hence, the Church has introduced the Babylonian management structure of majority vote control on the board and in the membership.</u>

As a result, the five-fold ministry members, gifted by God in Ephesians 4, in our midst are relegated to hireling status. For the most part, the Church no longer recognizes the offices of apostle and prophet. Therefore, we no longer receive the "setting in order" from the apostle, or "the admonition and encouragement of the prophet;" rather, in their place we hear the advice of the "prominent members of the community" who were elected by majority vote to the Church board. Much of the Church just cannot live with apostles and prophets, for apostles and prophets are not at all reticent to be quite vocal when they see unscriptural activity in the Church. Accordingly, those two offices have all but disappeared from the Church.

As a result, rather than structuring the Church to meet the Great Commission, many are structured for the comfort of their members. These churches have no concept of Christ on the cross conforming to the will of the Father; that commitment is like a fairy tale to the people in these churches. True submission to Godly authority as set forth in the Bible is something that we as Christians know precious little about.

How Church and Ministry Board Members are too often Selected

There is a way that seemeth right unto a man, but the end thereof are the ways of death
(Proverbs 14:12).

Business and professional people, because of their position in the community, are often called to sit on church/ministry boards. They are generally so selected because churches and ministries have deluded themselves into believing that "If these people are successful in the business and professional arena, they will help our church/ministry to be successful." Some churches and ministries even go further and take a prostitute's view by saying "If we put them on the board, they will be more likely to give to us."

Jesus did not ask the rich young ruler for his balance sheet nor did He ask him to sit on His board; rather, He tested the rich young ruler's commitment to God. When it became clear that the young man had no commitment, Jesus let him go. Jesus did not keep him just because of his position in the community.

Success in Babylon's business world is certainly not at the top of God's criteria for selecting church and ministry board members. Godly board members are the likes of the widow who gave all she had, Stephen, Joseph of Arimithea, Peter, James, and John. The single most important criteria in selecting church and ministry board members should be, "What is their daily walk with God in all areas of their lives?" The fact that they are ditch diggers or doctors should not even enter into the selection process.

110

Do not select church and ministry board members on the basis of who will impress men, rather, select them on the basis of who can best lead this ministry in service to God.

Proper Church Government Requires Spiritual Maturity

We have much to say about this, but it is hard to explain because you are slow to learn. In fact, though by this time you ought to be teachers, you need someone to teach you the elementary truths of God's word all over again. You need milk, not solid food! Anyone who lives on milk, being still an infant, is not acquainted with the teaching about righteousness. But solid food is for the mature, who by constant use have trained themselves to distinguish good from evil. Therefore let us leave the elementary teachings about Christ and go on to maturity, not laying again the foundation of repentance from acts that lead to death, and of faith in God, instruction about baptisms, the laying on of hands, the resurrection of the dead, and eternal judgment. And God permitting, we will do so (Hebrews 5:11-6:3 NIV emphasis added).

The Church needs to understand that salvation is just the first step in a walk toward God. We need to go beyond the elementary truths of God's Word, and receive instruction in the solid food of God's Word - then, through the constant use of that solid food of the Word in our everyday life, we will be able to distinguish good from evil. The Church should be the source of this solid food teaching and instruction in how to walk it out in everyday life.

However, the Church, in the main, has failed in this regard. Why? Because the Church has been so careful to not upset people (because when the people are upset, the numbers and the offerings go down) that it has compromised basic Bible doctrine in drafting its constitutions and by-laws. So the people, who are hungry for the things of God, have often had to find the solid food of the Word on their own or elsewhere - hence the rise in para-church ministries like Insight to Freedom.

The Church can regain its lost ground. The first step in that walk is to restore basic church doctrines in the church constitution and by-laws. Spiritual maturity can never be achieved with less than the fullness of the basic Church doctrines being adopted and taught - all the while knowing in the process that some, and maybe many, will leave the Church. Wouldn't it be interesting to see really what would happen to the people if the Church were to begin restoring the basic doctrines of God's Word in the everyday operations and teachings of the Church? Personally, I believe that the Church would be pleasantly surprised, for there is a great hunger in the people for the truth.

The Bible As
the Perfect Church Constitution

The Bible is the Perfect Church Constitution. The Bible already sets forth the entire relationship between man and God, tells Who God is, and the fullness of His dealings with man. Man cannot write any document that would add anything to, or improve upon the Bible, so why not use the Bible as our church Constitution? Certainly, no one can argue that the Bible is incomplete.

Drafting Church By-Laws

The first rule in drafting and adopting church by-laws is for the drafter to well remember that God's Word is clear that the Church is to be governed by Him through His anointed servants of the fine ministry as a theocracy, and not by man as a democracy. The Church is to be governed by the will of God, not by the fashion of man by majority vote at the time of the vote. A set of church by-laws should simply set forth how that church will fulfill the basic doctrines of the Bible in the life of that church.

By-laws are never to have the practical effect of emasculating basic scriptural doctrine for worship and church government as set forth in the Bible. By-laws need to track the Bible, and not the will of the people at the time. Praise God that Jesus, Moses, Isaiah, Jeremiah and millions of others did not bow to the will of the people, but gave their lives for the basic doctrines of the Word of God. We must be willing to do the same, or, God will pass us by and raise up a later generation that will serve God. The cost to us of our unwillingness to serve God will be that we will have forfeited walking with Him; and, the cost to our children will be that they will receive little, if any, Christian heritage from us - and they will have to find God on their own.

The reason that the Church has given so much weight to by-laws, rather than the Bible as its Constitution, is that man is more familiar with what he has written than he is with what God has written. This needs to be reversed, for when it is reversed the churches we have today will not even begin to contain all who will want to come.

The Five-Fold Ministry Form of Church Government Can Come Only Out of Relationships Ordained by God for Each Particular Church

Our relationship with God comes into being the moment we accept Jesus Christ as our Savior. From that point forward, we can begin to grow into the fullness of the measure of Christ, but only at the rate and to the depth at which we deepen our relationship with. Him. The same principle holds true concerning the form of church government to which we are willing to submit ourselves.

Neither a Pastor nor his people can just run out one day and say, "We are going to find an apostle, prophet, evangelist and teacher with whom our church can have a Five-Fold Ministry relationship." Rather, a Pastor and his people must diligently seek God first for men walking in the offices of the Five-Fold Ministry. A relationship will develop out of this seeking that will cause and allow God to sovereignly bring to the people those Five-Fold Ministry spiritual leaders that their particular church needs. The appointment of Five-Fold Ministry relationships to a particular church is designed in heaven, not in a board room by the prominent business and professional people who are the "shakers and movers" in the local church.

Becoming a Five-Fold Ministry Church Will Require Its Members to Forfeit "Control" of Their Church in Accordance With Ephesians Chapter 4

Shallow Christians have the need to preserve "control" in their church, while mature Christians desire to be governed in Church affairs by those whom God has given spiritual gifts to be apostles, prophets, evangelists, pastors and teachers. Ephesians 4:8 &11 - 16 (See page 107 of this Book) sets forth the manifold benefits that come with a Five-Fold Ministry governed church.

Beware of Wolves in The Five-Fold Ministry

For the gifts and calling of God are without repentance **(Rom 11:29).** Members of the Five-Fold Ministry are fallible, and can fall away from God just as can the rest of us. Even so, God will not repent of the gifts and callings He has placed on their and our lives. These wolves will often ply their God given Five-Fold Ministry gifts and callings for their own personal enrichment to the detriment of those they were meant to serve.

Symptoms of a wolf like behavior are: the lack of a servant's heart, while the wolf must have the most prominent part of the service; Jesus came for free, while a wolf comes for a minimum set fee; Jesus came on a donkey, while a wolf specifies first class air travel, an entourage of associates and a certain limousine for ground transportation; Jesus spent time alone with the woman at the well, while the wolf demands a guaranteed minimum crowd; Jesus never took up an offering, while for the wolf the offering is the most important part of the service; and, while Jesus spent time with the children, the wolf has no time to spend with "the little people."

SEE THE "APPENDIX " (beginning at Page 328) AT THE END OF THIS BOOK FOR A SAMPLE CHURCH FIVE- FOLD MINISTRY CONSTITUTION AND BY LAWS

BEING ABOVE OUR CIRCUMSTANCES

Even in darkness light dawns for the upright . . . .
(Psalm 112:4, NIV).

Though the circumstances of <u>the upright</u> appear to be disastrous, they can look to the dawning of the light of the Word for strength to carry them through those circumstances. Who are <u>the upright?</u> The upright:

> **Walk blameless**
> **Do what is righteous**
> **Speak the truth from their hearts**
> **Have no slander on their tongues**
> **Do their neighbor no wrong**
> **Cast no slur on their fellowman**
> **Despise a vile man**
> **Honor those who fear the Lord**
> **Keep their oath even when it hurts**
> **Lend their money without usury**
> **Do not accept a bribe against the innocent**

(The above is a condensation from Psalm 15:2-5 of the NIV).

<u>What Do We Desire Most in Life,</u>
<u>A Change in Circumstances or Christ?</u>

But seek ye first the kingdom of God, and his righteousness;
and all these things shall be added unto you
(Matthew 6:33).

If the focus of our life is on changing our circumstances rather than on developing an intimate relationship with God through Christ, no amount of changed circumstances will ever be satisfying to us. This is true because a concentration on circumstances is a concentration on flesh, and the flesh can never be satisfied.

But if we desire more to know about Christ than we do to change our circumstances, we will continually be fulfilled. This is true because God made us in His image, and we are fulfilled only when we seek to know more about Him.

Our Freedom Does Not
Depend Upon Our Circumstances

If the Son therefore shall make you
free, ye shall be free indeed
(John 8:36).

We all want to be free. Free from the pressures of cash flow, personnel problems, debt, etc. But, if we had all of the money in the world and were free of these pressures, would we necessarily be free? No.

The spiritual controls the natural. Unless we are free in the spiritual we shall never be free in the natural, regardless of our circumstances at the time. That is why he whom Jesus sets free is free indeed, regardless of our adverse circumstances at any given time.

An example is the thief on the cross who accepted Jesus as Savior just before he died. He, too, like Jesus, was naked and his physical body held captive to the cross by nails in his hands and feet - yet, salvation made him a free man before his death. His freedom did not depend upon his circumstances, neither does ours.

Compliments Vs. Flattery

A man that flattereth his neighbor
spreadeth a net for his feet
(Proverbs 29:5).

Compliments are based solely on facts and come from the servant's heart of the speaker. Flattery is not based on fact and comes from the desire of the speaker to get something for himself that he does not deserve. Flattery is deceit.

For someone to flatter us is for them to lay a net of deceit in front of our feet. If we are wise, we will see the net for what it is and avoid the net. But, if we are not wise we will step into the net by believing the flattery, and that will cause us to fall.

CONDEMNATION AND OVERCOMING IT

There is therefore now no condemnation
to them which are in
Christ Jesus, who walk not after the flesh,
but after the spirit
(Romans 8:1).

Condemnation occurs only <u>when we believe</u> Satan's lie that, "God cannot forgive us for what we did in the past; therefore, He does not love us." We overcome condemnation only when we choose to ask forgiveness for our sins and believe in faith that Jesus' blood washed away all of our sins.

The choice is ours.

KEEPING MATTERS IN CONFIDENCE

... and discover not a secret to another:
Lest he that heareth
it put thee to shame, and thine infamy turn not away
(Proverbs 25:9-10).

How many times have we been asked to keep a matter in confidence, and we just could not wait to tell the matter to someone else. This type of behavior is common to us all. The Psalmist said in *Psalm 103:14,* **For he knoweth our frame, he remembereth that we are dust.** Dust is not very stable.

Remember that dust frame of a man named Saul, who assisted in the murder of Stephen and only a few days later was leading people to salvation? What caused the change in him? He met Christ on the road to Damascus and submitted his life to Him.

Once we accept Jesus as Savior we, too, will have the power in us to **... discover not a secret to another...** If we will submit to that power, we will be faithful to both God and the person who gave us their confidence. But, if we are not submitted to Christ, our mouths will put us to shame and we shall forever be infamous in the eyes of the one with whom we broke confidence.

CONFRONTATION -

GODLY VS. UNGODLY

... all the congregation of the children of Israel
murmured against Moses and against Aaron ...
(Numbers 16:41).

And Nathan said to David, Thou art the man ...
(II Samuel 12:7).

Ungodly confrontation originates in pride and its purpose
is to elevate ourselves at the expense of humiliating others.
This is where the Israelites were coming from when they
murmured against Moses and Aaron. It was this ungodly
confrontation that caused God to bring a plague against Israel,
and 14,000 people died. Ungodly confrontation always carries
with it a penalty upon those causing the confrontation.

On the other hand, Godly confrontation originates out
of obedience to God's Word, and its purpose is to bring others
into knowing the love of Jesus Christ. When Nathan confronted
David with his sin, David repented and God allowed him to
remain as King of Israel. Godly confrontation always carries
with it the grace of God.

Confrontation should never be used lightly. It is one of
God's ways to bring His people into a closer walk with Him
through Jesus Christ.

Only By Pride
Cometh Contention . . .

Only by pride cometh contention . . .
(Proverbs 13:10).

The Word of God succinctly addresses the root of all issues in life, and contention is no exception. All contention comes from pride, nowhere else.

If two girls are in contention over a doll, the doll is not the problem, pride is. If a couple is in contention in their marriage, their marriage is not the problem, pride is. If two men are in contention over a business, the business is not the problem, pride is. If two professional people are in contention over a client, the client is not the problem, pride is. Contention is always only a symptom, and pride is always the cause of the contention.

Eliminating Contention

So, how do we eliminate contention? We eliminate contention only by recognizing and repenting for the sin of pride that caused the contention. When the pride is recognized and repented for, the symptoms of contention automatically disappear.

FINDING CONTENTMENT

There is that maketh himself rich, yet hath nothing; there is that maketh himself poor, yet hath great riches
(Proverbs 13:7).

Man was created by God in the image of God, not by the world in the image of the world. Therefore, man will find contentment only in the ways of God and not in the ways of the world. This is why success in the world's terms never brings contentment, it only breeds a lustful desire for more success.

There is absolutely no correlation between contentment and possessions. We have great contentment only when we become poor by giving of ourselves and our possessions to others. This is why I *Corinthians 3:19* states, ***for the wisdom of this world is foolishness with God.*** Hence, when we make ourselves poor by giving of ourselves and our possessions to others, we will find the great richness of contentment.

IDENTIFYING GODLY COUNSEL

The LORD by wisdom hath founded the earth; by
understanding hath he established the heavens.
By his knowledge the depths
are broken up, and the clouds drop down dew
(Proverbs 3:19-20).

How do we identify Godly counsel? Answer, ask the person giving the counsel to substantiate his counsel by several passages in the written Word of God. If he can do so, his counsel is Godly. If he cannot, his counsel is ungodly.

The Perfect Counsel

There is no wisdom nor understanding
nor counsel against the LORD
(Proverbs 21:30).

The perfect counsel in all matters is that counsel which comes directly from the Word of God. Why? Because no wisdom, understanding or counsel from any other source can ever prevail against the Lord. He and His counsel are perfect and are available to us simply for the asking *(Matthew 6:33).*

Refuse Ungodly Counsel

Cease, my son, to hear the instruction that
causeth to err from the words of knowledge
(Proverbs 19:27).

We must refuse to hear anyone's counsel that will cause us to act contrary to God's Word. We are not to give such counsel even a second thought.

How do we know what Godly Counsel is? Ask the person giving the counsel to substantiate his counsel by several passages in the written Word of God. If he can, his counsel is Godly; if he cannot, his counsel is ungodly.

The Counsel of Many

Without counsel purposes are disappointed: but in the multitude of counsellors they are established
(Proverbs 15:22).

God's Word states that all Christians are members in one body *(Romans 12:4).* Each of us is no more than a finger, ear, nose or toe. For that reason, if we are going to establish the purposes of God in our lives, we must seek the counsel of the other members in the body of Christ. Otherwise, His purposes for us will be disappointed.

No one Christian knows all of the wisdom of God. That is why we are to rely upon each other for counsel. It is through the balance of the counsel of many Godly people that God's purposes for our lives will be established.

Receive A Friend's Counsel

Iron sharpenth iron; so a man sharpeneth the countenance of his friend
(Proverbs 27:17).

The most valued friend is one who is willing to "speak his piece" to us. The question is, are we willing to listen? To listen and take heed is to be sharpened; but to ignore a friend's counsel is to go bluntly on in life following our blind pride, which comes before a fall.

A Counselor's First Responsibility

He that rebuketh a man afterwards shall find more
favor than he that flattereth with the tongue
(*Proverbs 28:23*).

A counselor's first responsibility begins even before he accepts the job. That responsibility is to ask the question, "Are you open to receiving correction?" If there is any reticence in the answer, we should decline to serve. Otherwise, we will be no more than a flatterer with the title "counselor." In the end, those who issue correction find favor and those who flatter find disfavor. Why should we set ourselves up for disfavor?

COURTESY

The poor useth entreaties;
but the rich answereth roughly
(Proverbs 18:23).

We have all seen the humble, soft speaking, poor man addressing the rich, and the loud mouth rich man addressing the poor. One is humbled by his circumstances and the other is prideful in his circumstances.

Pride has no room for courtesy, and it comes before a fall *(Proverbs 18:12)*. A man whose God is the Lord will be courteous to others. A man whose god is his riches will answer roughly and does not know the meaning of courtesy.

DEBT

If you fully obey the LORD your God and carefully follow all his commands I give you today, the LORD your God will set you high above all the nations on earth. All these blessings will come upon you and accompany you if you obey the LORD your God . . . : <u>The LORD will open the heavens, the storehouse of his bounty, to send rain on your land in season and to bless all the work of your hands. You will lend to many nations but will borrow from none. The LORD will make you the head, not the tail</u> . . . (Deut 28:1-2 &12-13 NIV emphasis added).

Preamble

Just as God has set in motion the physical laws of wind, tides, gravity and the precise movements of the planets, so did He set in motion certain spiritual laws that manifest themselves in the natural and spiritual realms of our lives. These spiritual laws are sometimes referred to as "the Ways of God." The purpose of the Ways of God are to bless us and free us from the entanglements of the world so that we can be free to serve Him when and as His Spirit directs.

On the other hand, the world, too, has its own set of ways, and we refer to the world's ways as "the ways of Babylon." The core purpose of the ways of Babylon is to have us to honor Babylon ahead of all else, including God. For instance, in Babylon's terms debt always includes interest and collateral. The word "interest" is not used in the Old Testament, rather, the word "usury" is often used; and we will discuss the meaning of "usury" later in this section on *DEBT*.

A past due debt in the world's terms means foreclosures and law suits - all being entanglements under the ways of Babylon. That is why Proverbs 22:7 states, ***The rich rule over the poor, and the borrower is servant to the lender*** (Prov 22:7 NIV). If you do not think the lender is your master, just miss a payment.

Why Are We in Debt?

There are four major groupings of people in debt:

First, are those who, for whatever reason, have not yet been able to break the several generation cycle of poverty into which they were born, and they are bound to debt just to exist day to day. It is these people that the Babylonian system charges unconsciousable interest rates like 25% or more;

Second, are those who through the expenses incurred by virtue of disease, accidents, natural disasters, sudden economic reversals, war, etc. had no participation in the cause of the debt, but nonetheless are bound to debt just to exist day to day;

Third, are those who incur debt to live beyond their means, and simply do not have the discipline to conduct themselves otherwise; and

Fourth, are those who determine to use their ordinary income to live within their means and work toward eliminating what debt they may have over as short a period of time as possible, knowing that to do so will cause them to sacrifice what many of their peers will not find acceptable.

How Do These Four Groups of People Become Debt Free?

However, there should be no poor among you, for in the land the LORD your God is giving you to possess as your inheritance, he will richly bless you, if only you fully obey the LORD your God and are careful to follow all these commands I am giving you today. For the LORD your God will bless you as he has promised, <u>and you will lend to many nations but will borrow from none.</u> You will rule over many nations but none will rule over you (Deuteronomy 15: 4-6 NIV emphasis added).

The above scripture sets forth the Way of God for all of His people to come out of debt. While the above scripture was written for the benefit of the Israelites who were about to cross over the Jordan and into the Promised Land, it is also serves as a type and shadow of New Testament people standing poised to walk out of debt and enter into the fullness of service in the kingdom of God... *if only you fully obey the LORD your God and are careful to follow all these commands I am giving you today. For the LORD your God will bless you as he has promised, and you will lend to many nations but will borrow from none.* Regardless of which of the above five debt groups we are in, the Way out of debt is the same.

Each of Us Has A Decision To Make.

We, in this generation, have a decision to make: Are we going to continue and pass on this legacy of "having to borrow" or, are we going to discipline ourselves and our children to "wean" ourselves and themselves off of debt so that we and they will be free to serve God unfettered by debt? Certainly, whether or not someone is in debt does not adversely affect their salvation; however, debt inhibits and, in some cases, may actually preclude our ability to respond to God's call on our life in a timely manner. So the issue of debt is not a situation where "it would be nice to be out of debt", rather, it is a fact that needs to be reckoned with if we and our future generations are to be free to serve God when and as He wills.

Not Borrowing/Rule or Relationship

(See David and his men eating shewbread in *I Samuel 21:1-6;* and See also Jesus and his disciples picking corn on the Sabbath in *Matthew 12:1-8.)*

We should not make "not borrowing" a rule, for if we make it a rule, "not borrowing" will become legalistic overnight. Rather, we should make "not borrowing" a part of our relationship with God based upon our respect for Him. Then, "not borrowing" will bring good fruit into our lives.

The Balance of Borrowing While Coming Out of Debt vs. Godly Priorities

Regardless of our situation at any given time, God loves us and knows that a period of time is needed for our life circumstances to transition from where they are to where He wants them to be. An initial step in that transition is to get our priorities in accordance with the order of the Ten Commandments i.e., worship, family, and then all other things, including not borrowing. Hence, there are priorities in our lives that may well take precedence for the moment over whether or not we should borrow. Some examples of those priorities are preservation of the family unit, honoring of the lender as our master and consolidation loans.

Preservation of the Family Unit

It would be optimum for us to make the decision to never borrow again; but the rigor of that discipline, added to the current friction that may already exist in our families, could be the straw that brakes the family unit. So borrowing may need to continue for a while to preserve the family unit, but such borrowing should always "be incurred with an eye towards the point when it is no more." Preserving the integrity of the family unit is certainly a priority over not borrowing. We should not make the decision to borrow or not to borrow until family stability has begun to take hold. But, at the same time, we must not allow family instability to serve as an excuse to borrow.

Honoring the Lender As Our Master

The rich ruleth over the poor, and the borrower is the servant to the lender (Proverbs 22:7).

When we borrow we make the lender our master, so he has authority over the way we handle our finances. If he tells us to borrow to pay him interest or principle, then we must do so. Yet, remember that we do not have to give the lender blind obedience. He is dealing with us from a Babylonian standpoint that respects negotiations. So in honoring our lender, we should not at all be reluctant to negotiate a better position for ourselves in the process of restructuring our debt.

Isaiah and Jeremiah well record how the Israelites' sin of impatience and covetousness caused them for a time to have to serve Babylon rather than God. Debt does the same to us. But, if we will return to God, He will return to us, take us out of the captivity of debt and into the freedom of a walk with Him.

Consolidation Loans

The mere making of the decision to take control of, and eventually get out of, debt is a step toward making Jesus our Master rather than the lender. The journey out of debt, as do all journeys, requires a first step. Consolidation loans may well be that first step. The benefit of consolidation loans is to lower payments and interest rates. Once this is achieved, we are on the way out of debt provided we keep our eyes on God as our source throughout the pay-out period.

Does Borrowing Place Us in A Better Position than God Desires for Us?

Some will say, "If I had not borrowed money and paid interest I would not have so-and-so today." However, if we had obeyed God and not borrowed, what would we have today out of obedience to His Word? We will never know. So let us not be presumptuous and believe that borrowing has put us ahead of where we would be if we had obeyed God's Word and not borrowed. Remember, He promises in *Deuteronomy 15:6 and 28:12* that if we will obey Him, we will not have to borrow.

Why Debt Workouts Are Extended and Painful

And now have I given all these lands into the hand of Nebuchadnezzar the king of Babylon, my servant; and the beasts of the field have I given him also to serve him. And all nations shall serve him, and his son, and his son's son, until the very time of his land come; and then many nations and great kings shall serve themselves of him
(Jeremiah 27:6-7 emphasis added).

. . . I will acknowledge them that are carried away captive of Judah, whom I have sent out of this place into the land of the Chaldeans for their good. For I will set mine eyes upon them for good, . . . and I will bring them again to this land . . .
(Jeremiah 24:5-6).

There is a saying, "We run into debt, but we will always crawl out." While this saying is worldly, it has spiritual parallels. Since the Israelites had run to their foreign gods, God sent the heathen King Nebuchadnezzar as His servant to take them captive, and He had them to crawl out of this slavery for the next 70 years. Our choice of a master other than God always brings the pain of slavery, *. . . until the very time of his land come . . .*

The fact of debt may be evidence of our having run to the lender as our master rather than Christ. God uses our creditors as His servants to rule over us during the period of the debt workout. This period of creditor rule is always painful and extends *. . . until the very time of his land come . . .*

However, this extended and painful period will be for our own good if we have a heart to learn. It is a time for reflection, returning to the basics and, most of all, returning to God. As we return to Him, He will set His eyes upon us for good and return us to our land by taking us out of debt. This procedure is extended and painful, but it indelibly places in our minds the servitude of debt vs. the goodness of God. Let us not have short memories of the pain of slavery and later return to debt.

Lending to Others

Many people say, "Well if I am not to borrow, then how can I lend?" The Bible addresses our lending to: (1) other nations *(Deuteronomy 15:6 and 28:12)*, and (2) to the needy *(Exodus 22:25)*.

(1) Lending to Other Nations

The term "other nations" as used in *Deuteronomy 15:6 and 28:12* means "a foreign nation, gentile heathen nation, people." Who are these people today? They are those who hear the Word of God about borrowing, and then decide to borrow in spite of the Word. It is proper to lend to them and collect interest.

(2) Lending to the Needy

Now, let us look for a moment at how a lending transaction is to be handled when we lend to the poor:

"If you lend money to one of my people among you who is needy, do not be like a moneylender; charge him no interest. If you take your neighbor's cloak as a pledge, return it to him by sunset, because his cloak is the only covering he has for his body. What else will he sleep in? When he cries out to me, I will hear, for I am compassionate (Exodus 22:25 - 27 NIV).

Obviously, God's ways make provision for us to lend to the poor, but not on interest. While the poor brother can pledge his cloak as collateral for the loan, the lender is to return the borrower's cloak to the borrower when the borrower needs it.

Obviously, God recognizes that some of his people will be poor and will have to borrow and, if others of us have substance, we are to lend to the brother who is poor - but not at all according to the world's way of lending.

Also, a lending brother has to respond to Deuteronomy 15:1-2, *At the end of every seven years you must cancel debts. This is how it is to be done: Every creditor shall cancel the loan he has made to his fellow Israelite. He shall not require payment from his fellow Israelite or brother, because the Lord's time for canceling debts has been proclaimed* (NIV emphasis added).

It would have been best if the generations before us had walked in the ways of God, earned their way out of debt and passed to us assets sufficient whereby we would not have to borrow for the "necessities" of life. However, that has just not happened; and, since we are living in the same manner as have our previous generations, the issue of debt in the world's terms has become an even more serious problem that adversely affects us more than we often realize.

The Real Cost of Borrowed Money

The real cost of borrowed money is measured in lost opportunity to spread the Gospel. As the following example hopefully depicts, every dollar paid in interest into our Babylonian system is a dollar lost to spreading the Gospel.

One July evening Donna and I were sitting in the Hillside Cathedral at the annual Fishnet Festival in Front Royal, Virginia. Larry Andes, the President of Fishnet and a good friend of ours, came on stage to encourage the approximately 16,000 people present to contribute to Fishnet's annual $750,000 budget.

Sitting there I prayed, "Why does he even have to encourage the people to give, why don't they just give?" I will never forget God's answer, "Because My people are in debt to the lender and cannot afford to give." I then remembered that each year, for several years, approximately 1,000 people had

134

been led to the Lord at Fishnet. It was then that the following equation came to my mind:

The Fishnet Equation

16,000 people in attendance at Fishnet divided by 4 people per family = 4,000 families

If only 3,000 of those 4,000 christian families owed $500/mo. in interest payments x 12 mos. = $18,000,000/yr. in interest paid by those 3,000 Christian families.

$18,000,000/yr. in interest payments divided by the $750,000 annual Fishnet budget = enough finances to conduct 24 annual Fishnets rather than only 1.

24 Fishnets x 1,000 average people saved per Fishnet = 24,000 people that could be saved rather than just 1,000.

Because those 3,000 christian families at Fishnet were in debt at the rate of $500 per mo. in interest each year, 23,000 people will have to hear the Gospel from some source other than Fishnet.

THE BODY OF CHRIST DOES NOT NEED MORE FINANCES, WE NEED ONLY TO USE WISELY THE RESOURCES WE HAVE ALREADY BEEN GIVEN.

Interest - A Super Expensive Tax Deduction

. . . and he that earneth wages earneth
wages to put it into a bag with holes
(Haggai 1:6).

Interest payments are widely touted as being beneficial to us as tax deductions. But what is our goal in business, to pay the lender or ourselves? It does not take a genius to figure out that for us to write off a dollar from our income for interest payments, we must first pay the whole dollar to the lender. Why not refrain from borrowing, pay the percentage of income tax on the dollar, and keep the after-tax portion of the dollar for ourselves? To write off $1 on taxes we have to first pay the whole $1 in interest to the lender, and we have zero left in our hand. Why not pay the tax of say .45 cents on the dollar, keep the remaining .55 cents for ourselves, and pay the lender zero?

Truly, to expend the effort to earn the dollar and then pay it all to the lender to get a tax deduction is to ... *earneth wages to put it into a bag with holes.* It is fashionable in Babylonian circles to boast about how much interest we pay. Would not it be intelligent to stop boasting, get out of debt, and not have to pay the lender anything?

Satan is ever so subtle in his control of our Babylonian system. He has even convinced many believers of his lie that it is beneficial to pay interest to the lender! Satan obviously would rather have the dollars paid in interest to a Babylonian system than for them to be given in offerings to God. I, too, believed this lie for a time.

Interest Payments Are as The Bite Of A Serpent

Unto a stranger thou mayest lend upon usury; but unto thy brother thou shalt not lend upon usury: that the Lord thy God may bless thee in all that thou settest thine hand to ...
(Deuteronomy 23:20).

The word "interest" is not used in the Bible, but the word "usury" is used in both the Old and the New Testaments. In neither is the word "usury" used kindly. The world money system has cleverly altered the meaning of the word "usury" to mean too much interest; while in the Hebrew and the Greek, usury means any interest at all.

In the Old Testament language of Hebrew, to charge usury is tantamount to the bite of a serpent, and a righteous man never charged usury to a brother *(Psalm 15:5)*. But a lender could charge usury to a "stranger," and a stranger was a person of the world who would not accept the ways of God.

A serpent's bite takes from us and gives us nothing in return just as do interest payments; i.e., they have no value. We spend our time laboring to earn money to pay interest, and have no value whatsoever in our hands to show for the interest payments. Just as a serpent's bite wastes our strength, so do interest payments make waste of our labors.

Endorsing Notes

Be not thou one of them that strikes hands, or of them that are sureties for debts (Proverbs 22:26).

A man void of understanding striketh hands, and becometh surety in the presence of his friend (Proverbs 17:18).

He that is surety for a stranger, shall smart for it: He that hateth suretyship is sure (Proverbs 11:15).

Take his garment that is surety for a stranger . . . (Proverbs 20:16).

Who needs to say more? (Also read "Godly Capital" at page 53)

MAKING DECISIONS BY THE BOOK

Anyone who lives on milk, still being an infant, is not acquainted with the teaching about righteousness. But solid food is for the mature, who by constant use, have trained themselves to distinguish good from evil. Therefore let us leave the elementary teachings about Christ and go on to maturity . . .
(Hebrews 5:13-14 & 6:1 NIV).

We Christians have a failing. For whatever reasons we have at the time, we are too often content to make decisions based only upon a milk-level knowledge of the Word. We are not willing to pay the required cost of diligence needed to seek spiritual maturity from the solid food of the word. So even through we are righteous through Christ, we do not have the spiritual maturity necessary to make righteous decisions.

God's people must learn the vast difference that exists between being made righteous by Christ versus walking in the righteousness of Christ. There is certainly no intent here to belittle our being made righteous by Christ, but we must understand that Jesus never meant for us to stop there. He means for us to mature beyond the elementary principle of salvation and proceed on into a daily walk of righteousness with Him.

And I heard another voice from heaven, saying, Come out of her (Babylon) *my people, that ye be not partakers of her sins, and that ye receive not of her plagues*
(Revelation 18:4 emphasis added).

The practical effect of our milk-level existence as Christians is that we make decisions just like the world (the Babylonians) does. Living proof of our milk-level existence is the divorce rate, adultery, church bickering and financial problems in Christian families today. These conditions also confirm the statement in

Revelation 18:4, that many of today's Christians are participating in Babylon's sins and receiving her plagues.

No wonder the world often views Christians as being hypocritical; we say we are Christians but, at the same time, we make decisions and live just like the Babylonians. It is easy to understand why so many in the world do not care to know our God!

That is why God is continually calling Christians *. . . my people . . .* out of the Babylonian ways of this world (Revelation 18:4). The way out is to seek the solid food of the Word of God, and to constantly use that Word in our everyday life so we can distinguish good from evil. Then we will know how to make decisions in a righteous manner.

The purpose of *Decisions By The Book* is to encourage people to constantly seek and apply the solid food of the Bible in your everyday decision making process. God did not write the Bible because he had nothing else to do. He wrote the Bible for us to live by in our home, church, government and work place. Now let us put the Bible to the use that God intended, and make all of our decisions based on the wisdom it contains.

The Proper Foundation for Decision Making

And thou shalt bind them (God's Word) for a sign upon thine hand, and they shall be as frontlets between thine eyes (Deuteronomy 6:8).

How often have we made decisions and did not know if they were right or wrong. We often say, "Well, I made the decision based on all of the information available at the time, and I hope it was correct."

God does not intend for us to "shoot in the dark" in our decision making process. Rather, He directed us to bind the Word on our hand and wear It in front of our eyes so that we can see the issues as He does. The Word of God is the foundation for proper decision making. When we view the issues to be decided through the eye of the Word, the insight of the Word will <u>always</u> grant to us the foundation to decide the issues correctly.

Making Decisions in the Midst of Confusion

For she said, if I may touch but his clothes,
I shall be whole
(Mark 5:28).

We have all experienced those times when confusion reigns and it seems impossible to make decisions in the chaos of the moment. Creditors are banging at the door, orders are not filled, construction is behind, equipment is breaking down, children are crying, the house is not clean, supper is not ready, the car is broken down and we are out of money.

Such was the scene when Jesus and His disciples walked into a certain city and a woman, who had been suffering a disease for 12 years, touched His garment. She knew that if she touched His garment, she would be healed. In the midst of this multitude of people who were yelling, pushing and shoving to get close to Jesus, this lady made the decision to focus on touching his garment and was healed.

We, too, need to learn to focus on Jesus in the midst of confusion. The peace resulting from our looking to Him will enable us to make proper decisions in the midst of the confusion of the moment.

Making Painful Decisions

For God so loved the world, that He gave His only
begotten son, that whosoever believeth in Him should
not perish, but have everlasting life (John 3:16).

No one, not even God, is exempt from making painful decisions. If God could make the excruciatingly painful decision to sacrifice His only Son for us, most certainly we can and should make the painful decisions that face us.

Approaching painful decisions is like taking a journey through the darkest night, because there is never a "good time" to make a painful decision. Delaying these decision only causes them to be more painful to make later. Make the decisions in the light of God's word, and move on in life knowing that His Word is working His Will in the matter.

Eliminating the Risk Factor in Decision Making

And it shall be, if thou wilt hearken unto all that I command thee, and wilt walk in my ways, and do that is right in my sight, to keep my statutes and commandments, as David my servant did; that I will be with thee, and build thee a sure house . . . .
(I Kings 11:38).

Where in God's Word did He ever require anyone to ever take a risk? Nowhere! To give obedience to God's Word is to eliminate the element of risk in decision making for our families, finances and ministry. We have strayed so far away from God's Word that we engage everyday in what we call "taking acceptable risks;" but not even the taking of "an acceptable risk" is pleasing to God. He has promised that if we will obey Him, He will *. . . build thee a sure house . . .*

God never meant for us to be subject to risk taking. Every step we take away from his Word is a step toward risk taking. It is a sin to leave the surety of God's Word for the sake of taking a risk to satisfy the desires of our flesh. Let us make our decisions according to His Word, and thereby eliminate the risk factor in decision making.

God, and not man, made the universe, so He gets to set the rules. Our man made rules, uncertain and ever changing as they are, provide for risk taking. But God's Word, His love letter to us, provides for certainty and the elimination of any risk factor in decision making. His will is that we *. . . prosper withersoever thou goest* *(Joshua 1:7)*, and have *. . . a sure house . . .* with no risk.

How Governmental and Court Decisions Are Made

The king's heart is in the hand of the LORD, as the rivers of water: he turneth it withersoever he will *(Proverbs 21:1).*

God uses everything for His own purposes including judges, zoning boards, administrative officers, etc. Now that we know the hearts of these officials are in the hand of God, and that He turns their hearts wheresoever He will, so let us offer prayers for those in authority a part of our diligent preparation to appear before them.

If our ways please the Lord, God will use the hearing officer to bless us, but that does not necessarily mean the case will be decided as we want at the time. Let us not pray to win or lose; rather, let us pray that God's will be done in the matter. Such willingness on our part to trust God leaves the matter in the hand of the Lord, right where the hearing officer's heart happens to be. Then the decision, whatever it may be, will be of God's choosing and that is the way we should want the decision to be made.

DEPRESSION OVERCOME

by Donna K. Deal

What you are about to read is the outcome of over 12 years of struggle with debt and corresponding depression. In order to explain how I recovered from depression I must give some preiminary testimony.

My personality during the time of our plunge into debt could be described as pessimistic, compromising, hesitating, conservative, slow to act. My motivational gift is mercy. Although having been a Christian from childhood, there was something spiritual in adult life missing and my husband and I experienced a Baptism of the Spirit a few years after we were married. From that time forward we began to walk a more committed Christian life.

Sadly, though, our personal characteristics had no time to undergo changes by the Spirit, and we impetuously overreacted by doing "good works." Good works, such as helping to financially support ministries, by investing in promising deals, coupled with our own greed and pride, quickly resulted in $6.5 million of debt.

So what then? We had committed our lives to the Lord and our life seemed to be falling apart. (That's the point!) Since our back was to the wall, in that there was no way out except suicide or bankruptcy or trust God, we chose to trust God. Little did I know that when I made a commitment of faith, God would chasten me by forcing me into a conflict that would prove me.

Now, my faith was not very great at this time. I knew Jesus was the Son of God and all those things we recite in the Apostles Creed, but I did not know how God interacted in a personal way with us. So, I just had a glimmer of hope that he would do what we were learning He said He would do. I look back on my beginning faith steps and realize that my hope was a culture in which faith seeds grew. As I dropped in more scriptural truths, my hope grew. The doubt seeds became less and less over a period of many years. My faith also grew as I saw God perform daily miracles. I once heard the story of a missionary who grew old, became ill and her family sought to bring her home to live out her last days. She refused saying about her ministry to people, "I have shown them how to live, now I will show them how to die." This made such an impression on me that I strove to be a good example to our two little girls. I really felt that I had 40 years left to live and I could stand anything for that long!

I encourage any of you who need hope and faith amidst great doubt and discouragement to water your hope with God's Word and prayer, and your faith will grow, too. For any of you in the place of "no hope" the source is the same, God will always supply the seed of hope if you will only desire to believe the scriptures and begin to pray as earnestly as you can.

My Period of Depression

The biggest thing with which I had to deal was depression. Over those 12 years there were days of heavy depression, and it took a long time for me to regain the health that stress took away. Mornings were difficult. I always wanted and needed more rest. I had less and less energy. A few hours up demanded more energy than I had, so I needed a nap; but rest was no cure. There were times, as I remember now, I could not take a deep breath. There was a knot in my chest. Headaches, chronic tiredness, restless and fearful nights marked many years. Looking back I see, however, that God kept us even then. Thankfully, John and I were never both depressed at the same time, so we could encourage each other. I see also that God had begun to set five patterns in my life that would effectively keep me from completely giving in to chronic depression and which would enable me to overcome a period of depression at any specific time. These five life patterns are:

1. Fellowshiping with God in a personal relationship;

2. Studying the Bible consistently in private
   and in groups;

3. Fellowshiping with growing Christians;

4. Helping other people; and

5. Being a doer of God's Word.

Keep these life patterns in mind as we discuss in some depth what depression is, how it enters our lives, and how to be victorious over it.

What Is Depression?

Depression is an unhealthy focus on myself and on my circumstances rather than on God and His Promises.

Several things may trigger depression. Depression can be the result of an organic problem and may then need to be medically treated.

Depression can be the result of continued over-activity which strains the emotions and the body. <u>Obeying God's laws of eating, resting and realistic activity need to be obeyed.</u> Years of depression stressed my physical body to the point that I had to labor to bring it back to health. I was not sick, but far from well.

Proper nutrition and exercise is sadly lacking in the Church. We are slovenly, overweight, self-indulgent and full of junk food. Sugar alone may trigger depression. To take care of the body machine is to extend a high quality of life in order to serve God. Take heed of and obey the cautions against over eating fast foods, fried foods, salt, sugar and white processed flour. I am responsible for the stewardship of my own body and for the nutritional health of my husband and children.

The depression epidemic spoken to here is a state of mind which affects the emotions and eventually the physical body. My emotions are telling me something. Stressful life circumstances coupled with a lack of knowledge of and trust in God can certainly trigger depression. In most of our situations we have allowed self-pity to dominate our minds in an unbalanced concentration on ME. Depression will squelch creativity, lower energy level, resist sleep, result in short temperedness, restrict deep-breathing, impede motivation and lower an already low self-esteem. In summary, depression is an unhealthy focus on myself and on my circumstances rather than on God and His Promises.

Lets Discuss the 5 Life Patterns in Relation to Depression:

First, fellowshiping with God in praise, thanksgiving, worship, prayer and fasting will build a strong spirit in a man; and he will be able to control what enters his mind as well as cast down evil thoughts that sneak into his life.

Second, studying the Bible consistently in private and with a group is the avenue through which the mind is transformed with God's mind. It is the avenue of group encouragement and prayer agreement which builds Godly life patterns and a basis for hope which yields faith.

Third, develop a circle of faith-filled friends who interact for social growth and provide a stage for laughter which brightens the soul with joy. Depression wants to be alone, do not let it! Be transparent and honest with these friends.

Fourth is to help someone else. This takes the focus from ME to another and puts the principle of sowing and reaping into action. Jesus Himself said *. . . **Inasmuch as ye have done it unto the least of these my brethren, ye have done it unto me** (Matthew 25:40).* We also know from scripture *. . . **It is more blessed to give than to receive** (Acts 20:35).* A giver with a purer motive always gains the most!

Fifth is to show Jesus that we love Him by obeying the Word - not just hearing Him. This life pattern encompasses great truths, a few of which I would like to draw to your attention because they have a definite relationship to depression.

Accept yourself as a person made in the image of God, you are special to Him. This is the basis upon which ones builds a healthy self-esteem. This is self-acceptance, not self-satisfaction which cripples spiritual growth. Do not be hard on yourself, remember God is not going to give up on you. However, I did not say be easy on yourself with excuses that will eventually deceive you. Strive to achieve healthy goals.

Be quick to forgive and receive forgiveness. Unresolved anger and a desire for justice above all else, out of balance, may lead to depression. One's imagination will have a field day with unforgiveness. To harbor ill feelings toward some one who offended you is self-pity.

Self-pity is a carnal response to an insult, a hurt or a rejection and is, therefore, a sinful response. If I harbor unforgiveness, it can easily lead to depression. To nurse feelings of rejection is a clear indication of an unforgiving spirit and an attitude of self-pity. Beware of such an infection in your life. *James 4:7* states, ***Submit yourselves therefore to God. Resist the devil, and he will flee from you.*** Repent and ask forgiveness.

Think, confess and act according to scriptural truths, for to do otherwise is to displease God and breed doubt and discouragement. Scripture reminds us that out of the heart the mouth speaks (Luke 6:45) and faith without works is dead (James 2:17,20,26). Our speech and our actions may tell on us and expose our carnal nature in spite of how much Bible we "know" and "recite." Indecision and procrastination will open doors to depression. Important in sidetracking any seeds of depression are (1) the attitude of expecting God to act in your life, and (2) patiently expecting Him to act abundantly on your behalf as you think, act and confess humbly according to His Word.

Jesus' words, *. . . **I will never leave thee, nor forsake thee** . . .* (Hebrews 13:5) free us from the clutches of depression. ***If the Son therefore shall make you free, ye shall be free indeed*** *(John 8:36).*

How Depression Enters Our Lives

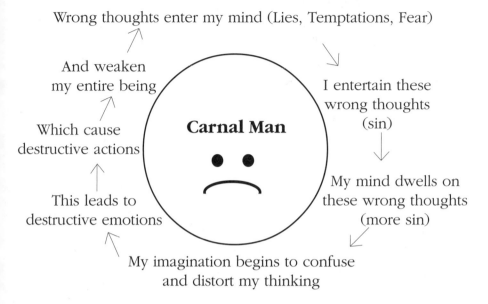

Wrong thoughts enter my mind (Lies, Temptations, Fear)

And weaken my entire being

I entertain these wrong thoughts (sin)

Which cause destructive actions

Carnal Man

My mind dwells on these wrong thoughts (more sin)

This leads to destructive emotions

My imagination begins to confuse and distort my thinking

How To Fight Depression

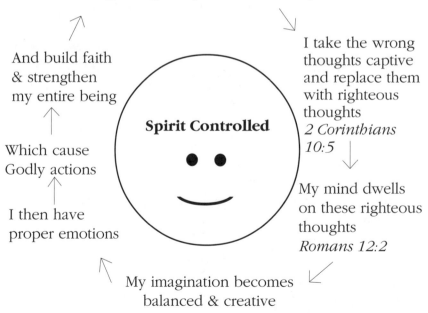

Wrong thoughts try to come into my mind

And build faith & strengthen my entire being

I take the wrong thoughts captive and replace them with righteous thoughts
2 Corinthians 10:5

Which cause Godly actions

Spirit Controlled

My mind dwells on these righteous thoughts
Romans 12:2

I then have proper emotions

My imagination becomes balanced & creative

How Depression Enters Our Lives

Man is a three part creation: spirit, soul and body. Depression enters our lives through the soul; therefore, it must be attacked in the soul. The soul is a blend of the mind, will and emotions. The depression process can be dissected to allow us to clearly see what happens between the mind, will and emotions and to then understand how the five life patterns will achieve victory.

"I am ever learning that life is most often a matter of choice determined by how yielded to God I want to be."

My will decides what I let into my mind through my senses. If a wrong thought (picture image) enters my mind and then I dwell on it, my imagination paints an even more vivid picture. Imagination is to the emotions what illustrations are to books. When this happens, I have allowed my imagination to run wild. James' discourse on the unbridled tongue closely compares with this runaway imagination. A spiritually growing person is soft and yielding to God's gentle conviction in this area and his conscience, filled with God's Spirit and the truth of God's Word, can ultimately gain victory over a wrong thought life.

Overcoming Depression

The five life patterns previously mentioned will establish in you signs of a growing and victorious Christian.

THE PATTERNS OF A GODLY WIFE

by Donna K. Deal

John says I never complained when we were millions of dollars in debt. However, I should add that I did have some mixed feelings about our problem! Ruth Graham summed up how I felt when she was asked in an interview, "Have you ever thought about divorcing Billy Graham?" She answered ". . . Divorce, no; kill, yes!"

1. Wives must forgive, encourage, and pray for their husbands, not berate and discourage them. Bridle your tongue. Do not push, manipulate or nag him.

2. Be a good homemaker and create a pleasant atmosphere. No one sees a flower in the vase if there is a dirty sock on the floor! No one has any excuse for sloppy living habits.

3. Learn to be thrifty. Eliminate things you do not need. Concentrate to make a few things go further: Example; clothes, cosmetics, food. Get rid of piles of clutter and excess. God does not bless poor management.

4. Take care of yourself. Be neat, clean, and smell good.

5. Consider making Life Goals. These would be character goals and things you would like to do in life. Pray over them and have God's heart in the matter. It is like reading a road map. If you do not know where you are going, you will not know how to get there; and, you also will not know when you get there!

THE PATTERNS OF A GODLY HUSBAND

by Donna K. Deal

Husbands, the following hints will make your home life even better!

1. Communicate eye to eye with your wife. She wants to hear from your heart how you feel about things. A woman generally appreciates more specific facts about a situation than a man does. So explain enough to satisfy her interest. Example: Explain what happened at the meeting so she will not have to drag it out of you.

2. Also, do not expect your wife to act a certain way today just because she acted that way yesterday. She may have changed a little!

3. To keep her from nagging you and to keep you from feeling guilty if there is a leaky faucet, there is only one thing to do. Fix it! Do not let molehills become mountains.

4. Be the leader of the home. Jesus was the ultimate leader to follow. He fed, healed, consoled, forgave, wept with, prayed for, taught, worked with and spent time with those he led. He washed their feet and gave His life for them.

5. Be a generous husband with money and time. A homemaker may need the security of a consistent amount to call her own when possible. This is not just the act of giving her the pay check and letting her pay the bills, etc. and whatever is left is hers. This also goes for time at home with family. Meetings and job demands need to be balanced, so the whole family can eat dinner together to form roots that today's lifestyle destroys. Say "no" to outside influences when possible. We have only one chance with a family. Let us make it successful. This also goes for a busy wife.

6. Husbands should lead devotions with the family in some way. Make God's Word interesting and applicable to their lives. Pray with your children everyday.

7. Be first to say "I'm sorry" whether you are right or wrong. Have no pride in the matter.

FROM DILIGENCE TO
MANIPULATION TO BURNOUT

Keep thy heart with all diligence:
for out of it are the issues of life
(Proverbs 4:23).

Our duty before God is simply to be diligent and place the outcome of all matters in His hands, not ours.

When we go beyond diligence to "make something happen," we have:

1. Left the safety of His hand and stolen a path into the field of manipulation;
2. Put our trust in our own hand which is by then ruled by the law of presumption;
3. Made ourselves responsible for the outcome of all matters before us; and
4. Entered into the area of witchcraft by attempting to manipulate the minds and circumstances of others.

If we will only be diligent, and then wait, He will bring about His plan in the entire matter. For us to "Make something happen" thwarts His plans for our lives and the lives of others.

On the other hand, the Babylonian system constantly demands that we use the power of our flesh to, "Make something happen." Babylon has no tolerance for patiently allowing God to bring things to pass in His time. So when diligence does not bring immediate results, we believe we are required to use our power of manipulation over people and events to "Make things happen." This constant use of manipulation, rather than living diligently before God, causes burnout. This can and does happen in the home, church, government and employment.

DILIGENCE VS. TALK

*In all labor there is profit: but the
talk of the lips tendeth only to penury
(Proverbs 14:23).*

We have all seen those who labor diligently and get the job done, but we have also seen those who talk and get nothing done. Diligence is profitable, but talk leads only to poverty.

Diligence Positions Us to Receive from God

*The sluggard craves and gets nothing, but the desires of
the diligent are fully satisfied* *(Proverbs 13:4 NIV).*

*And my God will meet all your needs according to His
glorious riches in Christ Jesus* *(Philippians 4:19 NIV).*

Our jobs are not our supply, God alone is our supply. Worship, family and work are meant by God, at least in part, to afford to us the opportunity to show ourselves diligent before Him.

Diligence in these areas positions us to receive His supply; the timing and amount of His supply are His alone to grant through the abundance of His grace to us.

GOD OFTEN USES THE NATURAL REALM
TO TRAIN US FOR THE SPIRITUAL REALM

And David said unto Saul, Thy servant kept his father's
sheep, and there came a lion, and a bear, and took a
lamb out of the flock: And I went out after him, and
smote him, and delivered it out of his mouth: and when
he arose against me, I caught him by his beard, and
smote him, and slew him. Thy servant slew both the lion
and the bear: and this uncircumcised Philistine shall be
as one of them, seeing he hath defied the armies of the
living God. David said moreover, The LORD that
delivered me out of the paw of the lion, and out of the
paw of the bear, he will deliver me out of the hand of
this Philistine. And Saul said unto David, Go, and the
LORD be with thee
(I Samuel 17:34-37).

Too often we believe that we are wasting our time by
working in a natural occupation rather than working in what
we perceive to be a "spiritual" capacity, but seldom is that the
case. When David, the shepherd boy, killed the lion and the
bear to protect a herd of sheep, he was in the process of being
prepared in the natural to fight a battle in the spiritual that
would forever alter the course of the Nation of Israel. It is good
that David did not think he was wasting his time as a shepherd,
and run away from home to work in the spiritual. Had he done
so, Israel's future would have been altered for many years.

In our exuberance to serve God, and in our desire to escape
the rigors of the world, we often do not consider that our current
worldly situation may well be a part of God's plan to train us for
service in the spiritual. That was God's plan in the lives of Joseph
and Moses in Egypt, and Peter and Paul in the New Testament,
and that is what may well be God's plan in our life today.

Remember the order of events in David's life:

David was disciplined as a shepherd boy by tending his father's sheep in the natural realm, and was then anointed by God in the spiritual realm to be King over God's sheep, Israel;

David was disciplined in faith when he killed the lion and the bear as a part of his shepherd's work in the natural realm, and then approaching Goliath, announced his certain death with words of faith; and

David was disciplined in submission to authority as he was pursued by Saul, who sought to kill him in the natural realm, and then ruled with Godly authority as King over Israel except in the matter of Uriah.

One of the most dangerous people in the kingdom of God is the person who knows they have been called by God, but has shunned the life experiences in the natural realm that God uses to teach us the disciplines we need to serve in His kingdom. This kind of person is one of the many who are called, but does not render himself fit to be chosen by God for service in the spiritual realm. We must never let our exuberance to serve God, or our desire to escape the rigors of the world, rob us from being trained in the natural realm for service in the spiritual realm. To do so is to be rebellious before God.

We must realize that God created both the natural and the spiritual, and He intends for us to live in both the natural and the spiritual in a balanced manner. Too often believers, especially charismatics, disdain the natural and attempt to live solely in the spiritual realm. That luxury is reserved for believers after death. Let us not waste our time wishing to be in the spiritual when God has a plan for us in the natural, for there is much discipline we need to learn in the natural so we can properly serve in the spiritual.

So what is the bottom line in the matter? Do not despise God working in your life through natural - worldly circumstances.

DISCIPLINING CHILDREN

*Chasten thy son while there is hope, and
let not thy soul spare for his crying*
(Proverbs 19:18).

The demands of our everyday life tend to pull us away from performing our responsibilities to our children, including the responsibility of disciplining them. How often have we said, "I don't like to scold my child because we have so little time together, and I want it to be a good time."

Disciplining our children is as necessary to their growth as is food; and, if we do not take the time to chasten them, both they and we will suffer for it later. Under no circumstances should we let their crying hinder our disciplining them. We would much rather hear our children cry from the application of discipline than from the guilt and sorrow that is certain to come later in their lives if we do not chasten them now.

Leaving Children to Themselves

. . . a child left to himself bringeth his mother to shame
(Proverbs 29:15).

When we leave our children to themselves, they will bring shame to their mother. To leave our children to themselves surrounded with many "things" is triple trouble. Not only will they bring shame to their mother, they will not know the value of time or money or the love of their parents.

What is the value of our time as parents spent away from home if it causes our children to bring shame to their mother and not appreciate what they have?

156

Children Leaving Home

*Unto the woman he said, I will greatly multiply thy
sorrow and thy conception;
in sorrow thou shalt bring forth children ...*
(Genesis 3:16).

A mother brings forth her children twice, first at birth
and again when they leave home. This is so because the cervix
in her womb and Godly authority in the home are much alike.
As the cervix keeps the child in the womb until the time is right,
so does Godly authority keep the child in the home until the
time is right.

In both instances the mother experiences pain because
the child wants to leave prematurely. If the mother allowed her
cervix to be prematurely opened or the child to prematurely
leave home, she would be placing her child in danger; yet, to
keep the child in the proper place causes her great pain. So
what does the mother do?

She patiently bears the pain while waiting for the child
to be brought forth. Although God designed the cervix to
expand, its expansion is brutally painful (so I am told); but,
once the child is born, the joy of birth obscures the pain of
delivery.

Likewise, even though God plans the time for the child
to leave the home, the child's leaving is extremely painful to the
mother. But, just as what happened at birth, when the child
leaves the home in the correct time and circumstance subject to
Godly authority, the mother's joy of watching her child make
their way out into life obscures the pain of their leaving.

DISCRETION

*He that keepeth his mouth keepeth his life: but he
that openeth wide his lips shall have destruction
(Proverbs 13:3).*

Pride is the lever that opens our mouth for the purpose
of impressing others. God never meant for us to impress anyone
with our mouths; rather, He meant for us to be discrete by
speaking slowly and being swift to hear *(James 1:19)*.

An indiscrete man cannot be trusted to keep his life or
carry on our affairs; but, he who is discrete will keep his life
and our business affairs.

The Sin Of Displaying New Christians

*He must not be a recent convert, or he may become
conceited and fall under the same judgement as the Devil*
(I Timothy 3:6 NIV).

While the above scripture concerns the qualifications of
deacons and elders, it also applies to how the body of Christ
should relate to new converts.

It is well to have a new convert announce his decision
before the church body, for that is scriptural. However, it is
wrong is for us to make a "show horse" out of him by giving
him public attention, or church duties, beyond the depth of his
walk in the Lord. Remember, he is a new convert in spiritual
diapers - not a seasoned Christian fit for spiritual battle.

The Church often violates its relationship with new
converts, especially in the matter of infamous, famous or wealthy
new converts. Too often, because of their notoriety and or wealth,
these new converts are paraded before the church as if they
were show horses.

What is our motive for putting on this horse show? Is it
to show the most recent notch in our spiritual six shooter; is it
in hope that the new convert will bring others of notoriety or
wealth into our midst; is it to show others how spiritually effective
we are or for some other spiritually immature reason; or, is it an
attempt to accumulate more finances for our church or ministry?
Regardless of why we do it, it is wrong to do, so let us no more
have any part in it.

Let us treat the new convert, regardless of his notoriety
or wealth, for what he is - a babe in Christ. Then, let us nurture
him to maturity so he can go where God wants him to go in
God's time.

THE WHOLE DUTY OF MAN

... Fear God and keep his commandments:
for this is the whole duty of man
(Ecclesiastes 12:13).

Solomon wrote the above scripture at the very end of his life. He had just written twelve chapters describing the futility of man pursuing money, women, power, wine and song. At the end of his life he turned around, looked at his past and concluded that the whole duty of man was to obey the whole Word of God.

Remember, Solomon had 1,400 chariots, 12,000 horsemen, piled silver in the streets of Jerusalem as if it were stone, billions in gold, 700 wives, 300 mistresses and a personal navy to collect the tribute paid to him each year. Yet, his summation on life was that the whole duty of man was to *... Fear God and keep his commandments ...*

It is a goal of business and professional people to make a profit, but it is also their duty to obey God's Word. A true man of God desires for profit to be made only as a result of his obedience to obey God's commandments, even in the most adverse economic climate. This desire will be realized because God is not bound even by time, much less a nation's economy *... and in the days of famine they shall be satisfied* (Psalm 37:19).

WHY ECONOMIES & GOVERNMENTS
RISE AND FALL

*Thou art worthy, O Lord, to receive glory and honour
and power; for thou hast created all things, and for
thy pleasure they are and were created*
(Revelation 4:11).

Economies and governments are created by God for His pleasure, to be used by Him at his pleasure. They are tools in God's hands by which He can bless us if we obey Him, or curse us if we disobey Him. Proof of this fact is well documented in the Bible as it relates to the history of the Nation of Israel *(Joshua 1:7&8).*

Economies and governments rise and fall in direct relationship to a nation's obedience/disobedience to God's Word *(Revelation Chapter 18).* Economic conditions and governmental decrees cannot even begin to impact a nation to the degree that will righteous obedience or disobedience to God, as the case may be.

Truly, the key to a strong economy and government is a nation's obedience to God's Word *(See the entire Bible).* If a nation's economy and government are failing, true repentance is the key to the restoration of that economy and government for... ***Return, ye backsliding children, and I will heal your backslidings ...*** *(Jeremiah 3:22).*

EMBARRASSMENT AND HUMILIATION
ARE INEVITABLE WHEN WE OBEY GOD

Now therefore, if ye will obey my voice indeed, and keep
my covenant, then ye shall be a peculiar treasure
unto me above all people . . .
(Exodus 19:5).

To determine to obey God is to ask to be embarrassed and humiliated in the eyes of the world. Just look at the lives of:

Jesus, in obedience to God, was beaten, flogged, convicted of crimes He did not commit and was crucified naked before the entire world;

Hosea, in obedience to God, married a prostitute *(Hosea 1:2)*;

Mary, in obedience to God, became pregnant by the Holy Spirit out of wedlock *(Luke 1:38)*;

Paul, in obedience to God, was publicly flogged three times, stoned, shipwrecked, and suffered cold, hunger and nakedness *(II Corinthians 11:23-28)*;

John, in obedience to God, was banished to the Isle of Patmos *(Revelation 1:9)*;

Jeremiah, in obedience to God, prophesied the fall of Jerusalem and was placed in mire up to his armpits *(Jeremiah 38:6)*; and

Others, in obedience to God, were stoned, sawn asunder, tempted, slain, wandered in animal skins, destitute, afflicted and tormented *(Hebrews 11:37)*.

So, when we are embarrassed/humiliated in the midst of obeying God, let us draw strength from Jesus, Hosea, Mary, Paul, John, Jeremiah and the others, and stand in obedience to the Word regardless of the price. To be embarrassed and humiliated for obeying God is to be in excellent company, and grants eternal benefits.

SILENCING OUR ENEMIES

***When a man's ways please the LORD, he maketh
even his enemies to be at peace with him***
(Proverbs 16:7).

The power of God in our every day lives is awesome. If
we will only please Him, He will cause our enemies to be at
peace with us. Now this does not mean we will not have
enemies, for if we walk according to the Word we will surely
have enemies; but God will cause them to be at peace with us
when we please Him.

So, to silence our enemies, let us not come against them;
rather, let us live our everyday lives in a manner pleasing to
God, and He will silence them for us.

ESCAPING INTO THE MINISTRY TO
AVOID THE RIGORS OF EVERYDAY LIFE

Behold, I send you forth as sheep in the midst of wolves:
be ye therefore wise as serpents, and harmless as doves
(Matthew 10:16).

We are supposed to be called into, and then chosen for, the ministry; ministry is not a place of escape from the rigors of the world. To try to avoid the rigors of everyday life by escaping into the ministry is concrete evidence of our having character deficiencies.

If we do make that escape, we can be sure that we will have to deal with those character deficiencies in the ministry, and we can be further assured that those deficiencies shall be dealt with more harshly in the ministry than in the world. The worst nightmare of any pastor is an irate church board backed by a voting congregation that views the pastor as their hireling.

Avoiding rigors of everyday life by escaping into the ministry did not cross Jesus' mind, His mind was set to the contrary. He said, I am sending my people into the midst of this ravenous world and, when they get there, I want them to be as wise as serpents and harmless as doves. Now, God does not expect us to enjoy the rigors of life, but nor does He want us to escape into the ministry to avoid them. He wants us to meet these problems head on.

We meet these rigors head on by recognizing that we are lambs sent into the midst of wolves, and we overcome the wolves by being wise as serpents and harmless as doves. As Christians we do not like being compared with serpents, but Christ is not comparing us with serpents; He is only saying be as wise as they are.

It is this wisdom that allows us, as lambs and doves, to constantly live in the presence of wolves. Once we can grasp that truth, we will no longer run from the rigors; rather, we shall use those rigors to strengthen our faith in Christ. As that faith grows, we will no longer have the desire to escape into the ministry - we will wait for our call and wait to be chosen for the ministry.

EFFECTIVE ESTATE PLANNING

***A good man leaveth an inheritance to his children's
children: and the wealth of the sinner is laid up
for the just***
(Proverbs 13:22).

A good man leaves his wealth to his childrens' children, but the wealth of the sinner is laid up for the just. This is true regardless of what is stated in the will and trust documents.

Why is this so? Because it is God who gives us the ***...power to get wealth...*** *(Deuteronomy 8:18),* but it is the degree of our relationship with Him that determines what will happen to our wealth *(Proverbs 13:22).*

FAITH

Now faith is the substance of things hoped for, the evidence of things not seen
(Hebrews 11:1 emphasis added).

What Is Faith?

Now faith is the substance of things hoped for (the person of Jesus) *and, the evidence of things not seen* (the Word of God, which is also the person of Christ). Faith is our submitting to the person of Christ in us so He can perform His will through us.

How Do We Receive Faith?

So then faith cometh by hearing, and hearing by the Word of God (Romans 10:17). We receive faith by continually listening to the Word of God. Well, what is the Word of God? It is the person of Christ *(John 1:14)*. So we receive faith by taking the person of Christ into ourselves through continually listening to the Word.

How Do We Make Faith Work for Us?

<u>Trust</u> in the Lord . . .
<u>Delight</u> thyself also in the Lord . . .
<u>Commit</u> thy way unto the Lord . . .
<u>Rest</u> in the Lord . . .
(Psalm 37:3-5 & 7 underlining added).

To make faith work for us, we must first trust in God; <u>then</u>, because we trust in Him, we can delight in Him; <u>then</u> because we trust and delight in Him, we can commit our matter to Him; and, <u>then</u>, because we trust, delight and commit in Him, we can rest knowing that He has already taken care of the matter, even before we ask Him to do so.

How Do We Balance Our Faith?

Faith is active in that it requires us to trust, delight and commit, but it is also passive in that it requires us to rest in peace. That is how faith is balanced. The shield of faith is held in place by our resting in peace while waiting for God to perform His Word *(See Psalm 37:3-5 & 7)*.

Faith, Boldness and Expectations
vs. Presumption and Demands

Now faith is the substance of things hoped for, the evidence of things not seen
(Hebrews 11:1).

In those days, there was no king in Israel, but every man did that which was right in his own eyes
(Judges 17:6).

Faith, boldness and expectations are fact. They are our knowing and believing that God means what His Word says and acting upon the integrity of that Word: presumption and demanding arise out of the flesh, and presume and make demands upon God without regard for His Holiness.

Faith, boldness and expectations are dependent upon God's Word: presumption and demands are dependent upon things other than God's Word.

Faith, boldness and expectations are born out of patience: presumption and demands are born out of impatience.

Having "Faith for" An Event vs. Having "Faith in" God:

. . . ye believe in God . . .
(John 14:1)

To have <u>faith for</u> money, healing, etc. is to look with one eye on God and the other eye on the expected event: to have <u>faith in</u>

God is to look at Him with both eyes, regardless of whether or not the expected event takes place.

To have <u>faith for</u> an event is to limit God to what we desire: but, to have <u>faith in</u> God is to leave the matter open to Him to benefit us exceedingly abundantly above what we can ask or think.

<u>It is His desire that we have faith in Him rather than for an event.</u> Faith in Him establishes a relationship with Him that causes Him to act on our behalf and afford to us what we need to serve Him.

FEAR

For God hath not given us the spirit of fear;
but of power, and of love, and of a sound mind
(2 Timothy 1:7).

He who is the Glory of Israel does not lie . . .
(I Samuel 15:29 NIV).

That by two immutable things, in which
it was impossible for God to lie . . .
(Hebrews 6:18).

You belong to your father, the devil, and you want
to carry out your father's desire. He was a murderer
from the beginning, not holding to the truth, for there
is no truth in him. When he lies, he speaks his native
language, for he is a liar and the father of lies
(John 8:44 NIV).

The Three Kinds of Fear

There are at least three kinds of fear: (1) reverent fear, (2) cautionary fear, and (3) the fear that comes from Satan.

Reverent fear is good, it is fear of the one true God, Our Father. It is reverence for our awesome God. This kind of fear is often mentioned in the Bible in the context of man recognizing the righteousness and power of God, and that man is but a vapor.

Cautionary fear is a safety mechanism placed in our lives by God to protect us from the hazards of this world. This kind of fear is good because it preserves our lives for service to Him. All of the great men in the Bible experienced this fear, and acted in respect to its warning; Joseph when he took Mary and Jesus to Egypt to escape Herod; David when he fled from Saul; Paul when he fled Damascus; and, Jesus when he often left the presence of the scribes and pharisees because His time had not yet come.

Fear from Satan is the type of fear which Satan uses in his attempt to take control of our lives. The symptoms of this kind of fear are often panic, lack of sleep, doubting God's promises, palpitating heart, sweating, and they come like a wave that appears for the moment to overwhelm us. This kind of fear is nothing more than a veneer covered lie of Satan. Satan's purpose for this veneer covered lie is to take control of our lives. He tries to effect this control of our lives by convincing us that his lie of fear is more powerful than God's promises; but, the truth is, the substance of this lie is no more than that of a balloon inflated by a child – 99.9% air and .1% spit.

Fear From Satan Is Always A Lie

God does not give to us a spirit of fear, nor does He lie. He cannot lie, it is impossible for Him to lie. On the other hand, Satan has no truth in him, lying is *. . . **his native language, for he is a liar and the father of lies*** *(John 8:44 NIV)*. So, by the truth stated in the word of God, we can be certain that the fear that comes from Satan has to be a lie.

We can recognize fear from Satan since it will invariably manifest itself as sudden panic. Whenever we feel this panic, we can be certain that we are in the process of being lied to by Satan. Fear from him is always a lie in disguise, and we should always recognize its substance as being that of a balloon. When we pop a balloon inflated by a child, what is left – nothing but air and spit. That is the substance of fear from Satan, 99.9% air and .1% spit. ***Be not afraid of sudden fear, neither of the desolation of the wicked, when it cometh*** *(Proverbs 3:25)*.

So, to allow fear from Satan to control us is to be led by air and spit rather than by the power and love of God and a sound mind from God. Satan wants to make us believe that his lie of fear is more powerful than are God's promises; and, he gains this control the moment we begin to act out of fear rather than in faith. So when the panic of fear comes against us, we should recognize it for what it is and begin to walk in the power and love of God, with a sound mind to allow God to accomplish His will in our lives.

171

Satan's Fear Brings with It A Snare

The fear of man bringeth a snare; but whoso putteth his trust in the LORD shall be safe
(Proverbs 29:25).

Genesis 3:1 states that Satan is the most subtle of all of the beasts of the field. His purpose is to gain control of our lives without our realizing it, and one of his most subtle weapons for accomplishing that purpose is the snare of his fear. We become ensnared by his lie of fear once we begin to let it control our actions.

An example of being ensnared by fear is the panic stricken behavior of a wild animal just after it has been ensnared in a trap. Once we submit to fear, our behavior is just as panic stricken as that of the ensnared animal. All Satan has to do then is to reel us into his kingdom through our fear controlled, frantic, and other ungodly behavior. Our actions will then evidence to the world that we have forgotten the promises of God, and are now being led to our doom by the father of all lies.

Satan's snare is to have us believe that this fear is a normal human reaction to an adverse situation. But, Jesus often proved this lie to be the lie that it is, i.e., the time when He fell asleep in the rear of the boat and a great storm came. His disciples were overcome with fear in the same boat and in the same storm, but Jesus kept on sleeping *(Luke 8:22-25)*. When He awoke, He exercised authority over the adversity and rebuked it into the pages of history. The snare that Satan's fear brings, unless we walk in God's Word, is that we will believe the lie of his fear, submit to it and not believe God's promises.

Satan's purpose for the snare of his fear is to keep us from entering the kingdom of God and His righteousness. If we believe his lie of fear, he will have succeeded in snaring us away from the promises of God. Satan's reward to us for taking the snare of his fear is to burden us with fear and anxiety. The best his fear has to offer is a snare and unwarranted anxiety.

172

Conquering the Fear that Comes From Satan

... Resist the Devil, and he will flee from you
(James 4:7 NIV).

Since Satan generated fear is a lie, we conquer it the same way we conquer Satan, rebuke fear and it will flee from us! How can we be sure of this? We can be sure because God is a God who cannot lie, and He says in *James 4:7* of his Word that if we will only rebuke Satan, he will flee from us.

Satan would have us to believe that he is all powerful, and that we are powerless against his lie of fear, but, the Prophet Isaiah saw Satan for the deceiver that he is and described him for who he is:

Those who see you stare at you, they ponder your fate:
"Is this the man who shook the earth and made
kingdoms tremble, the man who made the world
a desert, who overthrew its cities and would not
let his captives go home"
(Isaiah 14: 16-17 NIV)?

Isaiah's description of Satan should leave us confident that prevailing over his lie of fear is really no big deal.

The way for Satan's defeat in our lives has been well paved: first: when God defeated him by casting him out of heaven; second: when Jesus defeated him by walking out of the tomb; third: he has been defeated innumerable times by the angelic hosts on our behalf at God's direction without our even knowing about it; fourth: countless millions of times by Christians in the name of Jesus; fifth: countless millions of times by God on behalf of those who tithe according to Malachi 3:10; and sixth: IT IS NOW OUR TURN TO CONQUER fear BY REBUKING Satan IN THE NAME OF JESUS, AND he and his lie of fear WILL FLEE FROM US!

We should not let fear control us ever again, even for a minute. Christ came, He lives and Satan is defeated forever! Now claim your own personal victory over Satan and his lie of fear by rebuking him in the name of Jesus Christ!

173

ANSWERING A FOOL

***Answer not** a fool according to his folly,*
lest thou be like unto him.
***Answer** a fool according to his folly, lest he be*
wise in his own conceit
(Proverbs 26:4-5 emphasis added).

We will be confronted by fools from time to time and we must be careful how we answer their questions. We should not answer a fool in the same foolish manner that he asks a question, otherwise, we will be like him. But, if the circumstances permit, we should render a substantive answer to his foolish question, or he will be wise in his own conceit.

When confronted by a fool:

1. Do not try to get even *(Romans 12:19);*

2. Do not act hastily *(Proverbs 25:8);*

3. Consider your words *(I Samuel 3:19);* and

4. Do not become emotional *(Proverbs 14:17).*

Contending with A Fool

If a wise man contendeth with a foolish man,
whether he rage or laugh, there is no rest
(Proverbs 29:9).

We must learn that we will never be able to contend with a fool. A fool is a fool in the first place because he thinks he knows everything.

When we contend with a fool, whether in rage or in jest, there is no rest; we will have wasted our time, received no fulfillment for the effort and are disgusted to boot.

The Danger Of A Fool's Folly

Let a bear robbed of her whelps meet a man, rather than a fool in his folly
(Proverbs 17:12).

We who are caught robbing a bear's cubs get mauled by the bear, but the result of our being caught up in a fool's folly is even worse. (See also, *Controlling Our Temper,* at page 310)

FORGIVENESS

Put on therefore, as the elect of God, holy and beloved,
bowels of mercies, kindness, humbleness of mind,
meekness, longsuffering; Forbearing one another, and
forgiving one another, if any man have a quarrel
against any: even as Christ forgave you, so also do ye
(Colossians 3:12-13).

Introduction

To be unforgiving is to stand at the foot of the cross, look up at Jesus and tell Him, "You are not dying for me, I would rather have this bitterness than Your blood." That is why to be unforgiving is to pridefully reject the work of Christ's blood in our lives.

Christ wants us to reject our pride by taking upon ourselves kindness, humbleness, meekness and longsuffering just as He did. Then we will be able to forgive others as He forgave us.

What Is Forgiveness?

Forgiveness is God's gift of grace toward us. Forgiveness can be measured only by the sacrifice of Jesus, and is available to each and every one of us *(Ephesians 4:7).*

Forgiveness is the blood of Jesus Christ. **. . . Father, forgive them for they know not what they do . . .** *(Luke 23:34).* We need to look at forgiveness, not as a word, but as the blood of Jesus *(Colossians 1:20).*

Forgiveness is to be like Christ. **. . . even as Christ forgave you, so also do ye** *(Colossians 3:13).*

176

What Keeps Us from Forgiving Others?

Pride. *Only by pride cometh contention . . .* (*Proverbs 13:10*).

Why Is It Important For Us to Learn to Forgive?

We are directed to do so by scripture (*Colossians 3:12-13*).

Any root of bitterness defiles us before God (*Hebrews 12:15*). As righteousness has a root so does unforgiveness, and the root of righteousness shall not be moved (*Proverbs 12:3*).

We are in darkness if we hate our brother (*I John 2:9*).

Unforgiveness is a device that Satan uses to take advantage of us (*II Corinthians 2:10-11*).

If we regard iniquity (unforgiveness is a type of iniquity) in our heart, God will not hear our prayer (*Psalm 66:18*).

God does not want our offering until our heart is free of unforgiveness (*Matthew 5:23-24*).

Jesus taught us to pray that God would forgive us our trespasses as we forgive those who trespass against us (*Matthew 6:12*).

Jesus directed us to forgive one another seventy times seven (*Matthew 18:20-22*).

One of Jesus' last acts on the cross was to ask God to forgive those who were putting Him to death (*Luke 23:34*).

In the Lord's prayer, the requirement of forgiving others is positioned right next to the petition for our daily bread (*Matthew 6:12*).

How Do We Forgive Others?

Recognize that unforgiveness is a sin *(Luke 23:34);*

Repent before God for the unforgiveness *(Luke 13:3);* and

Go to the other person and ask his forgiveness for our having been unforgiving to him.

Bitterness, Resentment and Unforgiveness

. . . if any man have a quarrel against any: even as Christ forgave you, so also do ye (Colossians 3:13).

To have bitterness, resentment or unforgiveness is to stand at the foot of the cross and shout up to Jesus, "I would rather have this bitterness in my heart than your blood, so you are not dying for me." So for us to harbor bitterness is for us to reject the blood of Christ. Bitterness is never justified, it is always a sin.

Comment

Our willingness to forgive others is in direct proportion to our love of Jesus *(John 14:15).* Jesus is not any more our Shepherd than we are willing to forgive others.

CHOOSING FRIENDS AND ASSOCIATES

He that walketh with wise men shall be wise:
but a companion of fools shall be destroyed.
(Proverbs 13:20).

We are and will become like those with whom we choose to walk. If we walk with the wise, we will be wise; but if we walk with fools we shall be destroyed.

FINDING FULFILLMENT

There is that maketh himself rich, yet hath nothing:
there is that maketh himself poor, yet hath great riches
(Proverbs 13:7).

Man was created by God in the image of God, not by the world in the image of the world. Therefore, man will find fulfillment only in the Ways of God and not in the ways of the world. This is why success in the world's terms never brings fulfillment; rather, worldly success breeds only a lustful desire for more success.

There is no correlation between fulfillment and possessions. To the contrary, we have great fulfillment only when we give of ourselves and our possessions to others. Only when we make ourselves poor by giving of ourselves and our possessions to others, will we have the richness of fulfillment.

GIVING

*For God so loved the world, that he gave his only
begotten Son . . .*
(John 3:16).

Introduction

John 3:16 is the primary scripture in the Bible on giving.
It is also the focal scripture around which the entire Bible is
written.

The True Gift

*For God so loved the world, that he gave his only
begotten Son,*
that whosoever believeth in him should not perish,
but have everlasting life
(John 3:16).

In order to gain the proper perspective of giving, we
need first to consider some of what God has already given
to us:

1. His Son Jesus *(John 3:16);*
2. His love *(John 3:16);*
3. His grace *(Romans 1:7);*
4. His breath *(Genesis 2:7);*
5. His Holiness *(Hebrews 12:10);*
6. His image *(Genesis 1:26);*
7. His time *(Genesis 1:14);*
8. His word *(See entire Bible);*
9. His wisdom *(James 1:5);* and
10. His earth and all that is therein *(See entire Bible).*

Putting Finances in Proper Perspective

Obviously, God has given of Himself to us. In *Proverbs 8:11,* God stated the importance of wisdom over wealth when He said: ***For wisdom is better than rubies; and all things that may be desired are not to be compared to it.*** Money is way down on the list of what God has given to us. It has no place whatsoever in John 3:16. So let us never again look at giving just in terms of money. Let us always view our giving to God from the perspective of what God has given of Himself to us.

Since we are made in the image of God *(Genesis 1:26),* we should give of ourselves to God, just as He has given of Himself to us. Let us give Him:

1. Ourself and our family;
2. Our love;
3. Our repentance for sin;
4. Our very being and existence;
5. Our praise;
6. Our life to be molded into His image;
7. Our time in prayer, fasting, and the Word;
8. Our obedience to His Word;
9. Our willingness to seek His Wisdom; and
10. Our physical and financial substance.

As we begin to look on giving in terms of what God has given to us, money will take its proper position behind the very nature of God Himself. Then, we will have the faith to concentrate on the message we are to carry and know that God is never late in granting provision. It is not the primary responsibility of the husband, father, pastor or ministry head to raise money. Rather, it is their responsibility to, ***Fear God and keep HIs commandments: for this is the whole duty of man.*** *(See Ecclesiastes 12:13 and the lives of Abraham, Moses, Joshua, Ezra, Nehemiah, Jesus and Paul)* God always meets His obligations.

Today's Babylonian worldwide social and economic order has done to us what Pavlov did to his dog; we are very well conditioned to always think money simultaneously with being assigned a task, even though the task be assigned by God Himself. In short, Babylon has taught us well to think money before giving consideration to anything else, even God or the calling that He has put on our lives.

God gave to us His Son, who gave His life for us, which gave to us eternal life. Now, let us give love to Him as He gave love to us. When we love Him first, He will always provide our every need *(Philippians 4:19)*.

Giving of Finances

Now that we have put the giving of finances in its proper place, behind the love of God, let us look at the giving of finances:

Where Does Wealth Come From?

... for it is he that giveth thee the <u>power to get</u> wealth, that he may establish his covenant which he swore unto thy fathers, as it is this day
(Deuteronomy 8:18 emphasis added)

"<u>Power</u>" - means from giant lizards to good fruit: "<u>to get</u>" - means to create; our heart determines whether we will create giant Lizards (drug lords) or Christ-centered behavior (good fruit). ("Strong's Exhaustive Concordance" published 1985 by Baker Book House, Grand Rapids, Michigan).

Who Really Owns What We Give?

The silver is mine, and the gold is mine ... *(Haggai 2:8)*. We should never view giving from the perspective of how much do we want to keep? An example is the rich young ruler *(Matthew 19:21)*.

Do We Give to the Lord, the Church or the Ministry?

The Lord. **Take ye from among you an offering unto the LORD . . .** *(Exodus 35:5).*

Why Must We Give To The Lord?

1. Giving shows God that we honor Him *(Proverbs 3:9).*
2. Many days after we give, what we have given will be returned to us *(Ecclesiastes 11:1).*
3. Giving a tithe to God causes Him to open the windows of Heaven and pour out a blessing on us that we cannot hold *(Malachi 3:10).*
4. If we give, at least a tithe, God will rebuke the devourer for our sakes *(Malachi 3:11).*
5. If we draw out our soul to the hungry and satisfy their afflicted soul, the Lord will give to us guidance in our everyday lives *(Isaiah 58:10-11).*

What Should be Our Attitude When We Give?

The key to giving is to give as unto the Lord with a willing heart. In *Exodus 35: 5 & 21* the people were asked to give as unto the Lord with a willing heart. They gave so much that they were asked to stop giving.

What Should We Give to the Lord?

1. A sacrifice of praise *(Hebrews 13:15).*
2. The first fruits of our increase *(Proverbs 3:9-10).*
3. Only unblemished items *(Exodus 12:5).*
4. He that pities the poor lends to God, and He will pay him again *(Proverbs 19:17).*

How Much Should We Give to the Lord?

1. We should be willing to give all that we have *(Matthew 13:44)*.
2. We should give a least a tithe *(Malachi 3:10)*.
3. We should give out of our need *(Mark 12:38-44)*.
4. We should give as we are able according to what God has given to us *(Deuteronomy 16:17)*.
5. We should approach the collection plate with the same mind that Jesus had as He approached the cross on Calvary.

What Does God See Us As When We Do Not Give At Least A Tithe?

Thieves and robbers *(Malachi 3:8)*.

Why?

And all of the tithe of the land, whether of the seed of the land, or of the fruit of the tree, is the LORD'S: it is holy unto the LORD
(Leviticus 27:30).

The tithe belongs to God and is holy unto the Lord; therefore, we are thieves as to that portion of the tithe which we fail to give to God. To fail to tithe is the same as stealing out of the collection plate.

What Keeps Us from Giving?

Pride. Pride kept Sodom from strengthening the hand of the poor and needy *(Ezekiel 16:49)*.

Comments

I

When we think in terms of what the scriptures say about giving, we will focus on what God gave for us and to us; we will not focus on what we can get by giving. Our focus on giving to get leaves out Jesus and degrades the principle of giving to a "give and get syndrome."

II

The world says, "We must keep, amass, and continually acquire in order to gain." The Word says ***Give, and it shall be given unto you; good measure, pressed down, and shaken together, and running over, shall men give into your bosom. For with the same measure that ye mete withal it shall be measured to you again*** *(Luke 6:38).* Do not look at this scripture just in terms of money, look at it also in terms of love, time, wisdom, and the other intangibles in life.

III

There are many Christians who tithe faithfully and stay broke at the same time. They stay broke because balance is missing in their lives. The Word of God must be read as a whole and not picked apart to be used piece by piece when we deem it convenient. For instance, we can give all that we have but if we harbor bitterness, what good is the giving? *(I Corinthians 13:3)*

Fund Raising Campaigns

***And I, if I be lifted up from the
earth, will draw all men unto me***
(John 12:32).

186

In *John 12:32,* God established the most efficient fund raising campaign ever known to man when Jesus said ***And I, if I be lifted up from the earth, will draw all men unto me.*** When the wise men came to see Jesus, they worshiped Him first; then, they opened their treasures and presented gifts to Him *(Matthew 2:11).* God supplies funds through worship, which is our intimate time with Him. So, why do we waste our time putting together "efficient fund raising campaigns"? Answer, because we do not trust God to supply our need.

The churches and ministries that concentrate on worshiping God by lifting up Jesus, rather than concentrating on raising funds, will draw all men into their congregations and audiences. All the men have all the money. When Jesus has a man's heart, that man's pocketbook belongs to Jesus.

If we will simply teach people how to worship, out of that worship God will always supply us with all He wants us to have at the time. There is nothing wrong with telling of a need, but let the need be supplied out of worship and not out of hype and emotional fund raising campaigns. The churches and ministries that concentrate on telling the world about Jesus Christ, rather than concentrating on raising funds, will draw all men into their congregations and audiences.

The extent and consistency of true giving is guided by the level of our maturity in Jesus Christ. We must learn that telling the world about Jesus is the only true cure for all of the financial needs of every individual, business and ministry. A man will give with a willing heart as unto the Lord once he makes Christ the center of his life. Then, as he gives, God will bless him.

How many times are we approached by various organizations requesting donations. Then, comes the proverbial question, to whom should we give? The answer is to give to several rather than to just a few, for we know not what evil is in the recipients.

Certainly, when an organization gives us the "come on" that they are doing the most and are the most important to the work of God, we can dismiss them immediately. Such a "come one" is selling rather than telling, and that is manipulation which is as witchcraft.

The work of God requires many people and organizations working together for the common cause of Jesus Christ. So, let us be careful that we, *Give a portion to seven, and also to eight . . . (Ecclesiastes 11:2),* for then no one organization shall squander all of what we give.

Do Not Focus on Raising Money - Train Men to be Mature in the Word - Then They Will Give Without Being Asked to Do So

Pledge Cards, Matching Giving and Other Such Methods

Pledge cards, matching giving, and other such methods are signs of immaturity in the body of Christ, and there is no scriptural basis for their use. These man-made methods are born out of man's distrust of God to supply man's needs. To use these methods of raising funds carries us ahead of God's timing, causes a lack of peace in their use and does not produce maturity in the body of Christ.

The purpose of pledge cards is to **BIND** us in writing to do what we should already be doing out of a willing heart; the purpose of matching giving is to **EMOTIONALLY** encourage us to do what we should already be doing out of a willing heart; and, the purpose of other methods such as Founder's Clubs, $1,000 Clubs, $2,500 Clubs and President's Clubs is to play on our **PRIDE** which desires recognition. Actions growing out of **BONDAGE, EMOTION** and **PRIDE** do not produce maturity in the body of Christ. Neither does favoritism toward large givers, as it is sin *(James 2:1-4).* When we have a "partners meeting", we should not give the "big givers" the rooms with a waterfront view and the small givers the rooms with a view of the parking lot.

Maturity in Giving

Maturity in giving comes only as we gain insight into God's Word, so let us concentrate on teaching the Word and not increasing offerings. As we learn more of Jesus, the Holy Spirit will cause us to give with a willing heart, and the symptoms of immaturity in our lives will begin to disappear. Let us allow Christ in us to mature our hearts to give willingly as the Spirit directs.

The poor widow did not give out of bondage, emotion or pride; and Jesus saw the gift she made from a willing heart as being valued more than all the gifts from others. While the amount of her gift would make her a "partner," it certainly would not have entitled her to a membership in the Founder's or President's Club nor would it have entitled her to the "give always" bestowed on large donors. Yet, her willing-heart gift out of her need entitled her to an irrevocable place in the eternity of God's Word *(Mark 12:41-44)*.

It is the duty of the kingdom worker to plant the seed of the Word in the people. Then, the kingdom worker should tell of his needs and trust the Spirit to move on the people to meet those needs. The Word placed in the people will never return void; rather, it will afford to us exactly what we need. The God of this universe is certainly capable of directing His Spirit to move people to give to those who serve Him. He does not need or want our Babylonian pressure tactics to fund His purposes.

The Motive in Giving

Take heed that ye do not your alms before men, to be seen of them; otherwise ye have no reward of your Father which is in heaven
(Matthew 6:1).

Do we make gifts in such a manner that others will know what we have given or, do we make the gift in such a way that only God and the treasurer know what we have given?

If we give in any manner that draws attention to ourselves, our gift was made in vain and vanity is our only reward. Vain gifts draw attention to us and away from God. The heart that seeks glory for itself denies the glory of God. A gift from that kind of heart does not carry any Godly reward for the giver.

Why did we give the pew, window, car or dormitory? Was it to bring recognition to ourselves via a brass plaque bearing our name on the door, or our name being mentioned in the most favored level of givers in the next alumni magazine? Would we have made the gift but for the plaque or the "honorable" mention column?

Let us not be vain to the point of believing an object was given to glorify God when we really gave it to draw attention to ourselves. Such gifts are like putting a drop of gasoline into a gallon of drinking water, the whole gallon is polluted; neither the gas nor the water is now fit for its intended use. When the motive is wrong there is no reward in the giving. But when the giving is done to glorify the Most High God, our reward is to know that He is pleased with our motive.

Giving to the Poor

It is true that if we help the poor, they will take advantage of us. However, we should not let that fact deter us from helping the poor. After all, each time we sin we take advantage of the blood of Jesus Christ. Cornelius gave much alms to the poor, and God accepted those alms as a memorial before Him *(Acts 10:2-4)*. The very fact that Jesus had to die for our sins, is ample testimony of how we take advantage of Him daily. How fortunate we are that Jesus did not refuse to give His life for us when He knew that we would take advantage of Him.

The Hidden Agenda in Giving to the Rich

. . . and he that giveth to the rich, shall surely come to want
(Proverbs 22:16).

To give to the rich, expecting something in return, is sin. In such instances, are we so blind we do not realize the rich know why we are making the gift? We can voice all we want about the gift coming from our heart, but the rich know something is expected or hoped for in return.

Such giving is rewarded with poverty. This gift is not really a gift, it is promoted by a hidden agenda to hopefully obtain something from the rich. Such gifts are best described "as physical evidence of our hidden agenda."

God blesses tithes and offerings brought into the storehouse, but He detests gifts made to further hidden agendas; so do the rich and that is why the return on such gifts is poverty.

The Standard for Giving Finances

The character of Jesus Christ establishes the standard for our entire relationship with God. Unless and until we are willing to give as Jesus gave, we have not met God's standard for giving. When we are willing to give as Jesus gave, the Lord will be our Shepherd and we shall not want *(Psalm 23:1)*.

Instant Honor - Babylon's Reward for Giving

A man's gift maketh room for him,
and bringeth him before great men
(Proverbs 18:16).

A sure ticket to instant honor is to make gifts to "the right people" or "the right causes." We can be dumb as an ox, ugly as sin and reprobate as a jackass - but if we will only give the right amount of money to the right place at the right time, room will be made for us and we will be brought before great men. In other words, we will be given instant honor.

However, just remember that "what comes in an instant can go in an instant," and that applies to honor as well as the rest of life.

THE VALUE OF OUR GOD CONSCIOUSNESS

*The spirit of man is the candle of the LORD, searching
all the inward parts of the belly . . . For there shall
be no reward to the evil man: the candle of the of the
wicked shall be put out*
(Proverbs 20:27 & 24:20).

Our spirit (our God consciousness) is that part of us that communicates with God. God uses our consciousness as a candle to put light on the dark areas of our lives. Our God consciousness is His way of reminding us that He knows the truth, we are wrong and He has exposed our wrong to us.

We can become so wicked that God will snuff out our God consciousness. Thus, it is impossible for a man with God consciousness to understand the actions of a man without God consciousness, and vice versa. These men live in two entirely different worlds. The evil person has, by his actions caused God to snuff out his God consciousness.

Therefore, those of us with a God consciousness will never be able to comprehend the actions of Stalin, Nero, Hitler, Mao Te Sung, the drug lords and the like. Praise God we have God consciousness for it is the candle of the Lord searching the innermost parts of our being to give us the opportunity to choose righteousness over sin. If we are sensitive to the light of our spirit we will change our ways, and that is the value of our God consciousness.

God's Absolute Right
To Tell Us How To Live

I have made the earth, the man and the beast that are upon the ground, by my great power and by my outstretched arm, and have given it unto whom it seemed meet unto me
(Jeremiah 27:5).

God made the earth, man and beast, so He has the absolute right to tell us how to live; and He has stated in His Word how He wants us to live. To live contrary to God's Way is to deny ourselves the benefits of His Covenant with us. We can live contrary to His Word if we so choose but, when we do, we are locked in a sinful contest with the awesome power of God.

How Do We Know What God's Will Is For Our Life?

I beseech you therefore, brethren, by the mercies of God, that ye present your bodies a living sacrifice, holy, acceptable unto God, which is your reasonable service. And be not conformed to this world: but be ye transformed by the renewing of your mind, <u>that ye may prove what is that good, and acceptable, and perfect, will of God</u>
(Romans 12:1-2 emphasis added) .

If we will present ourselves as a living sacrifice acceptable to God, which is reasonable for God to expect; and not become conformed to the world, but be transformed by allowing Christ to renew our mind, we will know the will of God for ourselves, our family, business and professions.

How "Ye Were Healed"

Who his own self bare our sins in his own body on the
tree, that we, being dead to sins, should live unto
righteousness: by whose stripes ye were healed
(I Peter 2:24).

When God created Adam, he was without sin and his flesh was not subject to injury or disease by Satan or the world. But when he sinned, our flesh became destined to die, and Satan and the world constantly attempt to accelerate that death process through accidents and disease.

When Jesus came, He was God in the flesh. Because He was God, His flesh was not subject to sickness and disease by Satan and the world, but Jesus wanted to identify with us and take on our sin and disease. To do this, He had to submit His flesh to the world, and did so by allowing the stripes from the Roman whip to cut into His body. Just as His body was healed of those stripes in the resurrection, so were our bodies healed of our diseases and other infirmities at the same time.

However, while Christ has made our healing an actual fact, God has ordained that the healing does not become ours until we believe, in faith, that Jesus accomplished the healing for us. When we do, our healing is complete and and will then be manifested in our bodies in His time and way.

HIDING OURSELVES FROM EVIL

A prudent man forseeth the evil, and hideth himself:
but the simple pass on, and are punished
(Proverbs 22:3).

Wisdom dwells with prudence *(Proverbs 8:12)*, and it is this prudence from God that enables us to see evil before it overtakes us. When we see the evil coming, we are to hide ourselves from that evil. But if we do not prudently observe and hide from the evil, it will overtake us and we shall suffer the consequences.

Is Homosexuality Caused By Genetics?

And God Said, Let us make man in our image, after our likeness: and let them have dominion over the fish of the sea, and over the fowl of the air, and over the cattle, and over all the earth, and over every creeping thing that creepeth upon the earth. So God created man in his own image, in the image of God created he him; male and female created he them (Genesis 1:26-27).

If a man also lie with mankind, as he lieth with a woman, both of them have committed an abomination: they shall surely be put to death; their blood shall be upon them (Leviticus 20:13).

Homosexuality is a sin, it is not a matter of genetics. How do we know homosexuality is a sin? God, The Creator of all things, addressed homosexuality as sin in Leviticus 20:13, so that makes it sin and not genetics.

Now, all of the above having being said, God loves every homosexual just as much as He does the most righteous person on the face of the earth, and Jesus loves the homosexual so much that He willingly gave His life for that person.

If homosexuals will simply acknowledge their lifestyle as sin, and repent for it, Jesus will welcome them into his arms with great dignity and love that knows no end. He is waiting. Come!

HUMILITY IS PREPARATION
FOR HONOR

Before destruction the heart of man is
haughty, and before honor is humility
(Proverbs 18:12).

We like to be honored, but we do not like being humbled. If we are not humbled before we are honored, the honor will lead to haughtiness which will destroy us.

Jesus was humble unto death, and received honor in the resurrection;

Paul and ten of the twelve disciples were humbled in martyrdom, and honored by God;

David was humbled by being chased as a criminal by Saul, and honored as the King of Israel;

Joseph was humbled in an Egyptian jail, and was honored as the Prime Minister of Egypt;

As the list goes on and on.

INSIGHT TO FREEDOM

... The LORD is my shepherd, I shall not want
(Psalm 23:1) .

And I heard another voice from heaven, saying, Come
out of her (Babylon), my people, that ye be not
partakers of her sins, and that ye receive
not of her plagues
(Revelation 18:4 emphasis added).

... I shall not want does not mean that when the Lord is our Shepherd we will not have problems; rather, it means we shall not want for a proper relationship with the Lord in the midst of those problems. This Shepherd relationship will keep us from fearing evil as we walk in the valley of the shadow of death, and allow us to dine in peace in the presence of our enemies.

There are times in our lives when we pridefully turn our hearts away from the Lord as our Shepherd, and toward the lure of the world's social and economic order known as "Babylon." As we move in that direction, the Shepherd will call for us to come out of Babylon, for He does not want us to be partakers of her sins and suffer her plagues. He knows that once we are in Babylon, we will have difficulty in recognizing and answering His call for us to come out of Babylon.

We attain the insight to freedom from Babylon by learning principles from God's Word that will show us how to recognize and answer the Shepherd's call. The time and circumstances required for our individual journeys out of Babylon are different for each of us. They are dependent upon how long we pridefully insist upon doing what we want to do rather than what the Shepherd commands us to do. If we will only shed our pride and open our hearts to receive and apply the insight of the Word in our lives, the Shepherd will bring into being the circumstances necessary to take us out of Babylon and set us free.

JUSTIFYING OUR WRONG ACTIONS

All the ways of a man are clean in his own
eyes; but the Lord weigheth the spirits
(Proverbs 16:2).

As all of us know very well that we can justify almost anything we want, and to us what we have justified will be clean. Should not the fact that the act needs to be justified in the first place raise questions in our mind about the act? After all, is not justification the explanation of a wrong in a manner so as to make it appear to be right?

Obedience to the Word of God does not require justification because the Word is Christ. However, as we begin to move away from obeying the Word, and toward what we want to do, our pride requires that we justify our wrongful acts so as to give them the appearance of being righteous acts.

THE REAL TEST OF INTEGRITY

Test me, O Lord, and try me, examine
my heart and my mind . . .
(Psalm 26:2 NIV).

Our real test of integrity is to ask God to prove us. To make this request is to ask God to allow us to experience the depths of humility and the ultimate in joy. Such are the benefits of enduring the real test of integrity. Without requesting and enduring this test, let us not dare call ourselves Christians in the true sense of the word.

THE FRUIT OF LUST

IS A LEAN SOUL

They soon forgat his works;
they waited not for his counsel:
But lusted exceedingly in the wilderness,
and tempted God in the desert. And he gave them
their request; but sent leanness into their soul
(Psalm 106:13-15).

One of the most severe rebukes we can receive at the hand of God is for Him to let us have what we want. We too often call on Him to bless us rather than to counsel us. We lust exceedingly after material things and tempt Him with our sin. So, He gives us that for which we lust and, at the same time, sends leanness into our soul as the fruit of that lust.

MANIPULATION

Now the chief priests, and elders, and all the
council, sought false witness against Jesus,
to put him to death; But found none . . .
(Matthew 26:59-60).

Manipulation is one of the most common problems in our society. A manipulator is one who does not trust God for the outcome of a matter, so he attempts to deceitfully control facts, people and events to achieve his desired results.

While the manipulator may seem to succeed for a time, God's Word insures that his efforts will ultimately fail and will be exposed for the world to see. Proof of this is shown in *Matthew 26:59-60.* The whole world now knows how the chief priest, elders and whole council committed manipulative acts against Jesus in an effort to preserve their own political position.

Many people manipulate in the name of diligence. When do our actions move from being diligent to being manipulative? Answer, the moment we begin to not trust God for the outcome of the matter. It is our distrust of God's sovereignty that causes us to manipulate. Anyone who trusts God knows the difference between diligence and manipulation.

Once we learn to trust God we will no longer desire to manipulate, regardless of how great the threat to our position. To trust Him is to stand on the Truth, and the Truth insures that God's will is going to prevail in the matter. (See also *The Fallacy of Hype,* at page 37 and *Telling Vs. Selling* at page 38)

MARRIAGE, RECONCILIATION, DIVORCE AND MARRIAGE AFTER DIVORCE

Introduction

Only in the Word of God can we find:
The creation of marriage; the purpose of marriage;
His principles of marriage;
The causes of all of the problems in marriage;
The answers to all of the problems in marriage; and
The fulfillment of marriage *(see the entire Bible)*.

As we apply His Word in our lives, our marriage will be on the way to becoming equal to the marriage of Christ and the Church *(Ephesians 5:25)*.

Yet, there seems to be a range of opinions about marriage, divorce and remarriage that covers the entire spectrum of human imagination. Unfortunately, it is the self-will of those who have chosen to live outside of God's Word that has given rise to this vast spectrum of opinions. Given all of these opinions, most people could easily assume that no final authority governs marriage, divorce and remarriage.

But let there be no mistake, there is a final and absolute authority that governs every facet of marriage, divorce and remarriage. That authority is the Word of God. We must remember that man has opinions, but God has the truth; and, all of man's opinions that conflict with the Word are wrong. The Word is the absolute truth of and authority over marriage, divorce and remarriage.

When God created man, marriage and woman, He gave to us the inalienable right to choose how we want to live — within His Word or outside of His Word. If we choose to live within God's Word, we shall approach marriage, divorce and remarriage as does God; but, if we choose to live outside of His Word, we are left with only our personal opinions to govern our approach to these issues.

So, we must learn to be obedient to God and approach marriage, divorce and remarriage through the Word of God with no thought of our personal opinions. If we will, in time our marriage will become equal to the marriage of Christ and the Church (*Ephesians 5:25*).

The Creation of Man, Woman and Marriage

. . . it is not good that man should be alone;
I will make him an help meet for him; . . .
(Genesis 2:18).

The creation of man, woman and marriage became necessary when God spoke the words *. . . Let us make man in our image, according to our likeness . . . (Genesis 1:26).* Why? Because while the Father, Son and Holy Spirit are three separate entities, they are made one by their love relationship for the other. So man and woman, as separate entities, need a love relationship in which they, too, can become one; otherwise, their marrage will not be in the image and likeness of the Trinity.

God, in His infinite wisdom, chose to create Eve as Adam's help meet and for them to become one flesh through the help meet relationship of marriage; marriage being the love relationship through which husband and wife can become one flesh. That relationship was created when God spoke the words, *For this reason a man will leave his father and mother and be united to his wife, and they will become one flesh. (Genesis 2:24).* How they become one is a mystery known only to God, and the fulfillment thereof is most certainly enjoyed by husband and wife. This relationship of marriage is as much a part of God's creation as is the sun, moon, stars and oceans. Such is the power of God's spoken Word.

To place the creation of man and woman and marriage in its proper context, we need to understand that God created only three estates of oneness:

The Trinity - Christ and the Church - Husband and Wife.

205

Thus, we should accord to marriage the respect it deserves. Marriage is not a legal license to ecstasy or a convenience to man. It is that part of God's creation that was designed by Him to enable man and woman to become one flesh.

Marriage Belongs to God, Not to Man

. . . I will make him an help meet for him
(Genesis 2:18).

All of God's creation, including marriage, belongs to God. God gave us dominion over His creation, He did not give His creation to us *(Genesis 1:26-30 & Psalm 8:6).* He made us creation keepers, not creation owners. The creation owner designates who eats what in the garden. When Adam ate of the forbidden fruit he was, in effect, claiming the creation as His own and denying the authority of God over creation. Likewise, each time we act outside of God's Word in our marriage, we are claiming marriage as our own and denying the authority of God over our marriage.

Just as we have declared ourselves to be owners of God's creation, so have we declared ourselves to be owners of our marriage. And, just as we have no authority from God to pollute the earth, neither do we have the authority to pollute our marriage with divorce, strife and bitterness. That is why Jesus said in Matthew 19:6. . . **What, therefore, God has joined together, let no man put asunder.** From the beginning divorce was not God's will. Only as we begin to realize that God made us the keepers of our marriage, and not the owners, will our marriage begin to become what God intended.

Since marriage belongs to God, He has the authority to tell us how we are to conduct ourselves in marriage, and He does so in His Word. If we respect His Word, we will recognize that our marriage belongs to Him; otherwise, we will not. In any event, regardless of how we conduct ourselves in our marriage, our marriage still belongs to Him.

Preparation for Marriage

And ye fathers, provoke not your children to wrath: but bring them up in the nurture and admonition of the Lord (Ephesians 6:4).

Godly parents bring up their children in the nurture and admonition of God, and those children will be prepared for marriage. All other children will not be prepared for marriage. Hence, we see today's alarming divorce rate.

Think about it. How can children who do not know God enter into His creation of marriage and expect to be successful in that marriage? After all, when we go into another person's home, state or country, should not we first discover what is expected of us while we are there? Otherwise, our stay there might not at all be what we imagined, and at the first confrontation we will want to leave. The parallel in marriage is to divorce.

Preparation for marriage begins in the cradle, not at the time of engagement. To teach our children about God is to teach them about marriage. Why? Because, only as we begin to learn about the relationship of Christ and the Church, will we begin to understand the intimate relationship of marriage.

The depth of our relationship with our spouse is equal to the depth of our relationship with God. God is the Author of intimacy. He placed intimacy into marriage when He spoke the words *... I will make him an help meet for him ... (Genesis 2:18)*, and *... they shall be one flesh (Genesis 2:24)*. To enter into His creation of marriage and enjoy that creation to the fullest requires experience in yielding to the Creator.

As we learn more about the Creator we will begin to make decisions as He does. We will then be able to view our spouse as does the Creator, and not through our flesh. It is this spiritual insight that will insure the success of our marriage. Every moment spent with Him is a moment spent in preparation for marriage.

Nevertheless, it is never too late for us to prepare for marriage, even if we are already married. We must start preparing where we are, whether not yet married, married, or divorced.

The Irrevocable
Commitment Of Marriage

Husbands love your wives even as Christ also loved the
Church and gave himself for it . . . and the wife
see that she reverence her husband
(Ephesians 5:25 & 33).

Marriage is God's way of allowing man and woman to experience the joy and intimacy of being one with the other. This joy and intimacy brings with it the God given responsibility of irrevocable commitment to our marriage. If this commitment is lacking, joy will soon fade; intimacy will become repugnant; bitterness and strife will then enter; and, the marriage will be in jeopardy.

This irrevocable commitment requires that we lose the singleness of our identity as an individual by blending with the identity of our mate. The making of this commitment is akin to making concrete. The individual ingredients of sand, stone, water and cement each lose their separate identity and become one as concrete. These separate ingredients are much stronger by becoming one than they were individually.

Commitment is the cement in marriage. It is the ingredient in marriage that, when blended with the water of the Word, binds the husband and wife together to create a union that will last for a lifetime. In making concrete, the ingredients are removed from their former environments and blended together as one in a new environment. Likewise, the husband and wife leave the environment of their parents' homes and become a part of a new environment of marriage to serve a purpose designed by the Master Craftsman. It is the quality of commitment by the husband and wife to the marriage that determines if the Master's purpose for the marriage will be served.

Jesus spent His life preparing to become one with His bride. Because of His preparation, the elements of the world could not destroy Him or His marriage. Likewise, if our marriage is properly cemented together by our irrevocable commitment to it, the elements of the world will not prevail against our marriage. Then God's kingdom will come and His Will be done in our marriage and in the lives of our children for many generations.

The Sanctity of Marriage

Husbands love your wives as Christ also loved the Church and gave himself for it; . . . and the wife see that she reverence her husband (Ephesians 5:25 & 33).

The sanctity that God places on marriage is quite evident in *Ephesians 5:25-33*. There God directs the love relationship of every husband toward his wife to be the same as Christ's relationship with the Church, even to the point of the husband giving his life for his wife. Likewise, the wife is to reverence her husband. For God to compare the relationship of husband and wife with the relationship of Christ and the Church is concrete evidence of the sanctity that He places on marriage.

. . . and they shall be one flesh (Genesis 2:24).

Genesis 2:24 affirms the sanctity of marriage. How a man and woman become one flesh in marriage is a mystery known only to God. In any event, this one flesh pronouncement by God was the consummation of God's will that man be created in the image and likeness of Him. This consummation is true even though the husband and wife may be christians, christian and non-christian, or non-christians. Such is the power of God's spoken word.

Protecting the Sanctity of Marriage

. . . What therefore God has joined together, let not man put asunder (*Matthew 19:6*).

In Matthew 19:6, God granted the protection of His Word to the sanctity of marriage when Jesus stated**. . . *What therefore God has joined together, let not man put asunder.*** In *Malachi 2:16,* God clearly states He**. . . *hateth putting away* . . .** our marriage in divorce. Because of His respect for the sanctity of marriage, God goes on to state in *Malachi 2:16* that He considers divorce to be**. . . *violence* . . .** It is of paramount concern to God that the sanctity of marriage be preserved, even if it means the husband and wife must give their lives for the other. That is just what Jesus did for the Church, and God expects no less of us in our marriage.

People will often make the statement "not every marriage was meant to be" or "they should have never gotten married." These kinds of statements attack the sanctity of marriage. Whether the couple should have married or should stay married are not valid questions. They are married and God has made them one. Such statements cause husbands and wives to disregard the fact that God has made them one. These statements also deny the power of the Word to change the lives of husbands and wives and the course of their marriage.

Every marriage has its Gethsemanes but, as Jesus was greater than Gethsemane, so must we be greater too. The Godly way to preserve the sanctity of our marriage and overcome our marital Gethsemanes is to seek the will of God in the midst of the circumstances, **. . . *Father, if thou be willing, remove this cup from me: nevertheless, not my will, but thine, be done* (*Luke 22:42*).**

Then, as did Jesus, we are to act in accordance with God's will as shown in His Word. Jesus could have violated the sanctity of His marriage to the Church by jumping over the wall in Gethsemane and skipping town. But, because of His respect for the sanctity of His coming marriage to the Church, He stayed in the garden and proceeded to give His life for His wife. For us to do any less while in the Gethsemanes of our marriage would be to violate the sanctity of our marriage, and that would not be pleasing to God.

Marriage Does Not Create Problems

. . . it is not good that man should be alone;
I will make him an help meet for him
(Genesis 2:18).

Marriage does not create problems. Rather, problems in the marriage are caused by the husband and wife in the marriage. To say that marriage creates problems is to contradict God, for God said *. . . It is not good that man should be alone; . . . (Genesis 2:18).* God would not create a relationship (marriage) that causes problems. God is love, He is not a god of division. For instance, if a person has difficulty living as a Christian the problem is not in the person being a Christian; the problem is in the person. The same analogy holds true in marriage. The problems are in the people who are married, not in God's creation of marriage.

We bring problems into our marriage when and as we alienate ourselves from God. Most often these problems are in us long before we marry. Such problems are solved only when and as we become willing to be accountable to ourselves, God and our mate for our behavior in the marriage. For us to blame marriage for the problems in our marriage is for us to refuse to be accountable to ourselves, God and each other for our own shortcomings. Such behavior is to blame God, Who created marriage, for our own shortcomings.

This is one reason why we should submit to extensive counseling by our Pastor prior to marriage. Such counseling will reveal and resolve many of our personal problems and cause us to realize our accountability in marriage. Proper premarital counseling can save a us years of anguish and greatly reduce the possibility of our marriage ending in divorce.

It is the absolute duty of every Pastor to provide extensive premarital counseling to everyone he marries. Otherwise, he is accountable to the couple and to God for the breakdown in their marriage. The Pastor who does not give Godly counsel to those whom he is about to marry has shortchanged that couple, just as Aaron shortchanged the Israelites when he participated with them in making a golden calf *(Exodus Chapter 32)*.

We should look at the problems in our marriage through the eye of God's Word, and not through the eye of "self". The Word will reveal to us, without exception, that the problems in our marriage are in us, and not in God's creation of marriage.

Family Authority

Wives, submit yourselves unto your own husbands, as unto the Lord. For the husband is the head of the wife, even as Christ is the head of the church: and he is the savior of the body. Therefore as the church is subject unto Christ, so let the wives be to their own husbands in every thing. Husbands, love your wives, even as Christ also loved the church, and gave himself for it; That he might sanctify and cleanse it with the washing of water by the word. That he might present it to himself a glorious church, not having spot, or wrinkle, or any such thing; but that it should be holy and without blemish. So ought men to love their wives as their own bodies. He that loveth his wife loveth himself. For no man ever yet hated his own flesh; but nourisheth and cherisheth it, even as the Lord the church; For we are members of his body of his flesh, and of his bones. For this cause shall a man leave his father and mother, and shall be joined unto his wife, and they two shall be one flesh. This is a great mystery: but I speak concerning Christ and the church. Nevertheless let every one of you in particular so love his wife even as himself; and the wife see that she reverence her husband . . .

Children, obey your parents in the Lord: for this is right.
Honor thy father and mother; which is the first
commandment with promise; That it may be well with
thee and thou mayest live long on the earth. And, ye
fathers, provoke not your children to wrath: but bring
them up in the nurture and admonition of the Lord
(Ephesians 5:22-36 & 6:2-4).

"Taking the Cup" in Marriage

. . . O my Father, if it be possible, let this cup pass from
me: nevertheless, not as I will, but as Thou wilt
(Matthew 26:39).

Three times Jesus asked God to let the cup pass from Him, but each time He answered His own request by saying *. . . nevertheless, not as I will, but as Thou wilt.* It is no sin to ask God to remove the cup from us, but it is a sin to refuse to take the cup because we pridefully want our way in the matter. Praise God that Jesus made the decision to take the cup and please His Father.

Marriage often presents us with the opportunity to take the cup but, when faced with the cup, we often make statements like "It's not my fault, I didn't do anything wrong so why should I say I'm sorry"? Jesus did not do anything wrong either. But His willingness to take the cup allowed God to work His will in Jesus' life. When we are not willing to take the cup in marriage, God's plan for our life may well come to a halt until we determine to take the cup. In the meantime, at best, our life may well become a short-cut to mediocrity rather than a beacon of righteousness.

May all of us make the decision to "take the cup" in our marriage, for then we will be obedient to love and reverence each other as Christ loved the Church and gave Himself for it. This is pleasing to God and causes us to enjoy the fullness of our marriage as intended by God, and the fullness of His plan for our lives.

The Key Question in Solving Marital Problems

... nevertheless not as I will, but as thou wilt
(Matthew 6:39).

If we truly desire to resolve the problems in our marriage, the key question we need to answer is:

Who Do I Want to Please, God or Myself?

Our answer to this question will determine the future of our marriage. If we make the decision to please God, we will work toward resolving the problems in our marriage; but, if we make the decision to please self, our flesh will provide to us every conceivable excuse to "get our way" at the expense of our marriage. Some of us try to make the decision to please ourselves and God at the same time, but this decision leads only to greater confusion and frustration in our marriage.

The inevitable decision to please ourselves or God is not new or peculiar to today, it dates back to the creation. In the beginning God told Adam not to eat the forbidden fruit, but Adam and Eve saw that the tree was *... good ... pleasant and a tree to be desired ...* *(Genesis 3:6).* Therefore, they made the decision to do that which pleased self rather than please God by obeying His Word. The result of their decision was that they became separated from God. Because we are one with God and our mate, as we make decisions that separate us from God we automatically move away from loving Him and our mate.

Thus, as long as we make the decision to please ourselves rather than God, our relationship with our spouse will never enjoy the potential intended by God. Just as Christ gave His life for us, so must we be willing to give of ourselves to Him. The decision to please God rather than self is often more difficult than physical death. Could it be this is why Jesus sweat drops of blood in Gethsemane? But, once He made the decision to please God by offering Himself as a sacrifice, the sweating of blood ceased.

Three times Jesus asked God to let the cup pass from Him, but each time Jesus answered His own request by saying *. . . nevertheless not as I will, but as thou wilt (Matthew 26:39)*. It is not a sin to ask God to remove the cup from us, but it is a sin to refuse to take the cup by favoring ourselves over God or our spouse. Praise God that Jesus made the decision to take the cup and to please His Father rather than Himself. If we are to solve our marital problems we, too, must make the decision to please God and not ourselves.

We Must Identify the Problems our Marriage And Not Focus on the Symptoms

Ye blind guides which strain at a gnat,
and swallow a camel
(Matthew 23:24).

If persons experiencing marital problems knew how to identify the problems in their marriage, they could most often deal effectively with them. The majority of people suffering marital problems desperately want to have a fruitful marriage, they just cannot identify the problems. Therefore, they do not know how to overcome the problems.

We must learn that problems creep into our marriage only because we do not obey the spiritual principles given to us by God. If we will diligently study the Word, we will gain the spiritual insight needed to identify and correct the problems in our marriage. In the medical realm when the disease is properly diagnosed and treated in the person, the symptoms of the disease disappear. Likewise, in the marital realm, when the husband and wife study and follow the Word to identify and solve the problems in their marriage, the symptoms of their bad marriage will disappear.

People suffering marital problems most often place their entire attention on the symptoms rather than on the problems. Therefore, they never address the real problems in their marriage.

They think the symptoms of adultery, alcoholism, lack of communication, boredom, etc. are the problems in their marriage. As a result, these people are continually frustrated when they act and react to the symptoms, and matters just seem to get worse. The despair and frustration produced by not addressing the real problems in marriage must be one of the most exhausting, humiliating and exasperating experiences a human can suffer. Sadly, this despair and frustration leads to the death of over one-half of all marriages, divorce.

If we are to sort out symptoms and problems, we must remember that God created man in His own image, He created marriage in the image of the Trinity and Christ and the Church, and He established certain spiritual principles for us to follow in marriage. If we follow those principles, good fruit will become evident in our marriage. However, if we violate some or all of those spiritual principles, bad fruit will become evident in our marriage. When the bad fruit starts to become evident, we can focus on the bad fruit or we can focus on why the fruit is bad. To focus on the bad fruit is to focus on the symptoms, but to focus on why the fruit is bad is to focus on the problems.

Remember the scribes and pharisees that Jesus accused of being *. . . **blind guides, which strain at a gnat, and swallow a camel** (Matthew 23:24)?* These scribes and pharisees were always dealing with superficial issues and never with the real problems of the day. Such is the case of married people who deal with symptoms and not problems. The problems of a bad marriage are but as gnats, but the symptoms are as big as camels. If we will deal with the gnats in our marriage, the camels will go away.

One of the first questions commonly asked in marriage counseling is, "What's the problem in your marriage?" The answer is most often something like this:

"My husband is committing adultery!"

"My wife left me!"

"Twenty-eight years of marriage and he wants a divorce!"

"I just do not love him anymore!"

"Her folks will not keep their noses out of our business!"

Not one of these statements identifies any of the problems in the marriage, they all refer to symptoms of underlying problems. Alcohol, adultery, financial pressure, lack of communication, etc. never cause divorce, these are only symptoms of underlying problems. The same problems that caused the divorce caused the alcoholism, adultery, lack of communication, etc.

Over one-half of all men, women and children in our society today are living in a virtual marital no man's land of strife, divided authority over children, adultery and lack of self-worth. Divorce is not just of epidemic proportions, it is a national disaster. The real damage resulting from this disaster is the destruction of the family unit. This destruction can be avoided if husbands and wives experiencing marital difficulties will stop treating just the symptoms. If they will study the meat of God's Word, they will be able to discern good from evil. Then they will know how to identify and overcome the problems in their marraige and restoration will be on the way.

Loving our Mate Where They Are

Husbands, love your wives, even as Christ also loved the church, and gave himself for it; . . . and the wife see that she reverence her husband
(Ephesians 5:25-33).

Jesus' life, death and resurrection are irrefutable evidence that He loves us where we are. He made this message known in His life by giving Himself to us, in His death by giving Himself for us and in His resurrection by giving to us the power of His name. Likewise, every husband and wife should use their life to convey the message to each other that, "I love you where you are." God unmistakably places this responsibility upon every husband and wife with the words:

Husbands, love your wives, even as Christ also loved the church and gave himself for it; . . . and the wife see that she reverence her husband (Ephesians 5:25-33).

Unfortunately, some husbands and wives make it very difficult for their mates to love them, and Jesus had the same problem. He has every reason to stop loving His bride since we doubt Him, commit adultery on Him and our sins caused Him to be crucified; yet, He never uses any of these "reasons" to stop loving us. Jesus knows that if He stops loving us where we are, it will destroy His marriage relationship with us. He loves us where we are. Likewise, God expects every husband and wife to have that same kind of love for the other, regardless of where they are at the time.

We, in and of ourselves, are incapable of loving our spouse where they are. We can do so only through the love of Christ in us. The Apostle John speaks of this love in John 3:16 when he said **For God so loved the world that he gave his only begotten Son . . .** The depth of this love is also shown in *Song of Solomon 8:6. . . for love is strong as death . . .* and again in *8:7* **Many waters cannot quench love, neither can the floods drown it . . .** In *John 14:23* Jesus said if we love Him we will keep His Word, God will love us and Jesus and God will come and live in us. So, this whole process of being able to love our spouse where he is starts with our obeying the Word.

If we do not know the Word, then we cannot obey what we do not know. *Isaiah 33:6* sums the matter up well. . . **wisdom and knowledge are the stability of thy times . . .** Marital problems are symptoms of instability, i.e., a lack of the wisdom and knowledge of God in our everyday lives. Let us learn and obey the Word. Then the love of Christ will abide in us and we will have the stability to love and reverence our marriage partner where they are, just as Christ loves us where we are.

Accepting Accountability for Problems in Marriage

. . . Thou art the man . . .
(2 Samuel 12:7).

These spine chilling words were spoken by the Prophet Nathan to David concerning his affair with Bathsheba. God did not blame Satan or anything else for the problem; He placed accountability for the problem squarely on David's shoulders.

There is a great tendency for us to blame everyone and everything in sight for the problems in our marriage, and we often believe that Satan caused the pride problem. If in fact Satan has trespassed into our marriage, we should exercise our authority over him and cast him out of the marriage, *. . . Resist the devil and he will flee from you* *(James 4:7).* Satan is a problem in our marriage only if we allow him to be.

The longer we look at other people and things as the problem, the less likely we are to accept our accountability for the problems in our marriage. This behavior insures Satan's success in his self-avowed mission to keep us separated from Jesus Christ and wallowing in divorce, alimony, child support, fatherless homes, motherless homes, bitterness and strife. Let us not blame Satan or anything else for the problems in our marriage. We must learn to accept accountability for and correct our problem of pride that is causing problems in our marriage.

Why Husbands and Wives Do Not Communicate

Likewise, ye husbands, dwell with them (our wives)
according to knowledge, giving honor unto the wife,
as unto the weaker wessel, and being heirs together of
the grace of life; that your prayers be not hindered
(I Peter 3:7 emphasis added).

A husband who dwells with his wife *. . . **according to knowledge**. . .* has and practices the Godly trait of praying with his wife. Notice the last phrase of *I Peter 3:7, . . . **that your prayers be not hindered.*** Certainly a husband should, and often does, pray alone to God. But, if that husband does not also regularly pray with his wife, he is not walking in knowledge and his prayers will be hindered. When there is a lack of prayer, or there is hindered prayer, communication in the marriage becomes a casualty.

A man who walks in the knowledge of God is a humble man, and it is this humility before God that fosters joint prayer. But, when humility is lacking prayer is lacking, and when prayer is lacking communication is lacking.

Donna and I have counseled hundreds of couples with marriage problems, and most of them were Christians. However, there is one couple who has never asked for counsel; that is the couple who prays together every day. They pray, so they communicate, so they do not need counseling.

The Importance of Our Wife's Counsel

And the Lord God said, It is not good that man should be alone; I will make him an help meet for him
(Genesis 2:18).

Why did God make a help meet for man? Because Adam, standing alone, had no one with whom he could be one as the Father, Son and Holy Spirit are One. That is why God said, ***It is not good that he*** (Adam) ***be alone . . .*** So, God created Adam first, then marriage, and then Eve. He then brought Eve to Adam through the relationship of marriage *(Genesis 2:21-22)*. Now that they were one, God *. . . **called their name Adam, in the day when they were created.*** *(Genesis 5:2)*.

What does all of this have to do with listening to our wife? We are one with our mate and God at the same time; <u>so, if we do not have the patience to listen to our wife, we will not have the patience to listen to God.</u> This impatience leads to bad decision making. Our wife's advice may well be God's protection for us in the matter, so to ignore her advice may well be to ignore God's advice in the matter too. <u>We must never forget that a wife's caution to her husband may well be God's offer of a balanced life to her husband.</u>

There are two basic elements in every decision we make: (1) the raw data before us, and (2) the nature of the man making the decision. We mistakenly think that because our wife is not familiar with the raw data, she cannot be of any use to us in the decision making process. How wrong we are. Our wife knows our nature better than anyone; therefore, her advice gives balance to our nature which gives balance to our decision making. The real truth is that we do not include our wife in the decision making because we do not want to hear her say "no" or "wait." Thus, we often err in our decision making when we ignore her advice.

The way we (husbands) can correct this error is to:

1. Sit down with our wife at a time when there is peace and quiet;
2. Ask her to be blunt and tell us what she would change about us as a man and in our marriage; and
3. Pledge to our wife that we will listen and will not defend ourselves at any cost!

Remember, that while a wife's advice may not be correct from time to time, the issue is not the accuracy of her advice; rather, the issue is do we have the patience to listen to her.

If we will only have the "hutzpah" to ask our wife to expose us, our priorities will be in order and we will probably hear the answers to years of prayer in one brutal sitting. Of course, our wife is not always right, and we may be proper in acting contrary to her advice. But, if we will discipline ourselves to have the patience to take time to consider what our wife has to say, we will have the discipline to listen to God and keep our priorities in order. The only thing we can lose by patiently listening to our wife is a little bit of time and our pride.

Pride in the Husband and Wife is the Root Problem in Marriage

Only by pride cometh contention . . .
(Proverbs 13:10).

Only by pride comes contention and only by contention comes problems in our marriage. When we want our own way, we are prideful and cause contention. For us to reject pride is to eliminate the problems in our marriage. As light has no communion with darkness *(II Corinthians 6:14)*, neither can a Godly marriage have communion with pride *(See the entire Bible)*. Pride in the husband and wife is the root problem in marriage.

Contention is not of God, it grows out of the root problem of pride. Contention exists because we choose to be contentious. That moment in our lives when we first "wanted our way," is the very moment our pride opened the door for contention to enter into our lives.

Pride causes contention because it is our will demanding that we live contrary to God's Word. Since God created us and the earth, He gets to set the rules concerning how we are to live. Any attempt by us to live contrary to His Word brings us into contention with Him and our spouse.

Remember, we treat our spouse in direct relationship to our respect for God's Word. Therefore,to respect God's Word is to reject pride; to reject pride is to eliminate contention; and to eliminate contention is to eliminate the problems in our marriage. Of course, our rejection of pride is a growth process, it is not instantaneous.

Pride Is the Sin that Destroys Our Marriage

But your iniquities have separated between
you and your God, and your sins have hid
His face from you, that He will not hear
(Isaiah 59:2).

222

What is the sin of pride? **THE SIN OF PRIDE IS CHOOSING TO DO WHAT WE WANT TO DO RATHER THAN WHAT GOD TELLS US TO DO** *(Genesis 3:1-6)*. Sin separates us from God *(Isaiah 59:2)*, and as we are separated from God so are we separated from our spouse. This process of marital destruction is affirmed in *Proverbs 16:18*, **Pride goeth before destruction, and an haughty spirit before a fall.**

Pride is the most subtle of all sins. It is that part of us that causes us to believe that disobeying God's Word is . . . **good . . . pleasant . . .** and much to be . . . **desired . . .** *(Genesis 3:6)*. The same pride that caused the death of all flesh causes divorce, the death of marriage. As *Romans 6:23* well states, **For the wages of sin is death . . .** Pride is the sin that destroys our marriage.

Before pride could become a part of their lives, Adam and Eve had to choose to disobey God's Word. Their sin of pride was that they saw something good and pleasant which they desired more than they did to obey God's Word *(Genesis 3:6)*. This sin of pride caused them to be ashamed of their nakedness and separated them from God *(Genesis 3:10 & 3:23)*. The same sins that separate us from God separate us from our marriage partner.

For us to act out of pride in our marriage is for us to subject our marriage to a journey of sinful conduct. The way of this journey, unless it is cut short by repentance, is the death of our marriage - divorce. The journey is well mapped out in *James 1:14-15:*

But every man is tempted, when he is drawn away of his own lust, and enticed. Then when lust hath conceived, it bringeth forth sin: and sin, when it is finished, bringeth forth death.

The depth of all marriage problems is equal only to the thickness of the pride in the husband and wife. We must remember that problems in the marriage are not necessary because pride is not necessary. What is necessary is for us to obey the Word, then there will be no place for pride (problems) in our marriage.

We Choose to Have the Pride that Destroys Our Marriage

I call heaven and earth to record this day against you, that I have set before you life and death, blessing and cursing: therefore choose life, that both thou and thy seed may live
(Deuteronomy 30:19).

Before we can properly understand pride, we first have to realize that we choose to have the sin of pride in our lives. The real tragedy is that most often when we make the choice to have pride, we do not know that we are making a choice. This lack of knowledge is caused by our ignorance of God's Word.

To understand this choice factor we have to realize there are only two forces in this world that draw upon us: (1) Jesus Christ *(John 6:44 & 12:32)*, and (2) lust of the flesh *(James 1:14)*. Many times every day we must choose between being drawn to God by Jesus Christ or being drawn away from God by the lust of our flesh. There is no middle ground. Jesus put it very bluntly when He said *... because thou art luke warm, and neither cold nor hot, I will spue thee out of my mouth (Revelation 3:16).* To be drawn to God is righteousness, while to be drawn away from God by the lust of the flesh is sin. To succumb to the lust of the flesh is to tell God in pride, "I do not need you."

When we are experiencing problems in our marriage, we need to understand that we have a choice. We can repent for the sin of pride, be drawn to God through Christ, and watch our marriage problems disappear; or, we can renounce God, be drawn into sin by the lust of our flesh and watch the wages of sin go to work in our marriage and our lives. Just as we choose to allow pride into our lives, we can also choose to repent and cast pride out of our lives. As pride came by our choosing obedience to Christ, so is it cast out by our choosing to obey Him.

For instance, many people will say, "My husband and I just cannot work out our problems; it is just no use." Well, what these people are really saying is that they are not willing to make the commitment to choose Christ as the Lord of their lives. They would rather protect their pride and "save face" than to obey Christ. These people are focusing on the symptoms they see with their physical eye and are allowing those symptoms to control their lives. Their heart is not in the Word of God. Thank God that Jesus did not choose to "save His face" and act on what He could "see" at the whipping post and on the cross. He chose to take on our sins and thereby paid the price to solve every problem in our marriage. Now, let us choose to obey Him, rid ourselves of pride and thereby eliminate the problems in our marriage.

Pride Is Rejected Only Through Repentance - Not Through Just Feeling Sorry

... And Peter remembered the Word of the Lord; how he had said unto him, Before the cock crows, thou shalt deny me thrice. And Peter went out and wept bitterly
(Luke 22:61-62).

And he cast down the pieces of silver in the temple, and departed, and went and hanged himself
(Matthew 27:5).

To allow pride to stay in our marriage is to reject Christ in our marriage. As long as pride stays, problems will remain. We must acknowledge that we have pride, that pride is sin, repent for it and proceed on in our marriage in the love of Christ. Repentance is not just a word, it is a definite change in course of direction. To repent is to turn away from pride and toward righteousness, and that is the way we reject pride.

The stories of Peter and Judas exhibit the difference in true repentance and just feeling sorry. Peter repented for his pride and became the leader in the church of his day; but,

Judas was only sorry (not repentant) for what he had done and went out and hung himself. Repentance is a matter of the spirit, while feeling sorry is a matter of the flesh. If we truly want to restore our marriage we must learn the difference between repentance and feeling sorry for what we have done. Peace in our marriage is only repentance away.

The Character of Pride

The character of pride is subtle like a false messiah or false prophet. As the Word of God teaches us to recognize a false messiah or false prophet, it also gives to us the insight to identify the character of pride in our lives. Pride tells us that what it wants to do is *... good ... pleasant ...* and much to be *... desired ... (Genesis 3:6).* Pride always comes clothed in circumstances that cause us to first question and, very soon thereafter, doubt the Word of God *(Genesis 3:4-6).*

The character of pride is so subtle we are often offended by even the suggestion that certain of our actions are controlled by pride.

The character of pride is to make us believe the lust of the flesh is good and should be satisfied.

The character of pride is displayed by our will wanting to take the form of every human emotion and act that is in disobedience to God's Word. Pride is our desire to disobey God rather than to obey Him. This is called being *... drawn away of his own lust, and enticed (James 1:14).*

The character of pride is to refuse or neglect to study the Word. God desires that we study His Word to show ourselves *. . approved unto God, a workman that needeth not to be ashamed, rightly dividing the Word of truth (II Timothy 2:15).* When we meet this desire of God, we shall exhibit the love of God in our marriage, not the selfish character of Pride.

The character of pride is displayed by our will wanting to cause one or both of the parties in the marriage to "want to give up on the marriage" or "just not try anymore because it won't do any good." Jesus had every reason and justification of the flesh to utter those same words about His forthcoming marriage to the Church.

However, in spite of the circumstances that faced Him, He repelled the lusts of the flesh and obeyed the Word. . . . **but with God all things are possible.** *(Matthew 19:26),* even the resurrection of a marriage that looks to the parties to be a corpse. The choice is ours. Since God can resurrect the dead, He can certainly resurrect a dead marriage if we will only repent for our prideful character and allow the power of God to enter the marriage.

The character of pride is displayed by our will wanting to say, "I can never forgive my husband for what he did" or "I can never forgive my wife for what she did." Such statements are prideful in that they violate the Words spoken by Jesus on the cross, . . . ***Father, forgive them, for they know not what they do*** *(Luke 23:34).* When Jesus made this statement He was hanging naked before a city and was suspended by three nails on a cross. His entire body bore the scars of a Roman flogging, His beard had been plucked out, He had been spat upon, a crown of thorns was on His head, He was being ridiculed by the religious leaders of the time, His sole worldly possession was being gambled away and His mother and His Father were watching, He knew that when He died He was going to have to go to Hell for three days to be tormented by Satan.

All this time He was bearing the sins of the world. He had no pride in Him *(I Peter 2:22);* therefore, He could offer forgiveness to all. No husband or wife has ever suffered as Jesus was suffering when He was offering forgiveness to the very ones who were causing Him to suffer. No person has the right to refuse forgiveness to anyone. To refuse to forgive is not a right or privilege, it is a sin. It is to reject the blood of Christ. It is the sin of pride and there are no exceptions.

The character of pride is unwilling to accept accountability for wrongdoing. Those who will not accept accountability for wrongdoing are also the same persons who will refuse to forgive others.

The character of pride wants to make us believe that we can solve the problems in our marriage without the help of anyone or anything, including faith in the Word of God. By pride, a man's knowledge causes him to be puffed up, but his love of Jesus causes Jesus to be edified *(I Corinthians 8:1)*. Faith works by love *(Galatians 5:6),* and pride is the opposite of faith. Pride and faith cannot co-exist. God required Joshua to *... see ...* with his eye of faith the cities of Jericho and Ai as his, even before the battles began *(Joshua 6:2 and 8:1)*. Likewise, the Word of God requires a husband and a wife to use their eye of faith to *... see ..* a fruitful marriage beyond the problems that are before them.

The character of pride allows our will to have the same effect in our marriage as Samson's will had in his life. Samson's pride caused him to be blinded to the Word of God, bound him in sin and caused him to go around and around at the treadmill grinding grain and getting nowhere. In the end, while Samson was repenting for his sin of pride, everything around him was collapsing.

Such is the lot of many a believer whose marriage constantly goes around and around on the treadmill of their pride grinding out constant disagreement, bitterness and strife and getting nowhere. While he is repenting for his pride, he watches his family fall apart around him. God is pleased with and accepts the act of repentance by a repentant spouse, but the character of pride carries with it consequences that often travel far beyond the time of repentance. It is then that the repentant believer must accept the grace and love of God, and begin to intercede for those caught up in the consequences of his prideful behavior. *... The effectual fervent prayer of a righteous man availeth much (James 5:16).*

The character of pride demands, first subtly and then boastfully, to have its way. Love, care, concern and consideration for others are expressed only at a time that is convenient to pride. These feelings are inconsistent with pride and, when they are expressed by a prideful person, it is spiritually impossible for them to be genuine. David said *... neither will I offer* *burnt offerings unto the LORD my God of that which doth cost me nothing . . . (II Samuel 24:24).* Pride would say, "I shall not offer anything unless it does not cost me anything." Pride is us wanting our way just because we want our way.

The character of pride wants its way so much that we become blind to the destruction it is causing. The writer of Proverbs 16:18 stated the destructive character of pride very well when he said *Pride goeth before destruction . . .* Prideful tentacles of destruction extend outward from the person having the pride and they latch onto and try to destroy everyone they touch.

The character of pride is for us to deny that we are prideful. This denial is most often accomplished when we compare ourselves with our peers who are committing the same sins as we are. In our minds, because what we and our peers are doing is socially acceptable, we feel that we are "good people" and everything is okay. This behavior is glazed over by a putrefied humility which says, "I know I'm not perfect, but who is?"

The character of pride wants its way so much that it will cause us to distort the Bible to have our way. Any of us who pridefully want our way can interpret Scriptures to suit our pride. However, in the process of making such interpretations we bring upon ourselves the curses spelled out in the Bible for people who do such things.

The character of pride denies that God has anything to do with marriage beyond the marriage ceremony. Pride causes us to believe that God was in the ceremony only because we were washed, dressed right and married in a church building.

Finally, the character of pride is exhibited well in the story of the two thieves who were executed, one on each side of Christ. One was willing to acknowledge his pride *. . . for we receive the due reward of our deeds; but this man hath done nothing amiss (Luke 23:41),* and that man is spending eternity in Heaven with Jesus. At the same time, the other thief's pride would not let him admit his wrong, and he is spending eternity in Hell. In pride, he would rather go to Hell than admit he was wrong. Likewise, a prideful marriage partner would rather seek the death of his marriage, divorce, than to admit he is wrong. As light has no communion with darkness, prideful character has no place in a Godly marriage.

The Biblical Course of Action for the Abused Spouse

The ultimate in pride is for us to abuse another to satisfy the desire of our pride to have its way. God does not expect an abused spouse to sit idly by and take the abuse. The abused spouse is to treat the abusing spouse just as God treated the Israelites when they abused Him:

God's Action Toward Israel	The Abused Spouse's Action Toward Their Partner
1. God confronted the Israelites with their sin. He asked them to repent and told them of the judgment to come if they did not repent (*Isaiah 1:16-20*).	1. Confront the abusing spouse with his sin. Ask him to repent. Tell him the law will be called if it happens again.
2. When Israel did not repent and the abuse happened again, God's judgment was to send powerful nations against the Israelites to take them into captivity (*Isaiah 1:21-24*).	2. If the abuse continues, call upon the law to take the abusing spouse into custody. Have the law judge him to the fullest.
3. God always remained ready to forgive the Israelites as soon as they repented (*Isaiah 1:25-27*).	3. Always let the abusing spouse know he is loved and will be forgiven if he repents.

It is not up to us to "get even" or "punish" our spouse for his wrongdoing. This "get even" or "punish" syndrome is prideful behavior and works contrary to restoration. Jesus never had the desire to "get even" or "punish" anyone, but He did unmistakably teach that we will be held accountable (judged) for our actions.

As Jesus was hanging on the cross with nails through His hands and feet, He asked God to forgive those who were abusing

Him. So must the abused spouse forgive the abusing spouse. Yet, if the abuse continues, do not hesitate to use the courts of the land to the fullest extent provided by law. God has ordained the courts of the land to protect us from abuse.

For a marriage partner to raise his hand, fist or tongue against his spouse, or fail to support his spouse and children, is for him to pridefully rise up against the Word of God. At the moment of abuse, the abusing spouse forfeits all of his spiritual authority over the marriage, subjects himself to the judgment of God and man (the court system) and causes the abused spouse to call upon the law of the world for protection. The law is for the lawless and disobedient *(I Timothy 1:9)*. As righteousness begets righteousness, so does pride beget the judgment of God and man.

God's Will for People in Their Second or Later Marriage
(Ephesians 5:25-33 & III John 2)

Too often, people in their second or later marriage feel like second class citizens, and the attitude of many Christians toward these people certainly has not helped the matter. <u>God's will for men and women in their second or later marriage is the same as it is for men and women in their first marriage.</u> God expresses this desire clearly and unequivocally in *Ephesians 5:25-33* and again in *III John 2.*

In *Ephesians 5:25-33,* God states in unmistakable terms, that the husband is to love his wife as *. . . **Christ loved the Church and gave His life for it** . . .* and, He requires the wife *. . . **see that she reverence her husband.*** Obviously, there are no words of limitation in the *Ephesians 5* discourse that limit the love requirements of husband and wife for each other to only those who are in their first marriage. In *III John 2,* God states in unmistakable terms that, ***I wish above all things that thou mayest prosper and be in good health, even as thy soul prospereth.*** Again, there are no words here that limit this wish of God to only those who are in their first marriage. It is God's desire that His creation of marriage provide to every husband and wife, regardless of which marriage they are in at the time, the same joy that Christ experiences with the Church *(Ephesians 5:23).*

God knew, long before He created man, that man and woman would divorce. This is supported in *Matthew 19:8* where Jesus said that from the beginning God never desired for man and woman to divorce, but Moses permitted divorce because of the hardness of man's heart. As a matter of fact, in *Malachi 2:16,* God states that He *. . . hateth . . .* divorce. But, because God loves us, He sent Jesus to cleanse the hardness from our hearts and create a new heart within us so we would not desire divorce. He wants to write His Word in our hearts and be our God. He wants us to be His people regardless of which marriage we are in at the time *(Jeremiah 31:33).*

God looks at our heart, He does not count to see which marriage we are in at the time. He desires for us in our current marriage (regardless of whether it is our second, third, fourth, fifth or later marriage) exactly what He desired for us in our first marriage. Why? Because for husbands to love their wives and for wives to reverence their husbands fulfills His Word *(Ephesians 5:25-33).* If we are to receive God's desire for our current marriage, we must repent for our part in the break up of our previous marriage. Then we are to accept His forgiveness for our wrongdoing and proceed on in our current marriage expecting to receive the fullness of God's desire for us in this marriage. This is God's will for people in their second or later marriage.

Cain and Abel - The Story of the Two Husbands

Adam lay with his wife Eve, and she became pregnant and gave birth to Cain. She said, "with the help of the LORD I have brought forth a man." Later she gave birth to his brother Abel . . .
(Genesis 4:1-2 NIV).

Cain and Abel represent two different kinds of husbands, one negligent and the other diligent. Now, I do not know if either were married at the time that the scriptures recorded below were first spoken. Even so, their respective actions mirror those of countless millions of husbands and fathers.

232

... Now Abel kept flocks, and Cain worked the soil. In the course of time Cain brought some of the fruits of the soil as an offering to the LORD. But Abel brought fat portions from some of the firstborn of his flock. The LORD looked with favor on Abel and his offering, but on Cain and his offering he did not look with favor ...
(Genesis 4:2-5 NIV, emphasis added).

Abel kept sheep and Cain worked the soil. Abel, being diligent, was the example of Godliness and gave his best to God; but Cain, being negligent, was not diligent and gave to God only some of the fruits of the soil. So God looked with favor on Abel, but upon Cain with disfavor.

... So Cain was very angry, and his face was downcast
(Genesis 4:5 NIV).

A negligent husband and father is not happy with himself, so he becomes angry, and his countenance shows it.

Then the Lord said to Cain, "Why are you angry? Why is your face downcast? If you do what is right, will you not be accepted? But if you do not do what is right, sin is crouching at your door, it desires to have you, but you must master it" *(Genesis 4:6-7 NIV).*

God loves negligent husbands, and he desires for them to become diligent. His Word, if they will pay attention to it, asks the negligent husband three (3) questions:

1. Why are you angry?
2. Why is your countenance downcast? And
3. Don't you know that if you will do what is right, you will be accepted by God?

The Word reminds the negligent husband that if he does not do what is right, sin is crouching at the door of his family and desires to have his family; and, the Lord reminds this negligent husband that he can master the sin, if he will:

Now Cain said to his brother Abel, "Let's go out to the field." And while they were in the field, Cain attacked his brother Abel and killed him (Genesis 4:8 NIV).

But Cain, as the negligent husband did not desire to master the sin in his life, he let it kill part of his family.

Then the LORD said to Cain,
"Where is your brother Abel?"
"I don't know, he replied. Am I my brother's keeper?"
(Genesis 4:9 NIV)

So God asked Cain, where is your family? Cain's answer was, they are not my responsibility anymore.

The LORD said, "What have you done? Listen! Your brother's blood cries out to me from the ground . . ."
(Genesis 4:10 NIV).

So God asks the negligent husband, what have you done? Your wife and children call out to me in the midst of the pain you have caused them.

". . . Now you are under a curse and driven from the gound, which opened its mouth to receive your brother's blood from your hand. When you work the ground, it will no longer yield its crops for you. You will be a restless wanderer on the earth." Cain said to the LORD, "my punishment is more than I can bear."
(Genesis 4:11-13 NIV)

God reminds the negligent husband that his sin pollutes his family with all that is ungodly, and that righteousness calls out for judgment on him. God reminds him that his sin will cause his labors to be unfruitful, and, as long as he walks on the counsel of divorce, he will not receive the rest of God. But if he will repent and begin to seek God first, his family will be restored *(Matthew 6:33)*.

Habit Patterns

For repentance to be complete, two separate and distinct issues have to be addressed: (1) our sin, and (2) our habit patterns. Sin has been addressed at pages 1, 159, 277, 294 and 295. So now let us address habit patterns.

Sin establishes wrong habit patterns that must be changed. We can genuinely repent for the sin at the time but, if we do not change the habit patterns generated by the sin, the repentance is not complete.

To change the habit patterns we need simply to act upon our repentance for the sin, by walking in a righteous manner.

DIVORCE

For the LORD, the God of Israel saith that he hateth putting away (divorce)...
(Malachi 2:16 emphasis added).

... What therefore God hath joined together,
let not man put asunder
(Matthew 19:6).

... Moses, because of the hardness of your hearts
suffered you to put away your wives: but from
the beginning it was not so
(Matthew 19:8).

Thus saith the LORD, Where is the bill of your mother's
divorcement, whom I have put away? or which of my
creditors is it to whom I have sold you? Behold,
for your iniquities have ye sold yourselves,
and for your transgressions is your mother put away
(Isaiah 50:1).

Introduction

The above scriptures confirm that God does not look lightly upon divorce. Divorce represents the opposite of restoration, the mission of Jesus Christ. Divorce represents that which is not of God.

Even so, God loves us - divorced or married. Divorce limits, but does not prevent, His ability to use us in service to Him until we repent for our part in the divorce. (Please read *God's Will for People in Their Second or Later Marriage* at page 231)

The Pain of the Partner Who Does Not Want A Divorce

He will swallow up death in victory; and the Lord GOD
will wipe away tears from off all faces . . .
(Isaiah 25:8).

For us to properly relate to the partner who does not want a divorce, we must first understand the pain they suffer. The role of a partner who does not want a divorce must be one of the most devastating experiences a human can endure. <u>These partners say that the pain of rejection, humiliation and loneliness they endure is like a living death.</u> The shock of divorce, and all of its entanglements, often leaves these partners as if they were totally lost in a vast wilderness with no roads or sunlight. Certainly, many people reading this book have been there or are there now.

Let us see scripturally why the pain of divorce is so excruciating, and let us see how God has already provided a way for the pain to be removed from our lives. Then, we will look at other areas of practical concern to the partner who does not want a divorce.

Why Are Divorces Painful?

God is love, why does He let me suffer a divorce? He does not let us suffer, He does not even want us to suffer. We suffer divorce because sin is in the world, not because God is failing us in any regard. The pain of divorce is caused by sin, not by God.

The pain of divorce comes in three separate waves that strike in rapid succession, any one of which is devastating. <u>The three waves are rejection, humiliation and loneliness.</u> Jesus suffered all three in one day, just like the partner who does not want the divorce. He was <u>rejected</u> because of His intimacy with His father, just as we are rejected in divorce because of our intimacy with our spouse; He was <u>humiliated</u> at His trial and in its after effects, just as we are humiliated before our friends and in the divorce proceedings; and, on the cross He suffered the <u>loneliness</u> of being without the intimacy of His Father, just as we suffer the loneliness of being without the intimacy of our spouse. Jesus is very well acquainted with our pain. He knew it before we did.

Overcoming the Pain of Divorce

Just as Jesus overcame sin on the cross, He overcame pain in the resurrection. If we will accept the resurrection we, too, can overcome the pain. The resurrection was the manifestation of Jesus' faith that God would raise Him from the dead. If we will just have faith that God has removed our pain through the resurrection of Christ, the pain of divorce in our lives will ultimately disappear. As Jesus through faith overcame death, sin and pain, so can we. Jesus has done His part, now we must do ours.

I Don't Want A Divorce, What Should I Do?

... cast out first the beam out of thine own eye,
and then thou shalt see clearly to pull out the
mote that is in thy brother's eye
(Luke 6:42).

This is an extremely difficult question. Its difficulty is compounded since divorce is most often caused, at least in part, by both partners. So we really cannot tell this part-guilty party to act like a knight in shining armor and defend their integrity at all costs. Again, we must go to the Word for the answer in *Luke 6:42*.

The partner not wanting the divorce must first examine his own life to find his culpability in the other partner's act of seeking a divorce. Often, the best defense is a good offense against one's self. If this self-examination is to be accurate, it must be conducted in the light of the Word and not in the realm of personal opinions or self-justification; otherwise, the examination will only be a whitewash.

When we have used the Word to confirm our culpability, we must go to the other partner, confess our wrong (regardless of their wrongdoing), ask their forgiveness and commit to change our lives. Pride will attempt to enter here by telling us that the other partner is more at fault than are we. Resist that urge and it will flee from us. It is only our pride raising its ugly head. If we do not find that we have some culpability for the divorce proceedings, we should re-examine ourselves again. *(See Marital Reconciliation Requires A Journey Into Spiritual Maturity* at page 247)

The Use of A Lawyer in Divorce Proceedings

If this "Word examination" and entreaty to our spouse are not successful in causing a withdrawal of the divorce proceedings, then we should seek legal counsel. However, we must be very careful in what we instruct our attorney to do. We must never use a lawyer to circumvent our God-given duty to support our children and wife in a manner commensurate with our income. ***But if any provide not for his own, and specially for those of his own house, he hath denied the faith, and is worse than an infidel*** *(I Timothy 5:8).* Do not use a lawyer to seek "to get even." Vengeance belongs to God alone *(Psalm 94:1).* Only use a lawyer to get that which is just. If we are acting in accordance with the Word and the lawyer will not do what we tell him, fire him and get one who will.

Contesting the Divorce Action

Should we contest the divorce and if so, how? The abomination of no fault divorce laws has stripped partners who do not want a divorce from protecting their marriage against divorce. The Word response to no-fault divorce proceedings is to reiterate, at every available opportunity, the desire for reconciliation whether it be before our lawyer, the judge or our spouse.

Support and Alimony

Two apart will never live as cheaply as two together. The Word says in *I Timothy 5:8* that the husband is to provide for those in his own house. Now we get into the question of needs verses wants. When we have what we need, we have adequate provision. Wanting gets into lusting and lusting is sin *(I John 2:16)*.

As God said in *Isaiah 1:18,* **Come now, and let us reason together . . .** so must we attempt to reason with the partner seeking the divorce. Israel did not respond to the offer of guaranteed support from God, so God turned Israel over to the world for judgment *(See the Old Testament)*. Therefore if our partner will not "reason together" in matters of support and alimony, we must take him to the judge of the world and let the judge do the reasoning for us. As Moses established judges for the people of Israel *(Exodus 18:25-26),* so has God ordained the authorities today to settle our differences with our spouse when we cannot do so amicably *(Romans 13:1)*.

The Deceitful Divorce Decree

What therefore God hath joined together,
let not man put asunder
(Matthew 19:6).

Man in his physical eye looks at marriage as beginning at the altar and ending in death or the divorce court. His pride wants the divorce so much that he has deceived himself into believing that the divorce decree has severed the oneness of marriage. However, in God's eyes nothing is further from the truth. Here is why.

The Divorce Decree Does Not
Sever the Oneness of Marriage.

The husband and wife committed to marry, the clerk of court issued the marriage license and the pastor conducted the ceremony, but only God made them one *. . . and they shall be one flesh (Genesis 2:24 and Matthew 19:5-6)*. While the court has the authority to nullify the marriage license issued by its clerk, it has absolutely no authority to sever that which God has made one, . . . ***What therefore God hath joined together, let not man put asunder*** *(Matthew 19:6)*. There is absolutely no authority whatsoever in the Word to support the view that a decree of divorce issued by any court of law severs the oneness of marriage.

In further support of the contention that the decree of divorce does not sever the oneness of marriage, let us take another look at Matthew 19:9. In both the Old and New Testaments, the word "adultery" is reserved exclusively to describe an act of infidelity against the oneness relationship of husband and wife, and that of man and God. The Word makes it very clear that adultery can occur only when the oneness relationship exists. *Matthew 19:9* states clearly that when a spouse is divorced for any cause other than fornication, both the person seeking the divorce and the party later marrying the innocent spouse commit adultery upon their remarriage. Thus if remarriage after divorce (except on grounds of fornication) causes adultery, then the oneness of the former marriage was not severed by the divorce decree.

Marriage was created by God to allow man and woman to share the oneness that Christ enjoys with the Church. The divorce decree was pridefully contrived by man in his attempt to escape accountability to God and his spouse for breaking his marriage vows. Man's prideful divorce decrees will never succeed in putting asunder the oneness that God, in His wisdom and love, has created in marriage.

When Is the Oneness of Marriage Severed?

In further support that the decree of divorce does not sever the oneness of marriage, let us take another look at *Matthew 19:9*. In both the Old and the New Testaments, the word "adultery" is reserved exclusively to describe an act of infidelity against the oneness relationship of husband and wife, and that of man and God. The Word makes it very clear that adultery can occur only when the oneness relationship exists. *Matthew 19:9* states clearly that when a spouse is divorced for any cause other than fornication, both the person seeking the divorce and the party later marrying the innocent spouse commit adultery upon their remarriage. Thus, if remarriage after divorce (except on grounds of fornication) causes adultery, then the oneness of the former marriage was not severed by the divorce decree.

Marriage was created by God to allow man and woman to share the oneness that Christ enjoys with the Church. The divorce decree was pridefully contrived by man in his attempt to escape accountability to God and his spouse for breaking his marriage vows. Man's prideful divorce decrees will never succeed in putting asunder the oneness that God, in His infinite wisdom and love, has created in marriage.

The Word states clearly that the oneness of marriage is severed only upon:

> 1. The death of a spouse: ***The wife is bound by the law as long as her husband liveth; but if her husband be dead, she is at liberty to be married to whom she will; only in the Lord*** *(I Corinthians 7:39);* or

> 2. When a spouse commits fornication. ***And I say unto you, Whosoever shall put away his wife, except it be for fornication, and shall marry another, committeth adultery: and whoso marrieth her which is put away doth commit adultery*** *(Matthew 19:9).*

How Fornication Severs the Oneness of Marriage

The Greek word for fornication is "porneia" which is defined as harlotry (including adultery and incest), and the Greek word for harlotry is "porne" which is defined as idolatry. So to be a fornicator is to be in idolatry. While fornication is commonly referred to in connection with sexual sin, it may well reach beyond sex and into other areas of our lives. So the word . . . **"fornication"** . . . in Matt. 19:9 can be read as idolatry including adultery, incest, abuse and other such actions that have the effect of being an idol to the spouse committing those activities.

Thus, as the Israelites severed their oneness with God by worshiping other gods, so does the spouse committing fornication sever the oneness of the marriage. Notice, it is not the decree of divorce that severs the oneness of marriage; rather, it is the acts of fornication (idol worship) that sever the oneness of marriage.

Issues to be Reconciled by One Who Is Entertaining the Thought Of Divorce

Since fornication severs the oneness of marriage, is it grounds for divorce? <u>As can be seen from what is written below in this book, the fact that fornication may exist in a marriage does not necessarily grant to the other partner the clear-cut path to seek a divorce.</u> No one should ever make a decision concerning divorce without first filtering all of the facts and circumstances in the marriage through the Word of God.

Divorce is one of those matters that is between the person contemplating the divorce and God. Entertaining the thought of divorce is most personal. Let us not be critical or judgemental of those who unfortunately have to contemplate this decision.

Some of the issues that need to be worked through in this decision making process are:

1. Has the innocent party forgiven the guilty part?
2. Is the guilty party still in fornication?
3. What part, if any, did the aggrieved party have in causing the guilty part to enter into fornication?
4. And, most important of all, what does the innocent party believe is "right to do" before God, given all the circumstances at hand?

Christ in Gethsemane

. . . Father, if thou be willing, remove this cup from me: nevertheless not my will, but thine, be done (Luke 22:42).

243

While we cannot ignore the problems in our marriage, our focus, in determining whether or not to seek a divorce, must be on Christ and His decision making process in Gethsemane.

Remember that Jesus, too, is married-to us. Each time we are unfaithful to Him, we have another reason why God had to hand the cup to Him. Even so, Jesus did not refuse the cup; rather, He stated three times that obeying God's will was more important to Him than not obeying His Father.

What was in the cup? Along with all of the other sins in the world, there was also in the cup every reason anyone has ever had, or ever will use, as grounds for a divorce. Jesus was willing to take upon Himself every grief in every marriage that was to ever exist if that is what it would take to please God, and that is what it took. So, the mind of Christ was not on the grief in His marriage to us; rather, His mind was on the will of His Father for the marriage. That is the same mind-set we must have when we address the issue of what constitutes grounds for a divorce.

Jesus' focus was upon His Father, not upon the problems in His marriage to us. Jesus' mission was one of restoration, and He determined to accomplish that restoration. His sacrifice for His bride, the Church, set the pattern of sacrifice that is an absolute prerequisite to the restoration of every broken marriage. God is a merciful God, and He sent His Son to take away all of our sin. Sin is sin, wheter it be adultery, fornication, taking God's name in vain, stealing, covetousness, murder or whatever; Jesus washed it all away. God loves us and wants so very much to bless us in our present marriage. We must repent and proceed in our present marriage believing God for the promises of His Word in all areas of our lives, including the restoration of our marriage. God loves us! *(John 3:16)*

The whole matter is summed up well by our, ***Looking unto Jesus the author and finisher of our faith; who for the joy that was set before Him endured the cross,***

despising the shame, and is set down at the right hand of the throne of God *(Hebrews 12:2)*. The joy of the restoration of our marriage, in the midst of the humiliation that comes with a troubled marriage, overshadows the pain of the restoration process.

Is There Ever A
Time For Separation In Marriage?

(See the Books of Isaiah and Jeremiah)

Yes. When Israel became so wicked in adultery and fornication that God could not stand to look upon her, He had her vomited out of the land and taken in captivity to Babylon *(Jeremiah 24:1)*. God separated Israel from Himself for her own good *(Jeremiah 24:5)*. But we must remember that God's desire when He sent Israel away was to bring her back again with a new heart towards Him:

Thus saith the Lord, the God of Israel; Like these good figs, so will I acknowledge them that are carried away captive of Judah, whom I have sent out of this place into the land of the Chaldeans for their good. For I will set mine eyes upon them for good, and I will bring them again to this land; and I will build them, and not pull them down; and I will plant them, and not pluck them up. And I will give them an heart to know me, that I am the LORD; and they shall be my people, and I will be their God; for they shall return unto me with their whole heart *(Jeremiah 24:5-7)*.

The same process should take place in a troubled marriage. When a spouse becomes involved in abusive behavior, adultery, drugs, alcohol and other such acts, the time to separate may well have come. Separation is not to be viewed as a first step to divorce; rather, it is a means to stop the momentum toward divorce by affording to the errant spouse a time of reflection which will hopefully produce a repentant heart.

As God did not let Israel return until she had changed her ways, neither should the errant spouse be allowed to return until he had changed his ways. As the creation was not complete until the end of the day of rest, sometimes restoration cannot be made complete without a time of separation to afford a rest to the parties in the marriage. The parties desiring the restoration of their marriage should learn to pray *Jeremiah 24:5-7* for their errant spouse. This power of praying the Word into our marriage will cause the presence of God to come into the situation, and things will happen.

MARITAL RECONCILIATION REQUIRES
A JOURNEY INTO SPIRITUAL MATURITY

We have all too often heard the mournful cries for restoration by the person who does not want a divorce. Each cry is generated by the pain of rejection, humiliation and loneliness that attempt to drive the one crying into the depths of despair. This person's mind is frantically searching for an end to this pain; everything seems to be out of control, there is no peace in the family anymore, self confidence is very low - if not non-existent; uncertainty rules the day and there is no end to the friction. Hardly anything is understood anymore, life has been gutted, reason is nowhere to be found and purpose in life is most elusive.

These cries for restoration beg for some kind of an answer - any kind of an answer. As Job, the one crying, questions *. . . where then is my hope? Who can see any hope for me (Job 17:15 NIV emphasis added)?*

Then there is the obstinate spouse who, because of allowing the sin of pride to master him/her, talks only in circles, has become absolutely undependable, has no thought of the adverse consequences of his actions against the marriage and the family - and is selfishly thinking only of him/herself.

What do we tell this person who wants to restore the marriage, how do we counsel them? We must tell them that marital reconciliation requires a journey into spiritual maturity, and that journey begins in Matthew 6:33, *But seek ye first the kingdom of God, and his righteousness; and all these things shall be added unto you.*

The person then might ask, "Does this mean that if I travel this journey, the restoration of my marriage is guaranteed?" We must tell them, "No, it does not. But what it does mean is that by virtue of your walk through this journey, which lasts for a lifetime, you will please God by becoming more mature in Him each day."

It is the absolute desire of God's heart that every breach in every marriage be restored. However, at the same time, He will not violate the choice of the obstinate spouse to exercise his God given free will in a manner that will destroy the marriage. At first glance this does not seem God like or fair to the faithful spouse, but the reasons therefor lie in the depths of God's plan to require man to choose between God and the ways of the world.

How Does an Aggrieved Spouse
Respond to an Obstinate Spouse
While Attempting to Reconcile the Marriage?

If physical abuse is involved, please read the section entitled T*he Biblical Course Of Action For The Abused Spouse* at page 230, and act accordingly.

God gave to each of us the free will to choose what we will do with our life. We can choose to exercise that free will in the direction of righteousness and enjoy an excellent marriage, or we can choose to act against God's will and thereby set about to destroy our marriage and family. The latter is the course chosen by the obstinate spouse. How does the faithful spouse respond to that obstinate spouse?

The Role of Prayer in Marital Reconciliation

An obvious response for the aggrieved spouse is to pray a prayer similar to the following:

"Father, I acknowledge and repent for all of my faults in my marriage, and the part those faults have played in causing problems in my marriage. And I ask you for the wisdom, understanding and knowledge that I need to conduct myself in a Godly manner in the process of restoring my marriage.

And Father, I know without question that it is your will for my marriage to be reconciled, and it is obvious that my mate is not moving in that direction. So I pray that you will, in your time and in your way, bring those

circumstances into the life of my mate that will afford to him/her every opportunity to choose to turn toward You; for I know that in You lies the reconciliation of our marriage. I now take my hands off of my life mate and release my mate into your hands in all respects, keeping no part of my mate for myself. Enter into the life circumstances of my mate as only you can in order to afford to my mate every opportunity to return to You; for I know that only in You lies the restoration of our marriage. Amen."

The praying spouse, and those joining them in prayer for the marriage, can rest assured that God will be working in the life circumstances of the errant spouse in such a way to afford to the mate every opportunity to restore the marriage. Even so, as can be seen from the Cain and Able story mentioned below, God will not violate the choice of the errant spouse to destroy the marriage.

The Role of Faith in Marital Reconciliation?
vs.
The Free Will Choice of the Errant Spouse
To Destroy the Marriage

*Now faith is the substance of things hoped for,
the evidence of things not seen (Heb 11:1).*

It is the faith of the one standing for the marriage that establishes a spiritual life line for the marriage between the family and God. This faith for the marriage is not just a "wishful" thought in the spirit realm. Faith is a substantive relationship between the one exercising their faith and God, and that is why its very definition of faith includes the words *. . . substance . . .* and *. . . evidence . . .*

Now lets address the exercise of this role of faith on the one hand, and the free will choice of the errant spouse on the other - because they seem, and they are, directly contrary to one another. One or the other is going to determine the outcome of your marriage.

Then the LORD said to Cain, "Why are you angry? Why is your face downcast? If you do what is right, will you not be accepted? But if you do not do what is right, sin is crouching at your door; it desires to have you, but you must master it" (Genesis 4:6-7 NIV).

God was, in essence, saying to Cain, "I have given to you the free will to choose whether or not you will submit to the sin of pride in your life that is crouching at your door and desires to have your marriage; but you must... ***master it.***" Cain made the choice to allow the sin of pride... ***crouching at*** ... (his)... ***door*** ... to ... ***have*** ... him - and it did. And that is exactly the choice an errant spouse makes that furthers the process of destroying his marriage.

So what do we have here? A spouse praying in faith for the restoration of the marriage on the one hand, and the other spouse allowing the sin crouching at his door to have him - because he chose to fail to master it.

God always honors the prayer of faith. The spouse praying will see either the restoration of their marriage or, at the least, enjoy a much closer relationship with God. Prayers prayed for restoration, and faith strengthened in the process of believing God for the restoration, always bring eternal dividends to the one praying and those who were standing by in intercession.

Summary

Marital reconciliation requires a journey into spiritual maturity. Hopefully, your journey will end in a reconciliation but, if it does not, the journey will present you to God as one who has drawn closer to Him. Then, you will know the peace of God, and will know how to walk in His ways where you find yourself at the time. You will be prepared for the future, and God will honor you and your children.

MARRIAGE AFTER DIVORCE

(see the entire Bible)

The divorce decree is final, the issues of custody, support, alimony and property settlement have been decided and we are putting our lives back together. At some point in all of this we meet someone special and the possibility of marriage appears on the horizon. Next comes the question, what does God say about this?

This question has been before the Church as long as there has been a Church. Because of the extreme human emotions that are involved, the question never gets any easier. Furthermore, no one desires to offend the millions who have divorced and are remarried. Let us lay aside emotion and reticence for the moment and approach this issue from the Word.

If the previous marriage can be restored scripturally, we are not free to marry another; but, if the previous marriage cannot be restored scripturally, we are free to remarry. Why this answer? Because the purpose of Jesus' ministry was restoration and He expects no less of us *(John 3:16 and Ephesians 5:25-33)*. As He gave His life to restore man to God, so are we to concentrate all of our faith and efforts on restoring our marriage. We have a loving God who is full of grace, and He expects us to fully honor our covenant of marriage. But, if the marriage cannot be scripturally restored then we are free to remarry.

When Is Marital Reconciliation Scripturally Impossible?

Marital restoration is scripturally impossible in these instances: death, when one of the divorced spouses marries a third party, and unending fornication.

Obviously, the <u>death</u> of a spouse makes restoration of the marriage impossible, so nothing further need be said in such instance.

When a couple divorces and one of them marries another, the previous marriage cannot be restored. This is so because the spouse who married another is defiled as to their former partner and it would be wrong for that person to remarry their former spouse *(Deuteronomy 24:4)*. Thus, the unmarried partner out of the divorce is then free to marry.

Many people say this is Old Testament law and no longer applies since we are now under the New Testament. Well, Jesus said that He did not come to do away with the Old Testament, He came to fulfill it *(Matthew 5:17)*. We must understand that marriage is a covenant, not an agreement. A covenant is made out of love, while an agreement is made for reasons short of love. The word "covenant" comes from the Hebrew word "bryith" which means to become as one with another by walking between pieces of flesh, i.e., the covenant of marriage, becoming one flesh with another. The sanctity of marriage dictates that once the covenant is broken by divorce and a partner marries a third party, that the former covenant (marriage) cannot be restored.

However, if we have already divorced, married another spouse and then returned to our first spouse, do not let ourselves be condemned. The blood of Jesus washed that sin away too. Just repent. ***There is therefore now no condemnation to them which are in Christ Jesus, who walk not after the flesh, but after the spirit*** *(Romans 8:1)*. God loves us all and wants us to love Him too. God desires for us to experience in our current marriage what He wanted us to enjoy in our first marriage, but did not.

Apparent Unending Fornication

Fornication is idolatry and severs the oneness of marriage. When it is apparent that the severance will continue unended, the aggrieved spouse is free to remarry. When does the fornication become "apparent unended"? That is a matter exclusively between the aggrieved spouse and God, after much prayer, fasting and reading of the Word. For any of us to pass judgement on that person's decision, would be raw legalism.

WORRYING ABOUT DUE DATES

Take therefore no thought for the morrow:
for the morrow shall take thought for the
things of itself . . .
(Matthew 6:34).

How much time do we spend worrying about bills, note payments, and accounts that are coming due tomorrow when we do not have the money to pay them today. Would every man who made one cent or more from worrying about due dates please raise his hand!

To worry about due dates is to cast doubt on the ability of God to meet our every need. He does not want us to worry, He wants us to seek Him first *(Matthew. 6:33);* then, He will bring into our lives all of the "things" we need when He, in His wisdom, determines we need them.

Jesus once went into a city where the people did not believe in Him. As a result *. . . **He did not many mighty works there because of their unbelief** (Matthew 13:58).* The same happens in our lives when we become anxious about tomorrow, He cannot do mighty works in our lives. Hence, in part because we worry, the due dates come and go and the bills remain unpaid.

THERE ARE OPPORTUNITIES

IN MISTAKES

The steps of a good man are ordered by the LORD: and he delighteth in his way. Though he fall, he shall not be utterly cast down: for the LORD upholdeth him with his hand
(Psalm 37:23-24).

God knows that even good men, walking where He orders them to walk, will fall and make mistakes. But, so what! God will not let good men be utterly cast down. He will catch them in His hand and teach them from their mistakes.

Mistakes and flesh wounds have much in common, both look worse than they are. Given time they both will heal. If scar tissue results, the skin in the area of the wound is generally stronger than if the scar had not been suffered. Mistakes afford the opportunity to strengthen particular areas of our lives.

The discovery of a mistake is an opportunity to trust ourselves into the hands of God. His resolution of our mistakes is always loving and proper. He does not catch us in His hand to condemn us for our mistakes; rather, He catches us in His hand to hold us up so we can continue on in His service.

THE ATTEMPT TO SUBSTITUTE
BIBLE STUDY AND PRAYER
FOR OBEDIENCE

Let us hear the conclusion of the whole matter:
Fear God, and keep his commandments:
for this is the whole duty of man
(Ecclesiastes 12:13).

God knows the things in our lives that we do not want to surrender to Him. It is those very things that He uses to bring conviction upon us. It is the classic "God-man standoff." We will not give up on the thing, and He will not give up on us.

To break the deadlock, we vainly attempt to make our own feeble substitutions for obedience to the Word, even to the point of believing that if we study the Bible and pray enough we will not have to obey. It is like we try to bulldoze our way out of obedience through Bible study and prayer.

Quite often we begin this bulldozing not because obedience would be difficult, but because obeying will not allow us to have what we want. So, to bulldoze an "acceptable" back door out of obeying, we submerse ourselves in the pious activities of Bible study and prayer and delude ourselves into believing that God "will let us do it our way." Such activity is "religion" and not Christianity.

... Behold, to obey is better than sacrifice ...
(I Samuel 15:22).

How To Act When We Are Offended

*He that covereth a transgression seeketh love, but
he that repeateth a matter separateth very friends*
(Proverbs 17:9).

How should we act when we are offended? Should we talk about it to others or should we cover the offense by silence? If we tell, we seek division; but, if we cover the transgression by silence, we seek love.

To tell is to spread the effects of sin, but to keep silent is to seek love. Let us stop dwelling on the offense and begin to spread love by keeping silent. After all, what benefit have we ever received from telling of another's offense? But we have all benefitted from keeping silent.

WHAT DOES A PARENT DO WHEN THEIR SON-IN-LAW IS NOT HONORING THEIR DAUGHTER?

Likewise, ye husbands, dwell with them according to knowledge, giving honor unto the wife, as unto the weaker vessel, and as being heirs together of the grace of life; that your prayers be not hindered (I Peter 3:7).

How To Pray

As any parent of a married daughter knows, this is a most painful situation. The parents' pain is magnified as they suffer not only their own pain, but also the pain they know their daughter is suffering from not being honored by her husband.

It is God's knowledge that will teach the son-in-law how to dwell with their daughter in a manner that honors her. The parents' roles in this situation is to pray that God will grant His knowledge to their son-in-law; that the son-in-law will open his heart to receive that knowledge, and walk it out in his life. This simple prayer addresses every need the son-in-law has from being lazy - to salvation - to coming off drugs - to turning away from lust - to knowing the ways of God. One of God's names is *I AM THAT I AM, (Exodus 3:14)* which means My knowledge will be what the son-in-law needs when he needs it.

It is impossible for a son-in-law to have a problem that the knowledge of God cannot resolve. Every parent should remember that *. . . The effectual fervent prayer of a righteous man availeth much (James 5:16)*. Regardless of the symptoms present, the son-in-law is not honoring the daughter because he does not have the knowledge of God. If the parents are righteous, and pray fervently, God promises that the parents' prayer will avail much.

In the Case of Physical or Mental Abuse

Husbands, love your wives, even as Christ also loved the church, and gave himself for it
(Ephesians 5:25).

Clearly, a man is to love his wife as Christ loved the church; he is not to abuse her. When he does abuse her, he is certainly not affording to her the protection required of a husband. By abusing her, he has forced her to look elsewhere for protection. That elsewhere is either the law or family, or both. Why? Because a purpose of the law is to protect those under its authority, and one purpose of the family is to protect its members. So, if the daughter is being abused by the son-in-law, then her family should step forward and offer protection from that abuse.

And parents, this is not a time for you to, in your self righteousness, say to your daughter, "I told you so." That is the last thing your daughter needs to hear. What she needs it your comfort and protection blended with wisdom from the Word of God. She does not need your criticism.

(For a more in-depth study on the matter of abuse, see that section of this book entitled, *The Biblical Course of Action For The Abused Spouse,* at page 230.)

By What Authority Can the Parent Step Forward and Speak to the Son-In-Law About His Not Honoring Their Daughter?

And Moses' father in law said unto him, The thing that thou doest is not good. Thou wilt surely wear away, both thou, and this people that is with thee: for this thing is too heavy for thee; thou are not able to perform it thyself alone. Hearken now unto my voice, I will give thee counsel, and God shall be with thee
(Exodus 18:17-19).

If there was ever an area in our society that was taboo, it is the area of a father-in-law talking to his son-in-law about what the son-in-law is doing wrong in the marriage; and, even more so, telling the son-in-law how to do it right. Well, not too surprisingly, the Bible does not agree with the ways of our society.

Jethro, Moses father-in-law, saw that Moses was wearing himself out trying to judge the causes of 3,000,000 Israelites. He told Moses, his son-in-law, *The thing that thou doest is not good . . . Hearken now unto my voice, I will give thee counsel, and God shall be with thee.* In today's world, Jethro just dropped a bomb in the family. But in God's Way of doing things, Jethro saw his son in law being in need of sound advice, and he gave it to him. Notice, Jethro did not scream, yell or holler at Moses, nor did he call him names or use a few choice words. He spoke in a rational manner, addressed the issues at hand and wated for Moses response.

Without question, if Moses was exhausting himself trying to meet the needs of the Israelites, he was certainly not honoring his wife in many respects including not spending time with her or the children. This story of Jethro and Moses gives ample scriptural support for a father-in-law addressing the wrongs of his son-in-law that cause him not to honor his wife.

Do not wait for the "right time" to talk with your son-in-law, it most probably will not come. Speak as the situation demands. *Ointment and perfume rejoice the heart: so doth the sweetness of a man's friend by hearty counsel* (Proverbs 27:9). *Faithful are the wounds of a friend . . .* (Proverbs 27:6); and, *Iron sharpeneth iron; so a man sharpeneth the countenance of his friend* (Proverbs 27:17).

FINDING PEACE

There is that maketh himself rich, yet hath
nothing; there is that maketh himself poor,
yet hath great riches.
(Proverbs 13:7).

Man was created by God in the image of God, not by the world in the image of the world. Therefore, man will find peace only in the Way of God and not in the ways of the world. This is why success in the world's terms never brings peace; rather, worldly success breeds only a lustful desire for more success.

There is no correlation between peace and possessions. To the contrary, we have great peace only when we give of ourselves and our possessions to others. Hence, when we make ourselves poor by giving of ourselves and our possessions to others, we will have the richness of peace.

HELPING THE POOR

A devout man, and one that feared God with all his
house, which gave much alms to the people,
and prayed to God alway
(Acts 10:2).

It is true that if we help the poor, they will take advantage of us. However, we should not let that fact deter us from helping the poor. After all, each time we sin we take advantage of the blood of Jesus Christ. Cornelius gave much alms to the poor, and God accepted those alms as a memorial before Him *(Acts 10:4)*.

The very fact that Jesus had to die for our sins, is ample testimony of how we take advantage of Him daily; but that still does not keep Him from helping us today. How fortunate we are that Jesus did not refuse to give His life for us when He knew that we would take advantage of Him every time we sin. Likewise, we should always be eager to help the poor even though we know they will often take advantage of our care for them.

Now this certainly does not mean that we are not to be diligent in helping the poor. But it does mean if we are willing to take risks in investing our time and money to make money, then certainly we should be willing to take risks in helping the poor who, with us, are made in the image of God.

Taking Advantage Of The Poor

Rob not the poor, because he is poor, neither oppress the afflicted in the gate: For the LORD will plead their cause, and spoil the soul of those that spoiled them (Proverbs 22:22-23).

We have all driven through underprivileged neighborhoods and seen the kerosene prices posted in the small grocery stores; the interest rates charged by small loan companies; strategically located convenience stores charging high prices for items; the high pressure salesmen selling cars with more than 100,000 miles and financing them at exorbitant rates; and, the dilapidated apartments for rent at rates equal to more than the weekly salary of the tenant. When we have seen these things, we have seen advantage being taken of the poor and afflicted.

The owners of the above businesses and property might have the best lawyers, and judges often do not believe the defense of the poor; but, let us remember that the eternal lawyer of the poor and the afflicted is Jesus, and the eternal judge is God. Guess who will prevail in the end? No profit is worth a spoiled soul.

The poor have a special standing with Christ. They are as helpless in our Babylonian society as He was on the cross: as the poor are despised by the rich, so He was despised by those who crucified Him. To take advantage of the poor is to attempt to take advantage of Him. So the wages of taking advantage of the poor is a spoiled soul.

REAL POWER

For they got not the land in possession by their
own sword, neither did their own arm save them;
but thy right hand, and thine arm . . .
(Psalm 44:3).

In the world we look upon money and position as real power, but they are not so. The only real power in this world is the hand of God. God, not money and position, is supreme in all matters.

How many hurricanes have money and position started? Name two millionaires who lived in Jerusalem at the time of Christ. Now name the 12 disciples. Who had the most power, the two unknown millionaires or the 12 well known disciples who healed the sick, raised the dead, opened blind eyes and made the dumb to speak?

Real power is the hand of God. Money and position are simply tools He uses. Let us not misuse His tools and cause the real power of His hand to come against us; rather, let us remember it is the real power of His arm that provides to us what we need.

THE FOCUS OF RIGHTEOUS PRAYER

But seek ye first the kingdom of God,
and his righteousness; and all these things
shall be added unto you
(Matthew 6:33).

Why do we pray, to get things or seek the face of God? When the focus of our prayers is to get things, our eyes are not on God, rather, they are on the things we want. But when the purpose of our prayers is to seek the face of God, He will move His hand on our behalf in His time.

Prayer is not to be a time of begging for things or demanding our rights; rather, prayer is intended by God as a means whereby we can focus on and become intimate with Him as our Creator. The focus of prayer is to seek Him and His righteousness. When we have met this purpose, He will lovingly add unto us what He knows we need when He determines we need it.

Now, this does not mean that we are never to pray for things. It is often proper to pray for things and respectfully remind God of His Covenant with us, but only after we have first sought to be intimate with Him in worship.

Hindered Prayer

Likewise, ye husbands, dwell with them according to
knowledge, giving honour unto the wife, as unto the
weaker vessel, and as being heirs together of the grace
of life; that your prayers be not hindered
(I Peter 3:7).

If we do not treat our wives with respect, our prayers will be hindered; they will not even reach God. So let us respect our wives in obedience to His Word. Then He will hear and answer our prayers.

Prayers God Hears

For the eyes of the Lord are over the righteous,
and his ears are open unto their prayers; but
the face of the Lord is against them that do evil
(I Peter 3:12).

God's eyes and ears are attentive to the prayers of the righteous, so their prayers are heard by God. Who are the righteous?

. . . LORD, who may dwell in your sanctuary? Who may
live on your holy hill? He whose walk is blameless and
who does what is righteous, who speaks the truth from
his heart and has no slander on his tongue, who does
his neighbor no wrong and casts no slur on his
fellowman, who despises a vile man but honors those
who fear the LORD, who keeps his oath even when it
hurts, who lends his money without usury and does not
accept a bribe against the innocent. He who does these
things will never be shaken
(Psalm 15:1-5 NIV).

GOD'S ORDER OF PRIORITIES

Commandments 1-4 concern worshiping God;

Commandment 5 concerns the family; and

Commandments 6-10 concern everything else in life
(Exodus 20:1-10).

In the world we are taught that commerce is king, our family is to support us in the making of money, and business and Christianity do not mix. It is the daily lifestyle of these teachers and their students that make our families, government and economy so unstable and the church a social club.

God's priorities for our lives are the exact reverse. Worship Him first, take care of our family's spiritual and other needs second, and everything else, including commerce, comes in third place. God's Word does not change *(Malachi 3:6)*, but man does change in his quest to run his life according to his own priorities. Hence, God is still on the throne, Jesus is on His right hand, and commercial enterprises and civilizations come and go; but God will have the last word, not the shareholders.

What Is the Definition of the Word "Priority"?

In simple terms, we place in first priority that which we most want to do. We do those things first which we consider the most important; that which is most important to us is our God/god, as the case may be.

Improper Priorities Negate the Power of Faith in Our Lives:

The Word of God sets forth our priorities in the Ten Commandments *(Exodus 20:1-17)*, tells us that if we love God we will keep these priorities *(John 14:15)* and that faith works by love *(Galatians 5:6)*. Well, if we do not maintain our proper priorities, we do not love Him; and, if we do not love Him, there is nothing in us by which our faith can work.

Examples of Men of God Who Made Something Other Than God Their First Priority:

1. Abraham made having a son a priority over waiting on God, and Ishmael was born, look at the cost!
2. David made coveting Bathsheba's body a priority over obeying God, and his family was divided. Later he was chased out of Jerusalem by his own son-look at the cost!
3. Judas made receiving 30 pieces of silver a priority over loving Jesus-look at the cost!

What the Bible Has to Say About the Importance of Proper Priorities in the Family Realm?

The story of Moses and Zipporah is quite revealing. Moses had met God at the burning bush, and was on the way to Egypt when ... ***The LORD met him, and sought to kill him ...*** *(See Exodus 4:21-26)*. God commanded that all males be circumcised, but Zipporah obviously refused to allow Moses to circumcise their son. Moses, by bowing to Zipporaha's demands, was disobedient to God's commandment to have his son circumcised. Since Moses made meeting his wife's demands a priority above honoring God, God was going to kill him rather than permit him to lead God's people.

God was willing to allow 3 million people to stay in slavery rather than permit a man, who could not get his priorities straight in his own family, to lead His people out of slavery.

The Importance of A Husband Listening to A Wife's Advice:

We are one with our wives and God at the same time. How then can we say, "I am listening to the Lord, but I cannot, will not or have not the time to listen to my wife?" To not have the patience to listen to our wives is to have our priorities out of order. Still we are one with God and our wife at the same time. <u>Therefore, if we do not have the patience to listen to our wives, we will not have the patience to listen to God.</u> A wife's request of her husband to spend more time with her may well be God's offer to balance her husband's priorities.

<u>Following Is the Way We Husbands
Correct This Error:</u>

1. Sit down with our wives at a time when there is peace and quiet;
2. Ask her to be blunt and tell us what she would change about us as a man and in our marriage; and
3. Pledge to her that we will listen to her and will not defend ourselves at any cost!

If we men will have the "hutzpah" to do this, we will get our priorities straight and most probably hear the answer to years of our prayers in one brutal sitting. <u>Our wives are not always right, and at times we may be proper in acting contrary to their advice; but, if we will discipline ourselves to have the patience to consider what our wives have to say, we will have the discipline to keep our priorities in order.</u>

<u>Symptoms of the Work Overshadowing the Message</u>

All too often we become so wrapped up in the work God has committed to us that the work overshadows the message of Christ in our lives. Some common symptoms of this occurring are:

1. Shortage of finances;
2. Not enough hours in the day;
3. Lack of definite purpose;
4. Large turnover in supporters/income sources;
5. Anxiety and worry are prevalent;

6.   More discussions about funding the work, than about fulfilling the work;
7.   Financial commitments are made to make future expenditures "in so-called faith" when existing financial commitments are past due; and
8.   Desperate appeals and Madison Avenue techniques are devised to raise funds.

All of the Above Are Covered Up by Statements Like:

"Our supporters (income sources) are not as faithful as they used to be"; "God's people just do not care anymore"; "God will supply and in the meantime we must act in faith that He will"; and "Satan is after us to stop us."

The whole truth of the matter is that our priorities are out of order. The messenger (the occupation, profession, church or ministry) has become the first priority; the message the second priority. We must remember that to act ahead of God's timing is to make what we want to do a priority over what God wants us to do.

What Prevents Us from Maintaining Our Proper Priorities?

1.   Pride. Lucifer, because of pride, desired to be more like God than he did to obey God. Such is the fruit of pride. Therefore, he fell from Heaven.
2.   Over commitment. When we take on more than we have the time or the qualifications to perform, we begin to "give and take" in our priorities. We must learn to say 'NO". Even if people are disappointed at our having said "NO" to a request, they will respect our diligence to say "NO". The diligent... *shall stand before kings* ... *(Proverbs 22:29)*.
3.   Busy church work. Such activity often prevents us from having the time to worship God (Mary and Martha, *Luke 10:38-40*).

Husbands, our wives come before our jobs. God's Word directs that a husband should give his life for his wife as Christ gave His life for the church *(Ephesians 5:25)*.

If we husbands do not want our prayers to be hindered, we must learn to treat our wives with respect as the weaker partner, and as an heir with us in the gift of life *(I Peter 3:7)*.

Each time we commit a sin, we are making disobedience to God's Word a priority over obedience to His Word:

1. Either we have not taken the time to learn God's Word in the matter and are therefore acting in ignorance of God's Word; or
2. We knowingly and willfully disobey God's Word.

Symptoms vs. Problems

Because our priorities are out of order, we spend too much time treating, acting and reacting to symptoms rather than solving the problems in our lives. Why? Because we have not put the Word of God first in our lives. When we place the Word first in our lives, the wisdom, knowledge and understanding of the Word will cause us to look right through the symptoms and identify the problems. When we eliminate the problems, the symptoms will go away; but, if we insist on treating the symptoms, the problems will not go away. Proper priorities make the difference *(See the entire Bible)*.

Off Living on A Tangent

God never called a man into His service while the man was off living on a tangent. Rather, most of those called were engaged in the daily discipline of earning a livelihood when they were called. Moses was tending sheep; David was tending sheep; Paul was enforcing the religion of the day upon Christians; Gideon was threshing wheat; Peter, James and John were fishing; Matthew was collecting taxes; Elisha was plowing, etc.

Husbands

We should ask our wives, "What needs do you have that I am not meeting?"

Children

We must tell our children that we love them. Playing games, talking and spending time with our children can be more Holy than prayer, fasting and reading the Word.

Measuring The Depth Of Our Problems

The LORD is far from the wicked: but
he heareth the prayer of the righteous
(Proverbs 15:29).

The depth of our problems is equal to the distance we are away from Christ. So, to measure the depth of our problems, we need simply to study the Word and see how far away we are from walking with Him. The distance we are from Him is equal to the depth of our problems.

We solve our problems and close the gap between ourselves and Christ as we exercise a heart towards Him, not a heart intent on getting its own way.

THE KEY TO OVERCOMING
ALL OF OUR PROBLEMS

... The Lord is my shepherd, I shall not want....
Yea though I walk through the valley of the
shadow of death,
I will fear no evil: for thou art with me....
Thou preparest a table for me in the presence of mine
enemies ... (Psalm 23:1&4-5)

To walk through the valley of the shadow of death and eat in the presence of our enemies is to have problems. At the same time, the 23rd Psalm promises that if we will make the Lord our Shepherd, we will not want in the midst of those problems. This Psalm has a great deal more to say about focusing on the Lord in the midst of problems than it does about the problems. Why? Because we overcome our problems by focusing on God, not on the problems.

The key to overcoming all of our problems is for us to determine where our focus is going to be in the midst of the problems. Is our focus going to be on the problems or on seeking the Shepherd? If our focus is on the problems, then it is not on the Shepherd and we will be dealing with the problems on our own. But, if our focus is on seeking the Shepherd in the midst of the problems, we will fear no evil and partake of Him in peace in the presence of the problems. To focus on the Shepherd, and not on the problems, is the way we overcome all of our problems.

As long as we live in this world we will have problems, but we must be careful to focus on the Shepherd rather than on the problems. When we accept Christ as Savior, He gives to us the power to become sons of God. *(John 1:12)*. It is by our diligent and daily exercise of that power, through continuously seeking the Shepherd, that we overcome all of our problems.

PROFANITY

For by thy words thou shalt be justified and by thy
words thou shalt be condemned
(Matthew 12:37).

Words are very important. God created the universe with words, and then He created us in His image. So, our spoken words will have a cause and effect, just as did God's words. Our words will either justify us or condemn us, and they will have a postive or negative effect on those around us. Obviously we must be careful how we choose and use our words.

The word "profanity" is not in the Bible, but the word "profane" is often used. Profanity is simply verbalizing that which is profane. If we will look at several of the contexts in which "profane" is used in the Bible, we will then understand how we are actually condemning ourselves and adversely affecting others with our profanity:

Leviticus 18:21   To wound, bore,dissolve, profane, break, wedge, defile, pollute, prostitute, slay sorrow or stain;

Jeremiah 23:11   To soil or corrupt;

Ezekiel 44:23   To be common or to expose;

Matthew 12:5   To descecrate; and

I Timothy 1:9   To be heathenish or wicked.

Obviously, profanity is the exact opposite of righteousness. So whenever we use profanity we are condemning ourselves and creating a horrible environment for those around us, especially our wife and children if they happen to be present - and they often are. May this be the reason why that son or daughter, who was given much in material goods, does not respect you and has not turned out as you hoped? Our words condemn not only ourselves, but also those in front of whom we choose to use profanity.

PROSPERITY

Vs.

"JUST HAVING THINGS"

Are we prosperous, or do we just "have things?" The difference in the two is a walk with God through Christ. If we walk with God, our soul will be prosperous and we will enjoy prosperity even without things. But, if we "just have things," and do not have a walk with God, we cannot call ourselves prosperous.

God does not measure prosperity by the number or value of "things" we have; rather, He measures our prosperity by the depth of our relationship with Jesus Christ, His Son. To just have things and not have Christ, is to be . . . *wretched, pitiful, poor, blind and naked* (Revelation 3:17 NIV).

God's Only Measure of Prosperity

" . . . Man looks at the outward appearance,
but God looks at the heart"
(I Samuel 16:7 NIV).

God's only measure of our prosperity is the depth of our relationship with Christ. Although material wealth may be an outgrowth of our walk with God, by itself it is not even a factor to be considered in measuring true prosperity.

Jesus Christ did not have pocket money sufficient to pay the temple tax, or clothes on His back at the crucifixion, but who would dare have the audacity to even suggest that He was not prosperous? His prosperity was truly measured by His relationship with His Father, not by His lack of cash.

There is no question but that God wishes . . . *above all things that thou mayest prosper and be in health, even as thy soul prospereth* (III John 2). Let us not get hung up on the Babylonian connotation of the word "prosper;" let us

275

also consider God's connotation of the word "rich" as used in *Revelation 2:9*. ***I know your afflictions and your poverty - yet you are rich!* . . .** *(Revelation 2:9 NIV)*. Here God is not talking about a balance between "prosper" and "rich", rather, He is talking solely about the condition of our heart toward Him. ***"*. . . *man looks at the outward appearance, but God looks at the heart"*** *(I Samuel 16:7 NIV)*.

God loves rich people, and He wants us to have things. As a matter of fact, He desires to supply us with things more abundantly than we can ask or think. Even so, He does not measure our prosperity by our richness, things or abundance, but rather by our walk with Him.

THE SIN OF FOCUSING
ON PROSPERITY FIRST

For my people have committed two evils; they have
forsaken me the fountain of living waters,
and hewed them out cisterns, broken cisterns,
that can hold no water
(Jeremiah 2:13).

There is absolutely nothing evil about our desiring to be prosperous. What is evil is our making prosperity the cistern from which we pour our first drink. To pour our first drink from the cistern of prosperity is to make it a broken cistern that can hold no water.

The fountain of living waters, Jesus Christ, is the cistern from which we should always pour our first drink. The doctrine of prosperity, as all other doctrines, must always be placed <u>in its proper perspective behind the person of Jesus Christ</u>.

However, because we are flesh and since the subject of prosperity is appealing to the flesh, it is quite easy for a well intended and biblically based teaching on prosperity to be totally misinterpreted. Therefore, it is the duty of every teacher of any message on prosperity to cast that message in the context of seeking first Christ as the cistern from which we drink, and not in the context of, "If you are not prosperous, there is something wrong with your faith brother." The latter type message produces broken cisterns that cannot hold any water.

It is quite ironic for us as Christians to agree that intercessors are the real heros of Christianity and, at the same time, focus on spending so much time and effort in the Word to learn how to bring prosperity into our own lives. So let us focus first upon being a servant to Christ and, as a by-product of that focus, allow Him to bring that amount of prosperity into our lives that He desires for us to have *(Matthew 6:33).*

Protection From Those
Who Would Do Us Harm

*The angel of the LORD encampeth round about
them that fear him, and delivereth them
(Psalm 34:7).*

Each of us has been in situations where others have come against us to do us harm. Sometimes these actions take place in the form of lawsuits, slander, false charges, violence, etc; but, the Word promises that if we will fear God, the Angel of the Lord will encamp round about us and deliver us.

Our protection is not in us protecting ourselves, but rather in our fearing the Lord. It is the Lord who protects us, not we ourselves. We avail ourselves of His protection by fearing Him and keeping His Commandments. Our protection from those who would do us harm is a close relationship with Him.

Job is a splendid example of God's protection. He was *... a perfect and upright man, one that feared God, and eschewed evil (Job 1:8).* Satan's response to Job's protection by virtue of this relationship was *... Doth Job fear God for nought? Hast not thou made an hedge about him, and about his house, and about all that he hath on every side? Thou has blessed the work of his hands, and his substance is increased in the land (Job 1:9-10).* If we will only fear God as did Job we, too, can rely upon that same hedge for protection against those who would do us harm.

THE VALUE OF REBUKE

Poverty and shame shall be to him that refuseth
instruction: but he that regardeth reproof
shall be honoured
(Proverbs 13:18).

The last thing our flesh wants to hear is a rebuke after we have made a mistake, but to receive a rebuke for having made a mistake is Godly and will lead to honor. To refuse rebuke will lead to poverty and shame. Why? Because God honors Godliness, and judges ungodliness.

So, the value of rebuke is that it gives to us the opportunity to honor God when our flesh does not want to honor Him; and, with humility in our lives we will be honored.

THE FOUR ARENAS OF REPENTANCE

Let every soul be subject unto the higher powers. For there is no power but of God; the powers that be are ordained of God. Whosoever therefore resisteth the power, resisteth the ordinance of God: and they that resist shall receive to themselves damnation
(Romans 13:1-2).

God wants us to repent for our sin, and He has given us four arenas in which to do so. These four arenas are defined by the four areas of authority over our lives as established by God, and they are:

The first arena is the intimacy of worship between us and God but, if we resist the circumstances and do not repent here, then God will move our circumstances to:

The second arena is the privacy of the home but, if we resist the circumstances and do not repent here either, then God will move our circumstances to:

The third arena is the public eye of employment but, if we resist the circumstances and do not repent here either, then God will move our circumstances to:

The fourth arena is the public eye of the law.

God desires that we repent in private, but if we do not repent in private, He will judge us by placing us and our sin in the public arenas of employment and the law. Our rebellious attitude dictates who will know of our sin. God does not enjoy humiliating us in the public eye but, because He loves us, He would rather humiliate us publicly than allow us to continue in our rebellious ways. (See also "Habit Pattersn" at page 235)

REPENTANCE COMES FROM GODLY SORROW, NOT FROM JUST FEELING SORRY

For godly sorrow worketh repentance to salvation . . .
but the sorrow of the world worketh death
(II Corinthians 7:10).

Bring forth therefore fruits worthy of repentance . . .
(Luke 3:8)

There is just being sorry, and there is Godly sorrow which leads to repentance. Just being sorry does not carry with it any desire to change our lifestyle. On the other hand, Godly sorrow carries with it an eager desire to change our lifestyle which leads to repentance. Repentance is a sustained change of our lifestyle in that manner which is pleasing to God. The fruit of just being sorry is death, but the fruit of repentance is a Godly lifestyle.

REST

*And on the seventh day God ended his work which he
had made; and he rested on the seventh day
from all his work which he had made*
(Genesis 2:2).

God created the world in six days, but the creation was not complete until the end of the day of rest, and neither are we. If God saw the need to rest, then who are we not to rest? Until we rest, we are not complete in Him.

All that God expects us to do is to be diligent. To go beyond diligence is to cross over into manipulation, and that takes us out of rest. We need only to be diligent, and then rest in faith knowing that God will complete all matters not resolved by our diligence *(Hebrews 4:10-11).*

RETIREMENT

But seek ye first the kingdom of God, and his righteousness;
and all these things shall be added unto you
(Matthew 6:33).

To plan for retirement is Godly, but we should not make the plan a god. Our plan for retirement should include accepting responsibility for a greater effort in training ourselves and others in the things of God.

Retirement is the time in our lives when we can harvest the seeds of righteousness we planted in ourselves and others. If some of us did not plant those seeds in our earlier years, our retirement should be an exciting time of learning the things of God and restoring those relationships broken by the sins we committed in our earlier years.

If we focus ourselves in the above manner, God will add unto us the "things" we will need in retirement. The ultimate retirement plan is *Matthew 6:33,* **But seek ye first the Kingdom of God, and his righteousness, and all these things shall be added unto you.**

REVENGE

Say not thou, I will recompense evil; but
wait on the Lord, and he shall save thee
(Proverbs 20:22).

It takes Godly discipline to not take revenge when we have been wronged. If we will exercise Godly discipline, leave revenge to the Lord and wait on Him, He will take care of the wrong and save us from harm by the wrong.

Now this does not mean we cannot hold the one accountable who has wronged us, but it does mean we cannot take revenge against him for the wrong. To hold another accountable for his wrong is Godly, but to seek revenge is ungodly. Our hearts know the difference.

God Is More Concerned with Righteousness Than He Is with Taking Sides

". . . Are you for us or our enemies?"
"Neither," he replied,
"but as commander of the army of the LORD
I have now come."
(Joshua 5:13-14 NIV).

Shortly after Joshua led the Israelites across the Jordan River and was near Jericho, he saw a man dressed for battle standing in front of him. Joshua asked him... ***"Are you for us or our enemies?" "Neither", he replied "but as commander of the Army of the LORD I have now come."*** That Commander of the Army of the Lord was Jesus Christ. When He told Joshua ***"Neither"*** He was saying, "I am more concerned with righteousness, than I am with taking sides."

God does not focus on taking sides in a matter. Rather, His focus is on the higher plane of insuring that righteousness is done. Let us never again presume that God will lower Himself "to be on our side." Let us raise ourselves above that presumption and ask God that righteousness be done in the matter before us at the time.

RIGHTEOUSNESS AND THE UNRIGHTEOUS

In fact, though by this time you ought to be teachers, you need someone to teach you the elementary truths of God's Word all over again. You need milk, not solid food! Anyone who lives on milk, being still an infant, is not acquainted with the teaching about righteousness. But solid food is for the mature, who by constant use have trained themselves to distinguish good from evil (Hebrews 5:12-14 NIV).

God gave us His life when He breathed His breath into Adam, then He gave us salvation when He sacrificed His Son, and now He wants to give us His righteousness.

Righteousness is not a "thing" or a "state of being", it is God Himself. That is why one of His Hebrew names is "Jehovah-Tsiakenu" which means "The Lord Our Righteousness". Righteousness was manifested in the person of Jesus Christ, and God wants us to seek His righteousness so we can become a righteous people. *(Matthew 6:33).*

Righteousness comes from the Word of God to those who *. . . by constant use* (of the Word of God in their lives) *have trained themselves to distinguish good from evil* (Hebrews 5:14 NIV). *My tongue shall speak of thy word: for all thy commandments are righteousness* (Psalms 119:172).

It is God's desire that we prepare ourselves to be partakers of His Holiness *(Hebrews 12:10),* and His Holiness can rest only on a righteous people. This is why we are to seek first the kingdom of God and His righteousness, and He will then add to us all that we need to serve Him as a people Holy before Him *(Matthew 6:33).*

Why Are the Righteous Often Afflicted?

Many are the afflictions of the righteous: but the LORD
delivereth him out of them all
(Psalms 34:19).

If we will seek righteousness first, God will impart His righteousness into our spirit *(Matthew 6:33)*. This sharing of righteousness births an intimacy between God and us that is not conditioned or dependent upon our being in favorable circumstances. Righteousness is a God-man relationship that stands on its own, entirely independent of our circumstances.

Satan is insanely jealous of this righteous relationship between God and us. His avowed purpose is to pervert this relationship by making us believe that it is conditioned upon our circumstances. So he will afflict us with adverse circumstances to make us believe that the adversity is proof that we are not in a righteous relationship with God. Satan's goal in affliction is to make us doubt God's love for us.

Our defense to Satan's affliction, is the promise *. . . but the LORD delivereth him out of them all.* Implicit in that promise is that we must do our part and not allow the adversity to convince us that we are not in a righteous relationship with God.

For this reason we must be extremely careful in attempting to discern the cause of another's adversity. Their adversity may be the result of the consequences of sin, chastisement by God, or affliction at the hands of Satan. So let us be very careful before pronouncing what may well be the condemnatory statement of, "You are in trouble brother, what's wrong with your faith?"

To Take Our Eyes Off of the Righteous Relationship Will Cause Us to Become Double-minded

If any of you lack wisdom, let him ask of God, that
giveth to all men liberally, and upbraideth not; and it
shall be given him. But let him ask in faith, nothing
wavering. For he that wavereth is like a wave of the
sea driven with the wind and tossed. For let not

that man think that he shall receive anything of the Lord. A double minded man is unstable in all his ways (James 1:5-8).

If we allow Satan's afflictions to divert us from the righteous relationship we have with God, we will have become double minded and then cannot expect to receive anything from the Lord, including deliverance from the affliction. But, we can repent for that double mindedness and enjoy a new walk in righteousness. ***The steps of a good man are ordered by the LORD . . . Though he fall, he shall not be utterly cast down: for the LORD upholdeth him with His hand*** *(Psalms 37:23-24).*

A person after God's heart is definitely going to make mistakes, but God will not let him be cast down.

God Is More Concerned with Righteousness Than He Is with Taking Sides

. . . "Are you for us or our enemies?" "Neither," he replied, "but as commander of the army of the Lord I have now come" . . .
(Joshua 5:13-14 NIV).

Shortly after Joshua led the Israelites across the Jordan River and was near Jericho, he saw a man dressed for battle standing in front of him. Joshua asked him . . . ***"Are you for us or our enemies?" "Neither," he replied, "but as commander of the Army of the LORD I have now come"*** . . . That Commander of the Army of the Lord was Jesus Christ. When He told Joshua, **"Neither"** He was saying, "I am more concerned with righteousness than I am with taking sides."

God does not focus on taking sides in a matter; rather His focus is on the higher plane of insuring that righteousness is done. Let us never again presume that God will lower Himself to "be on our side." Let us raise ourselves above that presumption and ask God that righteousness be done in the matter before us at the time. If we walk in righteousness, we are on His side.

SEEK GOD FIRST

But seek ye first the kingdom of God, and His righteousness; and all these things shall be added unto you (*Matthew 6:33*).

What Is the kingdom of God and His Righteousness?

The kingdom of God Is Jesus Christ

1. *For the kingdom of God is not meat and drink; but righteousness, and peace, and joy in the Holy Ghost* (*Romans 14:17*).
2. *. . . behold, the kingdom of God is within you* (*Luke 17:21*).
3. *. . . My kingdom is not of this world . . .* (*John 18:36*).

God's Righteousness Is the Character of Christ

In the Greek the word "righteousness", as used in Matthew 6:33, means "character" i.e., the character of Christ.

Why Seek First the kingdom of God and His Righteousness?

1. We are directed to do so by scripture (*Matthew 6:33*)
2. Our sins have separated us from God and have caused Him to hide His face from us (*Isaiah 59:2*).
3. We shall find God if we seek Him (*Matthew 7:7-8*).
4. God looks for those who seek Him (*Psalms 14:2*).
5. Those *. . . that seek the Lord shall not want any good thing* (*Psalms 34:10*).
6. God does not forsake those who seek Him (*Psalms 9:10*).
7. God grants the exceeding greatness of His power to those who believe in Him, and His fullness to those who love Him (*Ephesians 1:19; 3:19*).

Comments

I

Jesus has appointed unto us the same kingdom of God that God appointed unto Him. Therefore, unless we seek that kingdom first, we will not know what Jesus has appointed unto us *(Luke 22:29)*. God is our shield . . .

II

Fear not, Abram: I am thy shield and thy exceeding great reward (Genesis 15:1). Every thought, word and deed made within the Word has the protection of the Word.

An example of seeking first the kingdom of God and His righteousness is the story of the woman suffering the issue of blood:

> *For she said within herself, if I may but touch his garment, I shall be made whole* *(Matthew 9:21).*

How Do We Seek/Touch God?

> *. . . Verily, I say unto you, Except ye be converted, and become as little children, ye shall not enter into the kingdom of Heaven. (Matthew 18:3)*

What keeps us from seeking first the kingdom of God and His righteousness?

1. Pride. ***The wicked, through the pride of his countenance, will not seek after God: God is not in all his thoughts.** (Psalms 10:4)*
2. Sodom was destroyed by God, because Sodom had:
   Pride;
   Fullness of bread;
   Abundance of idleness;
   Failed to strengthen the hand of the poor;
   Haughtiness; and
   Committed abomination before God.
   (Ezekiel 16:49-50)

Obviously, the people of Sodom were not seeking first the kingdom of God and His righteousness.

What Are the Consequences for Not Seeking First the kingdom of God and His Righteousness?

1. The imagination of our hearts is evil from our youth *(Gen. 8:21)*. Unless we seek first the kingdom of God and His righteousness, we will be controlled by the evil imagination of our hearts.
2. If we seek God we will be found of Him; but if we forsake Him, we will be cut off forever. *I Chronicles 28:9)*
3. If we seek things, we will make the things we seek our idol. *(Psalms 115:4-8)*
4. We create an Ishmael each time we seek first anything other than God. *(Genesis 16:1-4)*

How Do We Seek First the Kingdom of God and His Righteousness?

1. Prayer and fasting (Daniel 10:3)
2. Meditating on the Word of God day and night *(Joshua 1:8)*
3. With all our heart and soul *(Deuteronomy 4:29)*
4. Set our heart to seek God *(II Chronicles 11:16)*
5. Set our whole desire to seek God *(II Chronicles 15:14-15)*
6. Early *(Proverbs 8:17)*
7. Continuously (I Chronicles 16:11)
8. Moses sought God so earnestly through prayer that God had to tell Moses, **Now therefore let me alone . . .** *(Exodus 32:10)*
9. The Israelites so earnestly sought God that they agreed **. . . That whosoever would not seek the LORD God of Israel should be put to death, whether small or great, man or woman** *(II Chronicles 15:13)*.
10. Set the Lord always before us *(Psalms 16:8)*

What Should be Our Attitude When We Seek the Lord?

1. Rejoicing... *let the heart of them rejoice that seek the Lord.* (*I Chronicles 16:10*).
2. Praising... *they shall praise the Lord that seek him*... (*Psalms 22:26*).

Comments

I

In Ezra it took several years to rebuild the Temple in Jerusalem, while in Nehemiah it took only 52 days to rebuild the wall around that entire city. Why? Because it takes longer for our hearts (the Temple) to mature in the Word of God than it does for God to change our outward circumstances (the wall).

II

In the world's system we are instructed that we must seek first to earn the things we need. This traditional humanistic instruction causes us to rely upon ourselves, and not upon God, to supply our need. By exercising such traditions, we have made the Word of God of no effect in our lives (*Matthew 15:6*). The only way to reverse this lifestyle is to seek God first, not things (*Matthew 6:33*).

FORFEITING THE PRIVILEGE
OF SERVING GOD

And now I have given all these lands into the hand of Nebuchadnezzar the King of Babylon, my servant; and the beast of the field have I given him also to serve him. and all nations shall serve him, and his son, and his son's son, until the very time of his land come . . .
(Jeremiah 27:6-7 emphasis added).

The Israelites wandered so far away from God that He appointed the heathen King Nebuchadnezzar of Babylon to be His servant to take the Israelites captive. God directed the Israelites, through the Prophet Jeremiah, to serve Nebuchadnezzar rather than God. Their sins caused them to forfeit the privilege of serving God . . . ***until the very time of his land come . . .*** They now had to serve Nebuchadnezzar the Babylonian king until God determined to deliver them.

The same happens to us when we become so entangled in the "things of the world" and wander away from God. Of course, once we repent and have walked out our repentance over a period of time, God will restore to us the privilege of serving Him. In the meantime, our sins will have caused us to forfeit the privilege of serving God. Extended debt workouts are a splendid example of our having forfeited the privilege of serving God, we have to serve the lender instead. But, these "periods in Babylon" are not all bad. They can be used by us, if we so will, to learn the Godly discipline of patience. It is in this manner that the discipline of patience learned in serving Babylon is later used to serve God.

For instance, the Internal Revenue Service and certain other creditors will demand that we cease tithing until they are paid in full. Since the lender is our master, we must do as he demands and cease tithing. But the sting of that rebuke will cause us not to borrow, the next time we will pay cash.

THE WISDOM OF SILENCE

Even a fool, when he holdeth his peace, is counted wise: and he that shutteth his lips is esteemed a man of understanding
(Proverbs 17:28).

The desire to speak quickly is ever present, but the ability to keep silent is prudent. The choice here is, are we to speak quickly and be counted a fool, or are we to remain silent until the proper time and be counted wise?

CAN WE MASTER SIN?

"... it (sin) ***desires to have you, but you must master it"***
(Genesis 4:7 NIV). So we can make the choice to master sin or submit to sin. To master it is to be righteous, but to submit to sin is unrighteousness.

Sin

"... But if you do not do what is right, sin is crouching at your door; it desires to have you, but you must master it"
(Genesis 4:7 NIV).

What Is Sin?

To properly understand sin, we need first to understand righteousness. Righteousness is of God, and sin is all of that which is not of God.

Why Do We Commit Sin?

And when the woman saw that the tree was <u>good</u> for food, and that it was <u>pleasant</u> to the eyes, and a tree <u>to be desired</u> to make one wise, she took of the fruit thereof, and did eat, and gave also unto husband with her; and he did eat
(Genesis 3:6 emphasis added).

The terms ***"good," "pleasant"*** and ***"to be desired"*** are all appealing to the desires of the flesh. As Eve, whenever we act upon that which is appealing to the flesh, we open the door for sin to come into our lives; but that door is closed when we master sin by acting according to the Word of God.

Sin Has Cords That Bind Us

Cords enslave us and we become the servant of sin. *His own iniquities shall take the wicked himself, and he shall be holden with the cords of his sins* (*Proverbs 5:22*).

How Are We Set Free From Sin?

The slave of sin is set free only by repentance through Christ. Sin's cords are so strong that only the righteous blood of Jesus, the Son of God, can wash them from us; and He will do so simply for the genuine asking.

To turn away from righteousness and towards evil is to invite sin to crouch at our door with all lf its devilish desire to have us, *. . . but you* (we) *must master it* (Genesis 4:7 NIV).

THE PENALTY

FOR SLOTHFULNESS

*He also that is slothful in his work is brother
to him that is a great waster*
(Proverbs 18:9).

Slothfulness is a great waste. It is an attitude which pervades not just one area, but all areas of our lives. To permit slothfulness is to permit waste, and one of the penalties for waste is for us to go broke.

WE ARE AND BECOME
WHAT WE SPEAK

A man's belly shall be satisfied with the fruit of his
mouth; and with the increase of his lips
shall he be filled
(Proverbs 18:20).

This scripture is a two-edged sword, it cuts both ways - good and bad. It causes us to remember that our belly is like a seed bag and our mouth is the seed selector.

If our lips speak hate, envy and strife, that fruit of our lips will fill our belly. On the other hand, if our lips speak Godly matters, our belly shall be filled with the fruit of the things of God. The choice is ours, we are what we speak.

Spiritual Deficiency -
The Sole Cause
Of All Of Our Problems

(See the entire Bible)

When the Israelites were in right relationship with God, they prospered; but, when that relationship was deficient, they suffered a multitude of problems. The same holds true for us today.

The circumstances that we call problems in life are not problems at all, rather, they are just symptoms of our wrong relationship with God. If we will only come into a right relationship with God, the adverse symptoms in our lives will disappear as a by-product of that right relationship.

This was proven true in the life of Jesus. He was responsible for the financial support of His mother, the 12 disciples and their families, lived in enemy occupied territory and had no visible means of support. Yet, Jesus never had a financial problem because He enjoyed a proper relationship with His Father. So can we.

Financial, marital and other problems will not go away if we acquire more money, another spouse, etc.; rather, they are resolved only by our repenting for our deficient relationship with God, and then living in accordance with the repentance. For instance, when we are broke, the last thing we need is money; what we really need is to turn from our ways and develop a proper relationship with God. As we do, God will supply all of our needs through Christ Jesus *(Philippians 4:19)*. (See also *Chastisement* at page 101)

HOW TO ACHIEVE STABILITY
IN OUR LIFE

And wisdom and knowledge shall be the
stability of thy times . . .
(Isaiah 33:6).

We desire to achieve stability in our lives, but it seems to be ever so elusive. This elusiveness is brought about in great part by our own frantic behavior in striving to achieve stability. It seems that the harder we strive to achieve stability, the less stability we have.

Stability will continue to elude us as long as <u>we strive</u> to achieve it. We enjoy stability only when we allow the wisdom and knowledge of God's Word to govern our lives. That is why divorce, bankruptcy, church splits, poor government and unemployment are never a problem; they are only symptoms of our failure to exercise Godly wisdom and knowledge in those areas of our lives.

Our lives, and the lives of those under our authority, are no more stable than our daily exercise of the wisdom and knowledge of God. So let us take our hands off of the steering wheel of our lives and allow the wisdom and knowledge found in His Word to guide us into stability. God does not require us to become supermen, He only requires us to be diligent, and He will do the rest. To trust Him to do the rest is to achieve stability.

SUBMISSION

by Donna K. Deal

When a couple becomes one at the time of their marriage it is important to note that this is how God sees them and what He intends. The oneness is in the heart of God but probably not in the hearts of the newlyweds! We marry to get our needs met. Therein lies the struggle. Each partner is supposed to grow in God to look to the needs of the other with God as ultimate source.

By faith, God gives Christian couples the <u>power and instruction</u> to become one in spirit, soul and body. This process takes a <u>lifetime of commitment</u> to each other and <u>yielding</u> to the Spirit's teaching and guidance. If we wish to grow together into that special oneness, the wife must take her role of submission in attitude and action and the husband his roll of headship in love and deed. The Bible links the roles of headship and submission with the Christ-like fruit of love and service. When <u>mutual</u> and genuine love and service permeate the roles of husband and wife, the most wonderful marriage relationship can be the result.

Do any of these complaints sound familiar?
"I say anything to keep peace in the house."
"I don't care anymore."
"I'm tied of trying."
"My spouse uses tricks to manipulate me and tells little lies."
"There is a communication breakdown."
"We don't share things like we used to."
"We're growing apart."
"We don't pray together."
"I get/give the silent treatment."
"Our discussions lead to arguments."
If our answer is "yes", then there is some room for improvement in our relationship and the first place to look is the dual relationship of headship and submission.

Before we go further, let's check scripture to see what instructions God has given to the wife and then the husband.

Responsibilities of A Wife

1 Peter 3:4 - develop a gentle and quite spirit

Genesis 2:18 - be a helper to your husband

Ephesians 5:33 - respect your husband

Proverbs 31:25 - be a woman of strength and dignity and have no fear of old age

Proverbs 15:7, 31:26 - speak wisely with kindness

Deuteronomy 6:7 - nurture the children in morality

Titus 2:5 - be a good housekeeper and homemaker

Matthew 19:6 - partners for life

Responsibilities of A Husband

Micah 6:8 - do justly, love mercy and walk humbly with your God

Ephesians 5:31 - leave your father and mother for your wife

Ephesians 5:28 - love your wife as you love yourself

I Timothy 3:2-4 - be committed only to her in the marriage

Ephesians 5:29 - provide for your wife and children, protect family against evil

Matthew 19:6 - married for life

Joshua 24:15 ... ***as for me and my house, we will serve the LORD.*** Lead by Example.

The marriage relationship and the resulting family is a vehicle through which God reveals Himself. His desire is the harmony and intimacy He originally set in the Garden of Eden. Our Christian marriage should reflect Christ to the world. What does your marriage reflect?

To capsule scripture:
>The husband
>>has responsibility over his domain for protection, direction and provision, harmony and Godliness, walks with God daily, nurtures children as they mature, comforts wife and disciplines children - building security, love and trust
>
>The wife
>>helps her husband and supports and respects him sets the tone of the family life and builds the nest nurtures the younger children - morality, obedience

Submission

We shall continue by defining the word "submission". It means:

1. obedience with a humble attitude
2. deferring to the decision or judgment of another
3. willingly putting ourself under the authority of another.

I have made up a personal definition whereby the word defines itself. First though, I would like to change the spelling to "Supmission" and give the definition as: <u>one who supports the mission</u> or undergirds the plan of God for our marriage. Husbands, do you have a mission for your family? Do you and your wife know where you want your family to be in future years?

Let's check these scriptures and see what the Bible says concerning both submission and authority.

>***. . . Your desire will be for your husband, and he will rule over you*** *(Genesis 3:16 NIV)*.

302

(Ephesians 5:22 and 25 NIV) - **Wives, submit to your husbands as unto the Lord . . . Husbands, love your wives just as Christ loved the Church and gave Himself up for her . . .**

(Colossians 3:18-19) - **Wives, submit unto your own husbands . . . Husbands love your wives – and do not be bitter toward them.** (another balance)

(Romans 13:1 NIV) - **. . . Everyone must subject himself to the governing authorities . . .**

(James 3:17 NIV) - **But the wisdom that comes from heaven is first of all pure; peace-loving, considerate, submissive, full of mercy and good fruit, impartial and sincere. Peacemakers who sow peace raise a harvest of righteousness.**

(Hebrews 13:17 NIV) - **Obey your leaders and submit to their authority.** (everyone submits to somebody).

(I Timothy 2:11 NIV) - **A woman should learn in quietness and full submission.** (denotes an attitude that promotes great wisdom).

Why Should I be Submissive?

God has told me I am to have a meek and quiet spirit which means a desire and willingness to obey Him, and accept what God gives me knowing that He has my best interest in mind. I trust that God only gives me directives/circumstances that are for my good, even if I cannot see it at the time. Submissive may be defined as power under control (Moses)! Meekness never diminishes my worth but instead develops my strength and dignity. I can only submit honorably if I am first strong in faith. Without honor, I am a doormat.

Following this belief or philosophy, and because I am a woman of faith, three things happen:

1. I am free to fit into rather than fight the leadership my husband offers. I am not threatened by him. I can do what he asks with a loving attitude and give myself to him. I am at peace with myself, my husband, children and my God.

303

2. As I lovingly defer to my husband, I am free from bearing his responsibilities and am able to carry out my own responsibilities. He becomes responsible for the decisions he makes, whether wise or foolish. This enables him to grow as a person, feel more masculine, protective and tender. My husband has the freedom to hear from God and become the man God wants him to be.

3. When I defer my will to my husband, I show the children by example how to obey authority. When I relinquish the temptation to undermine my husband to prove a point, the attitude of peace and trust are seen by the family. As a wife and mother, I am more loving, tender - unlike a woman who is irritated at not getting her way. Submission is God's path for a wife to serve her husband. The proof of real love is the willingness to serve another. Didn't Christ set the example for us. Who wants to be great? Let him serve.

Rebellion and Control

Question: What is the opposite of submission? It is helpful to grasp a word's meaning by seeing the opposite. The opposite of submission is rebellion. Rebellion being the open, organized resistance to authority; it is insubordination; it is mutiny, it is a defiance of lawful authority; and worse yet - it is a **HARDENED HEART!**

Question: What are signs of rebellion in a marriage? Signs of rebellion might be open verbal fighting, manipulation, pushing and nagging, a haughty or proud attitude, scoffing, insolence, acts that undermine. For a wife to rebel against a husband's authority and win the battle to control the family, is to lose. When a wife gets ungodly control over her husband she risks disdain, loss of respect, etc. She cannot be the helpmate to him. She also loses respect for him and endangers further maturity of the marriage. Some men may give up leadership easily and things appear to be peaceful. This is not real harmony. It is not the recipe for a vital and growing marriage relationship like that of Christ and the Church.

Leadership

General Norman Schwartzkoff once said that he . . . "did not have a good definition of a leader, but he knew one when he saw one!" Take a look a Jesus. He is the ultimate leader. We must take our example from him - not some coach, world leader or CEO. Matthew 20:25-28 and John 13:4-14 show us true leadership. Jesus acted out the true example of leadership as He served the disciples by washing their feet thereby portraying a leader as one who serves. This is the position of the husband. <u>To be the head of the house is to serve the household in strength under God by protecting, providing for and communicating together with his wife to make harmonious and Godly decisions.</u>

Leadership and authority in a Christian go hand in hand with love - God's love. To lead without love is disharmony at best and hell at worst. Since a man is designed to be strong and lead, he will naturally take his stand in order to "win" over his wife. To lead without love can go two ways - bitter fighting or bitter silence. A man will either fight his wife or withdraw from her.

This marriage cannot fulfill God's intention of oneness. Man was created to lead, provide, protect. Paul's relationship with his churches is a fine example also. Paul led the churches, provided spiritual needs and protected against outside influences that would replace freedom with legalism. When a husband has God's power flowing through him, he can be all God intended in action and attitude. As he submits to the Lord, he stands in Godly authority for his wife and family.

A Noble Woman

Having seen what a man's role is, let's see what a woman's role is. A wife was created to respond to the husband, nurture and influence the children in morality. A wife sets the tone of the home. The helpmate relationship is not a demeaning role. *John 14:16* speaks of the Spirit as a helpmate, and God is my helper in *Psalm 70;* so this is a highly exalted role. A wife must not be disloyal in any way to her husband because he needs her respect and honor. She should endeavor to stand beside him thus helping to create harmony in the family. When she is asked for advice she can either give it or not.

It is Godly for both to have part in decision making. This exhibits mutual respect and openness between a couple.

If a husband is not reacting well to his wife and seems stubborn, perhaps he is reacting to a wrong attitude he senses in her. A wife must not push or command in words or tone of voice. Respectful, and humble disagreement can move mountains! A man also reacts to a wife's resistance. If the wife's attitude is Godly, he has reason and opportunity to move into leadership and become a powerful man of God. Unfortunately, some men do not have a heart for God; nevertheless, a Godly wife can draw him in patience and perseverance. Even if the husband never knows Jesus as Lord, a wife's approach will make the home more Godly than if she persists in pushing, resisting and generally being unlovely! (Abuse is addressed in another place.)

The Real Liberated Woman

In *Proverbs 31:10-31,* God shows us how rich and rewarding a Godly woman's life can be. God has not cursed us with roles that produce conflict, rather, we are blessed when we operate within these roles of submission and headship. We produce conflict as we fight God's way. If we are in a position of conflict rather than blessing, we need to consider ways to change. This life is not a dress rehearsal where we get another chance. This is it. We must make the effort to please God.

How to Effect Change

The Bible gives us the only way to effect Godly change:
1. Justification - receiving Jesus in new birth and exchanging our sins for His righteousness - a free gift.
2. Sanctification - walking daily with the Lord, devouring His Word and submitting attitudes, thoughts, old habits, emotions, and deeds to the Spirit to allow holiness to change us - growth over a lifetime.
3. Spiritual Fruit - reflecting the character of Christ and responding in service to others *Romans 1 - 7* explains how we are dead in Christ once and for all, are raised in new life without penalty of sin and have the power now to choose righteousness in our life.

In order to have a **S E C U R E** marriage relationship consider the following acrostic:

S - Share - Give of ourself in time, activities, concern, ideas, innermost thoughts, spiritual walk, family objectives and career goals. Jesus shared all that the Father had with His friends. Communication is vital to a living relationship.

E - Edify - Build up, encourage, and support our spouse. Seek to know our spouse well so as to fulfill his needs and give understanding. Restore a broken spirit with edifying words found in scripture.

C - Commitment - Dedicate ourselves to purity, provision and protection of each other and of our families.

U - Uphold - Our foundation to hold up the marriage relationship is our relationship with Christ. Do not neglect praise, worship, fasting, meditation in scripture and fervent study of God's word.

R - Recreational time. Hurray! A vacation every year for relaxation, recuperation, restoration and realigning is a must. Special days, afternoons, each week should be allotted to something fun. Build traditions and memories.

E - Emotional well being - Physical contact is a God given need from the gentle touch of your hand or playful punch to marriage intimacy. If we think we have success in all other areas and fail here, we have actually failed to bring warmth, comfort, calm from fears and deep security to our spouse and our family. None of this can be accomplished without the power of the Holy Spirit.

Husbands, seek to be like Jesus. Your wife will be happy to take her position of support beside you. What was Jesus like? He fed, healed, consoled, forgave, wept with, prayed for, taught, worked with, and spent time with those he lead. He washed their feet and gave His life for them.

Wives, be like Jesus; He was loyal and submitted totally to, Father, God.

Allow God To Supply Our Need

And

How To Tell That A Certain Supply Is From The Lord

But my God shall supply all your need according to his riches in glory by Christ Jesus (Philippians 4:19).

To accept the supply for our need from any source other than God evidences that we are impatient and not content to wait upon Him. On the other hand, to allow God to supply all of our need requires that we will first have to be content in whatsoever state we find ourselves *(Hebrews 13.5)*. This contentment will allow us to patiently wait upon God to supply our every need in His time.

Now comes the question, "How can we know that a certain supply for our need is from the Lord?" Answer, God will never supply our need in any manner that violates His Word *(See the entire Bible)*. One thing for sure, God will never supply our need in any manner that places us in bondage. Why? Because Jesus came to set us free, and God will not thwart Jesus' purpose for coming by placing us in bondage to supply our need. (See also *Debt* at page 127)

HONORABLE SWEAT VS. STRIVING SWEAT

*Peter saith unto him, Thou shalt never wash
my feet. Jesus answered him, If I wash
thee not, thou hast no part with me*
(John 13:8).

There is honorable sweat and there is striving sweat. Honorable sweat occurs when we work diligently in the attitude of a humble servant of God allowing His power to govern our daily activities. On the other hand, striving sweat occurs when we strive in our own power to get through our daily activities, while refusing to allow the power of God into our lives.

Sweat turns from striving to honorable the moment we cease from striving and let the power of God into our lives.

CONTROLLING OUR TEMPER

He that is soon angry dealeth foolishly . . .
(Proverbs 14:17).

Temper is not something God gives to us, rather, it is our impatience asserting its way against the Godliness in our lives. Whenever we allow impatience to prevail, we deal foolishly. So, to not control our temper is to be a fool.

All temper can be controlled. The issue that we have to decide is, do we want Godly patience to overcome ungodly impatience in our lives? If we allow God's will to have its way, we will control our temper; otherwise, our temper will prevail and we will continue conducting ourselves in a foolish manner.

But let patience have her perfect work, that ye may be perfect and entire, wanting nothing (James 1:4). After all, we are much more becoming as Godly people rather than a fool.

NOT ENOUGH TIME

***And on the seventh day God ended his work which he
had made; and he rested on the seventh day from all his
work which he had made***
(Genesis 2:2).

God manufactured the world in six days, but the creation
was not complete until the end of the day of rest, and neither
are we. If God saw the need to rest, then who are we not to
rest? He knew what He was doing when He made the day 24
hours long. If 24 hours is not time enough for us, God is not at
fault, we are.

So, let us enter into the rest of God *(Hebrews 4:3),* then
we will always, have enough time to do all that God desires for
us to do.

COMPREHENDING THE WAYS OF GOD

And the light shineth in darkness;
and the darkness comprehended it not
(John 1:5).

"*...darkness...*" as mentioned in *John 1:5,* does not apply just to unbelievers, it also applies to believers. We, as believers, are in darkness anytime we do not comprehend the light of God's Word in any particular situation, and all of us have those times in our lives?

As light is painful to our eyes when we have been in darkness, so is the light of the Word often painful to our lives when we begin to see that light. But, if we will only walk in the light we have at the time, He will take away the pain and we will begin to comprehend His ways.

WEALTH

But seek first His kingdom and His righteousness, and
all these things will be given to you as well
(Matt 6:33 NIV).

God is very much in favor of His people having wealth,
provided it is not the focus of their lives. He means for wealth
to be our servant, not our master.

The Power to Get Wealth

But thou shalt remember the LORD thy God:
for it is he that giveth thee power to get wealth,
that he may establish his covenant which
he swore unto our fathers . . .
(Deuteronomy 8:18 emphasis added).

The power to get whatever wealth we have comes from
God, and not from our working 18 hour days. God loves our
diligence, but He does not honor our "burning out."

The words "power" and "get" are the key words in
Deuteronomy 8:18. The word "power" in the Hebrew language
means the force to create large lizards or good fruit, and the
word "get" means "to create." (See *Strongs Exhaustive
Concordance,* published by Baker Book House, Grand Rapids,
Michigan 1985.)

As *Deuteronomy 8:18* states, God gives to all of us the
. . . power to get . . . wealth for the purpose of establishing His
Covenant on this earth; but He lets each of us determine how
we will use that *. . . power to get . . .* We must each ask ourself
the question, am I using this *. . . power to get . . .* to create large
lizards or to establish the good fruit of God's Covenant?

Wealth Gained by Diligence Increases, but Wealth Gained by Vanity Diminishes

Wealth gotten by vanity shall be diminished: but he that gathereth by labor shall increase
(Proverbs 13:11).

God does not reward those who act out of vanity, but He does reward the diligent. So, that which we acquire by vanity will be lost, but that which we acquire by diligence shall increase.

Why is this so? Because both vanity and diligence are conditions of the heart; and it is by the condition of our heart that God blesses us or judges us, as the case may be. To be judged for being vain is to be diminished; to be blessed for being diligent is to be increased.

The Magnetism of Wealth

The poor is hated even of his own neighbor: but the rich hath many friends
(Proverbs 14:20).

Wealth is a powerful magnet that draws friends like spoiled meat draws flies: but, as the flies leave when the meat is gone, so will those friends leave when the wealth is gone.

ON FRIENDS AND GOING BROKE

The poor is hated even of his own neighbor:
but the rich hath many friends
(Proverbs 14:20).

Wealth draws friends like spoiled meat draws flies. But, as the flies leave when the meat is gone, so will those kinds of friends leave when the wealth is gone.

THE WISDOM OF GOD

Get wisdom, get understanding: forget it not; neither decline from the words of my mouth. Forsake her not, and she shall preserve thee: . . . Wisdom is the principal thing; therefore get wisdom: and with all thy getting get understanding
(Proverbs 4:5-7).

What Is the Wisdom of God?

The wisdom of God is the sum total of the character traits of Jesus Christ . . . *and of Christ; In whom are hid all the treasures of wisdom and knowledge* (Colossians 2:3).

. . . *Christ the power of God, and the Wisdom of God*
(I Corinthians 1:24).

What Does It Mean to Have the Wisdom of God?

To have the wisdom of God is to know and do what Christ would do if He were in our circumstances.

What Keeps Us from Learning that the Wisdom of God Is the Principle Thing?

Pride. Our love of self/pride causes us to be self-reliant rather than to fear God. The fear of God is the beginning of wisdom (Proverbs 1:7).

What Are the Penalties for Not Seeking the Wisdom of God As the Principle Thing?

He that sins against wisdom, sins against his own soul *(Proverbs 8:36)*.

We are considered by God to be rebellious if we do not have wisdom *(Isaiah 30:1)*.

Unless we build a house with the wisdom of God, the house is built in vain *(Psalm 127:1)*.

Without the wisdom of God we shall be destroyed, God will forget us, reject us and not allow us to be His ministers *(Hosea 4:6)*.

God will grant our requests and send leanness into our soul *(Psalm 106:15)*.

Where and How Do We Acquire the Wisdom of God?

By accepting Jesus Christ as our Savior. In Christ are hidden all the treasures of wisdom and knowledge *(Colossians 2:3)*.

Wisdom comes through meditation in the Word of God day and night *(Joshua 1:8)*.

If we seek wisdom as silver and as hidden treasure, then we shall understand the fear of the Lord *(Proverbs 2:4-5)*.

Ask God for wisdom, and He will give it to us liberally *(I Kings 3:5-14 & James 1:5)*.

Wisdom comes through the counsel of many men of God *(Proverbs 15:22)*.

The Spirit of God fills us with wisdom of heart to do all manner of works that God has called us to perform *(Exodus 35:35)*.

What Are the Benefits of Having the Wisdom of God?

Wisdom will promote us and give to us honor, an ornament of grace and a crown of glory *(Proverbs 4:8-9)*.

We who have wisdom shall eat the labor of our hands, we shall be happy, and it shall be well with us *(Psalm 128:2)*.

My fruit is better than gold, yea, than fine gold; . . . That I may cause those that love me to inherit substance; and I will fill their treasures. *(Proverbs 8:19-21)*.

When we have the wisdom of God, He causes our enemies to be at peace with us *(Proverbs 16:7)*.

By wisdom, princes rule *(Proverbs 8:16)*.

Through wisdom is an house builded; and by understanding the house is established; and by knowledge shall the chambers be filled with all precious and pleasant riches *(Proverbs 24:3-4)*.

And wisdom and knowledge shall be the stability of thy times . . . *(Isaiah 33:6)*.

The Wisdom of God vs. the Wisdom of Babylon:

The wisdom of this world is foolishness with God . . . *(I Corinthians 3:19)*.

There is a way which seemeth right unto a man, but the ways and thereof are the ways of death *(Proverbs 14:12)*.

For my thoughts are not your thoughts, neither are your ways my ways ... so are my ways higher than your ways, and my thoughts than your thoughts (Isaiah 55:8-9).

It is better to trust in the Lord than in men and princes *(Psalm 118:8-9)*.

The Lord does not see as a man sees *(I Samuel 16:7)*.

Because thou saith, I am rich, and increased with goods, and have need of nothing; and knowest not that thou art wretched, and miserable, and poor, and blind, and naked ... (Revelation 3:17).

When Solomon asked for wisdom he received, as a by-product of that asking, wealth enough to become the wealthiest king of his time *(I Kings 3:5-14)*. Solomon became so wealthy that silver became as piles of stone in the streets of Jerusalem *(I Kings 10:27)*.

What The Scriptures Say About Going To The "Money Man"

The wisdom of the world is that everyone must go to the "money man." However, there is no record in the Bible of God ever sending His people to the world to ask for money to serve God; i.e., Solomon, the world came to him *(I Kings 10:23- 27)*. The queen of the south came from the utmost parts of the earth to hear the wisdom of Solomon *(Luke 11:31)*.

Comment

God first supplies the wisdom, then the people and then the money *(see the entire Bible)*.

The Preparation of Man in the Wisdom of God

During the last supper, Jesus <u>took</u> the bread, <u>blessed</u> it, <u>broke</u> it, and gave it to His disciples *(Matthew 26:26)*. God uses the same process to prepare a man in, and with, the wisdom of God in that He:

> **Takes,** chooses, and ordains us to go and bring forth fruit *(John 15:16);*

> **Blesses** us with vision through the Holy Spirit *(Genesis Chapter 15);*

> **Breaks** us through chastisement to teach us His wisdom *(Psalm 119:71);* and

> **Gives** us to the world as His vessels *(Acts 1:8).*

Why Many Are Called but Few Are Chosen

Too many of us want to jump right into God's work for our lives as soon as we receive the vision of our calling. In our impatience we do not understand that we have only been called, we have not yet been chosen. The time period between our being called and being chosen is a period of preparation in the wisdom, understanding and knowledge of God. If we become impatient before being chosen, we will render ourselves unworthy to be chosen. Hence, *. . . for many be called, but few chosen (Matthew 22:14).*

When God was directing the Israelites in the construction of the Tabernacle *(Exodus Chapter 35)*, He called the man who would oversee the construction of the instruments of worship in the Tabernacle. Then God *. . . filled him with the spirit of God, in wisdom, in understanding, and in knowledge, and in all manner of workmanship; . . . with wisdom of heart, to work all manner of work; . . . (Exodus 35:31&35).* Anyone who wants to be used as an instrument of worship in service to God may receive this same wisdom, understanding and knowledge by simply asking God for it *(James 1:5)*. As we learn wisdom, so do we become eligible to be chosen.

WHAT IS WORRY?

Take therefore no thought for the morrow: for the morrow shall take thought for the things of itself...
(Matthew 6:34).

To know what worry is, we must first understand what faith is. Faith is our submitting to the person of Christ in us so He can perform His will through us *(see the entire Bible).*

Worry is the opposite of faith, it is our refusal to trust God. Therefore, to *... tale thought for the morrow ...* is to worry, and to worry is to deny the Holiness and power of God *(Numbers 20:12).* That is why worry is sin.

UNEQUALLY YOKED

*Be ye not unequally yoked together with unbelievers:
for what fellowship hath righteousness with
unrighteousness; and what communion hath light
with darkness*
(II Corinthians 6:14)?

Introduction

To be unequally yoked is to be in that kind of relationship with others that allows the darkness in them to overshadow God's light in us.

What Is the Definition of the Term "Unequally Yoked"?

"To associate discordantly." (<u>Strong's Exhaustive Concordance</u>, Reprinted 1985 by Baker Book House Company, Grand Rapids, Michigan.

The yoke we take is the authority to which we submit. If we choose Jesus' yoke, Jesus is the authority to whom we will be obedient; however, if we choose the "things of the world" as our yoke, we will be discordantly associated with the ways of the world.

Why Do We Become Unequally Yoked with Others?

<u>Pride.</u> We think we know more than God knows and, therefore, form relationships for expediency sake, even though they are unequally yoked relationships.

Some Examples of Unequally Yoked Relationships Are:

1. Believers covenanting with unbelievers in marriage, business, etc.;
2. Debt/suretyship; and
3. Partnerships and corporations that are not organized in accordance with God's Word.

Contrary to popular belief, Christians can become unequally yoked to one another. Such unequally yoked relationships can be averted only if the final authority in all matters is granted to the person in the relationship to whom God gave the vision for the mission at hand (Moses at the Red Sea & Jesus making the decision to go to Jerusalem).

Comment

Unequally yoked relationships cause God to withhold His provision from us *(Abraham & Lot in Genesis 13:9-18)*. It was only after Abraham and Lot separated that God could give the promised land to Abraham.

Double-Mindedness/Expectations - Examples of Being Unequally Yoked

If a husband and wife are not careful, they can unwittingly allow their expectations of the other to cause them to become double-minded before God. This double-mindedness occurs when we desire to serve God but, at the same time, see our expectations of the other go unmet. So to satisfy those unwarranted expectations, we turn away from God as our source and launch out to meet those expectations. At this point the husband and wife have become unequally yoked to each other in that God has become secondary and meeting our spouse's expectations have become primary *(Moses and Zipporah in Exodus 4:21-26)*. This double-minded husband and wife cannot expect to receive anything of the Lord *(James 1:6-8)*.

Husbands and wives must learn to give all of their expectations to the Lord and not use them as an encumbrance upon each other. It is the Lord who is the source of our supply, not our expectations. The Lord may well supply a wife's needs through her husband, but God is the ultimate supplier of all of our needs.

How Do We Create and Terminate Unequally Yoked Relationships?

Unequally yoked relationships are created in two ways: (1) the yoke we put on ourselves, and (2) the yoke we put on others. In both cases they are terminated by our:

1. Recognizing that the relationship violates God's Word *(Abraham and Lot);*
2. Repenting for having made the relationship *(Luke 13:3);*
3. Asking the other person in the relationship to forgive us for our part in the creation of the relationship *(Colossians 3:12-13);*
4. Honoring all obligations arising out of the relationship *(Joshua Chapter 9);* and
5. Taking the time to seek the wisdom of God in the matter. Then allow the Word of God to accomplish the will of God in our lives. God's Word prospers in the thing wheresoever He sends It *(Isaiah 55:11).*

How Do We Avoid Becoming Unequally Yoked?

By establishing our relationships in accordance with God's Word (See the entire Bible).

Authority and responsibility must always remain equal:

1. When Jesus gave to us all power (authority) in Heaven and Earth, He also gave to us all of the responsibility to teach all nations about Him *(Matthew 28:18-20).*
2. When God gave to Moses the responsibility to lead the Israelites out of Egypt, He also gave to him the authority to accomplish the mission *(Exodus Chapters 3-4).*
3. When God gave to Joshua the responsibility to lead the Israelites into the Promised Land, He also gave to him the authority to accomplish the mission*(Joshua Chapter 1).*

4. Following are two examples from the Word of God evidencing what happened when the man of God gave up or shared his authority over a mission but, at the same time, kept the entire responsibility for the mission:

a) Abraham and Lot *(Genesis 13:9-18);* Abraham and Lot began quarreling and Abraham gave Lot the best half of all that he had; and

b) Moses and Aaron *(Exodus 32:1-10);* Aaron made the golden calf while Moses was in the mountain praying.

Comments

I

As long as we make Christ our yoke we shall receive each and every provision we need, when and as we need it, to carry out God's will for us. However, if we choose the "things" of the world as our yoke, we shall be their bond slave to be buffeted by them at the whim and fancy of the world.

II

When the one with whom we are unequally yoked is enduring chastisement, suffering the consequences of having acted outside of God's Word, or suffering tribulation at the hand of Satan, we shall also be caught up in and suffer from those same circumstances. Thus, an unequally yoked relationship may well cause us to fall short of God's calling in our life.

Selling As Yoking

The story of the rich young ruler *(John 3:1-21)* is quite revealing about our high pressure "sales" economy. Note that Jesus did not attempt to "sell" the young man on believing Him, even though his soul was at stake. Jesus was not about to unequally yoke the young man by trying to make him believe the Word; rather, He told the young man the Word and let him make up his mind. Jesus had a good Product, It did not need to be sold.

So, why do we unequally yoke our customers by giving them a "sales pitch" to <u>make</u> them buy our product? Why don't we just "tell" them about our product and let them make up their own mind in the matter. After all, if the Lord wants our customer to purchase our product, He is well able to cause the sale to close without our "selling." If He does not want our customer to buy our product, we should not thwart His purpose in their lives and ours by "selling." Is what we have to sell so inferior that it needs to be "sold," or are we so distrustful of God that we do not trust Him to "close the sale"?

Fund Raising As Yoking

High-pressure pleas for donations/offerings, regardless of the reason for the plea, create unequally yoked relationships.

The Primary Purpose for Severing Unequally Yoked Relationships

... Let there be no strife ... for we be brethren. Is not the whole land before thee? separate thyself, I pray thee, from me: if thou wilt take the left hand, then I will go to the right; or if thou depart to the right hand, then I will go to the left
(Genesis 13:8-9).

God told Abraham to leave his kindred and country, and go unto a land that He would show him. Abraham, in an act of unrighteousness, broke God's Word, took Lot (his nephew) and made him a partner in his sheep herding business.

Some years later, because of contention between Abraham and Lot and their employees, it became necessary for Abraham to move towards breaking up their business. Genesis 13:8 shows that Abraham was not trying to make the best deal for himself in the break-up; rather, his primary purpose was to terminate the unequally yoked business relationship so as to preserve their spiritual relationship as brothers. That is the mark of a Godly man. To Abraham ending an unequally yoked relationship, in order to preserve his relationship with God, was more important than making a good deal. He knew that as long as he and Lot were unequally yoked, they could not be brothers and serve God as God desired.

In Genesis 13:11, Lot showed where his heart was when he choose the lush green Jordan Valley and left the desert to Abraham. But, look down four verses later to verse 14 . . . *after that Lot was separated from him . . .* Since Lot was now separated from Abrabam, God could give the entire promised land to Abraham. The man of God knows that righteousness, and not economics, is the primary purpose in severing unequally yoked relationships. Such behavior by a man of God allows God to bless that man of God.

APPENDIX TO
DECISIONS BY THE BOOK

This Appendix to *Decisions by the Book* contains sample drafts of what:

A church Constitution might look like when a church adopts the Bible as it's Constitution; and

A set of church By-Laws might look like when the church has chosen to be governed by the Five-Fold Ministry pursuant to Ephesians Chapter 4.

The following Constitution and By-Laws are not meant to be final for any one person's persuasion or for the operation of any particular church. Rather, this Constitution and By-Laws are in draft form and will vary for any given person or church depending upon where the person or the church is in their walk with God at any given time. With the above in mind, please feel free to use any or all of the following in any regards that will advance the cause of Jesus Christ.

However, it must be emphasized that we are never to be in a hurry to adopt a Five-Fold Ministry form of church government. Depending on the circumstances at the time, it may well take more than a year for a church to process toward adopting that form of government. And, in some instances, it may be best for whatever reason that a particular church body to not adopt the Five-Fold Ministry form of church government. In any event, if it is your church's desire to adopt this form of church government, please always do so in patience, decency and good order.

No church or ministry should use all or any portion of the following Constitution and By-Laws without first having an attorney at law, licensed to practice law in the jurisdiction where those documents are to be used, to review these documents (or any portions thereof being used) for content and compliance with all federal, state and local laws, rules and regulations.

THE CONSTITUTION OF

(Insert Corporate Name of Church)

(A State of _____ religious corporation)

(Insert Address of Church)

WHEREAS, the Bible undisputably sets forth the entirety of the intimate relationship that God desires with man, and the way that God has provided through Christ for man to enter into that relationship. Therefore, it is incumbent upon this Church to adopt the Bible as its Constitution and conduct all of its affairs in accordance with the Bible;

WHEREAS, this Church has always been governed by the majority rule of the voting members of its Membership;

WHEREAS, on _____, 200_, at a duly called and held Meeting of the Membership of this Church, the necessary percentage of the voting Members of the Membership of this Church voted to: (1) adopt the Bible as the Constitution of this Church; (2) dispense with the democratic government in this Church; and, (3) for this Church to be thereafter governed by a Five-Fold Ministry form of church government as provided in Ephesians 4:7-16;

WHEREAS, the Bible is now the most authoritative ruling document that this Church has to define and establish its purpose, guide and govern all of its affairs and otherwise conduct its daily operations as a Church. Accordingly, all other documents that are created by anyone concerning the purpose, governance and operation of this Church, including the By-Laws of this Church, can serve no higher purpose than to explain how the teachings of the Bible ought to be interpreted and applied in the governance of this Church in all of its affairs; and

THEREFORE, the Apostle, Prophet, Pastor, Evangelist and Teacher serving as the Five-Fold Ministry of this Church, as set forth in Ephesians Chapter 4, will now and hereafter have the final responsibility and accountability to God for the ultimate direction and leadership of this church. Accordingly, together they will have the final authority in the interpretation of God's Word as it relates to all Church matters of all kinds and nature whatsoever.

The Church Secretary executes this document to affirm to the world the lawful and favorable vote of the Membership of this Church at a duly called and held Membership Meeting on _____, 200_, to adopt all of the foregoing.

In affirmation of all of the above, the undersigned have all set forth their signatures herein below:

Pastor & Chief Elder and Local Elders	**Members of the Five - Fold Ministry:**
Pastor & Chief Elder	Pastor
Local Elder	Apostle
Local Elder	Prophet
Local Elder	Evangelist
Local Elder	Teacher
Church Secretary	

THE BY LAWS OF

(Insert Corporate Name of Church)
(A State of _____ religious corporation)
(Insert Address of Church)

PREAMBLE:

Whereas, on _____, 200__, the Membership of *(Insert Corporate   Name of Church)* _____, Incorporated, voted to adopt the Bible as its Constitution, and to no longer be governed by the vote of its Members. This makes the Bible the most authoritative ruling document in this Church. Therefore, the Bible will at all times hereafter define and establish the purpose of this Church, and guide and govern all of its affairs including the conduct of its daily operations as a Church. All other documents that are created relative to the governance of this Church, including these By-Laws, can serve no higher purpose than to set forth that the members of the Five Fold Ministry serving this Church will ultimately determine how the teachings of the Bible are to be hereafter interpreted and applied in all of the governmental, ministerial and other affairs of this Church;

Whereas, in the due exercise of the responsibility and authority conferred by the Bible upon the Pastor and Chief Elder of this Church, the Pastor and Chief Elder of this Church has appointed the undersigned Local Elders of this Church to serve as such as provided in these By-Laws; and

Whereas, in the performance of their responsibilities to this Church, the members of the Five-Fold Ministry currently serving this Church and the current Local Elders of this Church (selected and serving as such at the pleasure of the Pastor and Chief Elder of this Church) have all executed these By-Laws to evidence their agreement with and the adoption of these By-

332

Laws, all in accordance with the Constitution of this Church effective _____, 200_.

NOW, THEREFORE, THESE BY LAWS OF
(Insert Corporate Name) ,
INCORPORATED

ARTICLE 1

THE PURPOSE OF THESE BY LAWS

The purpose of these By Laws is to set forth this Church's interpretation and application of the Bible in the governance of all of the affairs of this Church by the members of the Five-Fold Ministry and Presbytery serving this Church.

ARTICLE 2

DEFINITIONS

The terms below are defined as follows for use in these By Laws:

"_____ *(Insert the Corporate Name of Church)*_____, Incorporated,*" is defined as *(Insert Corporate Name of Church)*, Incorporated, a State of _____religious corporation conducting its affairs principally at _____ *(Insert Address of Church)*_____, and elsewhere as this Church deems proper from time to time.

"***this Church***" is defined as _____ *(Insert the Corporate Name of Church)*
"***Membership***" is defined as the collective term for all of the persons who have been and will be accepted by this Church as Members of this Church in accordance with these By Laws.

333

"**Elders**" shall mean those persons whom the Pastor and Chief Elder of this Church has chosen and designated in writing to serve in the role and office of "Elder" in this Church, and to whom the Five Fold Ministry of this Church has given its approval to serve as such.

"*Member*" is defined as each individual person who has requested membership in this Church, met the qualifications for membership in this Church as determined by the Presbytery from time to time and has been accepted into the membership of this Church by the Pastor and Chief Elder of this Church.

"*Pastor and Chief Elder*" is used herein to mean the one and the same person who will at the same time, as is set forth in these By Laws, serve as both the Pastor and the Chief Elder of this Church. The Pastor and the Chief Elder of this Church at the time of the adoption of these By Laws, is

_____.

"*Presbytery*" is a collective term which includes the Pastor and Chief Elder and all other Elders of this Church acting together at the time as the governing body of this Church.

"**Five-Fold Ministry**" shall mean those persons, collectively, walking in the Five-Fold Ministry offices of Apostle, Prophet, Pastor, Teacher and Evangelist (the Pastor and Chief Elder of this Church being the "Pastor" member of the Five-Fold Ministry serving this Church at the time) whom the Pastor and Chief Elder of this Church recognizes, and has designated in writing, for being gifted and consistently operating in those offices and have been called of God to serve this Church in the capacities of those offices as set forth hereinafter in these By Laws.

It is hereby noted and acknowledged, that one person serving in the Five-Fold Ministry may, at one and the same time, walk/serve in more than one of the five offices of the Five-Fold Ministry. If that is recognized to be the case of a particular individual serving in the Five-Fold Ministry of this Church, it is to be so noted by the Church Secretary in the records of the Five-Fold Ministry members serving this Church, and the same must be acknowledged in writing by at least the other three of the other persons then serving this Church in a Five-Fold Ministry capacity.

ARTICLE 3

THE GOVERNANCE OF _____ *(Insert Corporate Name of Church)*

Section 1 - The Singular Office of Pastor and Chief Elder

A. The Authority and Responsibility of the Pastor and Chief Elder: The Pastor and Chief Elder is one in the same office. The Pastor and Chief Elder will serve this Church as the first among equals of the Elders of this Church. His primary responsibility is to give order and direction to the entirety of the work of this Church. Subject to the objection of all but one of the members of the Five-Fold Ministry serving this Church at the time, the Pastor and Chief Elder will have final authority in all decision making in the Church, notwithstanding the opinion of all of the other Elders and persons in positions of authority of this Church to the contrary.

B. Qualifications for the Pastor and Chief Elder: The Pastor and Chief Elder must be called of God to be the Pastor and Chief Elder of this Church, meet the qualifications for an Elder as set forth in I Tim. 3:1-7 and Titus 1:6-9, and always carry well the mantle of leadership that God has placed upon him to be the Pastor and Chief Elder of this Church.

C. The Term of Office of the Pastor and Chief Elder:
The Pastor and Chief Elder will remain in that office for such period of time that the Pastor and Chief Elder, and all but one member of the Five-Fold Ministry serving this Church at the time, will determine from time to time.

D. Selection of a New Pastor and Chief Elder: A new Pastor and Chief Elder will be selected by the then Pastor and Chief Elder of this Church after due consultation with the Presbytery and the Five-Fold Ministry, and with the consent of all but one of the members of the Five-Fold Ministry.

E. Death or Resignation of the Pastor and Chief Elder: In the event that the Pastor and Chief Elder dies in office or resigns his office, his replacement will be timely selected by a two-thirds (2/3) majority vote of the Elders after consultation with the Five-Fold Ministry, and with the consent of all but one of the members of the Five-Fold Ministry then serving this Church at the time.

F. Pastor and Chief Elder Who Has Become Unable or Unfit to Serve: In the event that it should become the decision of all but one of the members of the Five-Fold Ministry serving this Church at the time, after consultation with the Presbytery, that the Pastor and Chief Elder has become unable or unfit to serve this Church as Pastor and Chief Elder, then those members of the Five-Fold Ministry making such decision can require of the Pastor and Chief Elder that he step down from his office under such terms and conditions as all but one of the members of the Five-Fold Ministry serving this Church should determine at the time.

G. Interim Pastor and Chief Elder: If for any reason the Pastor and Chief Elder is no longer in his office, and his replacement has not yet been selected as required by these By Laws, a two-thirds(2/3) majority vote of the Elders, and with the consent of all but one of the members of the Five-Fold Ministry then serving this Church at the time, may select from among the Elders of this Church, an Elder to be the Interim Pastor and Chief Elder to serve as such until a full-time Pastor and Chief Elder can be selected as provided in these By Laws. The Interim Pastor and Chief Elder will have the same authority and responsibilities as are accorded to the full-time Pastor and Chief Elder.

H.   **Ordination of the Pastor and Chief Elder:** Whenever a Pastor and Chief Elder is selected as provided in these By Laws, he will be timely ordained as such by the Presbytery and the members of the Five-Fold Ministry then serving this Church at the time.

I.   Specific Authority and Responsibilities of the Pastor and Chief Elder: The Pastor and Chief Elder will have the Authority and Responsibility to:

1.   Discern, formulate, communicate and oversee the implementation of his overall vision, purpose and direction for this Church;

2.   After due consultation with the Presbytery and the Five-Fold Ministry, and the concurrence of all but one of the members of the Five-Fold Ministry, render the final decision on any interpretation of the Bible and these By Laws;

3.   Serve as the spiritual overseer of this Church;

4.   Provide for the pastoral care of this Church either personally and/or through the Elders, Five-Fold Ministry and pastoral staff and in such other and further persons and positions (employee and/or voluntary) pursuant to such terms and conditions as the Pastor and Chief Elder deems in his sole discretion to be proper to provide for the spiritual health and growth of this Church, and to insure the fulfillment of the overall vision, purpose and direction of this Church;

5. After consultation with the then existing Elders and the members of the Five-Fold Ministry then serving this Church at the time, select and appoint those men who are to serve as Elders of this Church, for such term(s) and with such duties as the Pastor and Chief Elder determines from time to time. The Pastor and Chief Elder will also have the authority to, as a member of the Presbytery, and in his own right as the Pastor and Chief Elder, ordain Elders for this Church. He will also have the authority to ordain and commission persons to be Pastors in this and other churches, and to remove an Elder of this Church from office at anytime for any cause that he deems appropriate at the time;

6. After consultation with the Presbytery, and the members of the Five-Fold Ministry serving this Church at the time, designate in writing to the Elders and to the Secretary of this Church those members of the Five-Fold Ministry who are to serve this Church, including identifying the particular Five-Fold Ministry office in which each designated member of the Five-Fold Ministry is to serve this Church;

7. After consultation with the Elders, appoint Deacons and Deaconesses and all such other and further positions of ministries of help, including the duties attendant to each position, as are in his sole opinion to implement and bring to fulfillment the vision and outreaches of this Church in an orderly manner. The Pastor and Chief Elder will also have the authority to remove a Deacon, Deaconess or any other position of ministries of helps at anytime for any cause he deems appropriate at the time;

8. Create such boards and committees as he deems appropriate from time to time, staff and assign such duties, responsibilities and authority to those boards and committees as he deems appropriate, and dissolve any and all such boards and committees when and if he deems it appropriate to do so;

9. At any time, and in his sole discretion, call and preside as Chairman over meetings of the Membership, the Presbytery, the Elders, the Deacons and Deaconesses and all other boards and committees of this Church, and designate who will preside in his absence as the chairman over any/all such meetings;

10. Serve as the corporate President of *(Insert Corporate Name of Church)* , Incorporated;

11. Appoint the Secretary, Treasurer and all other corporate officers of *(Insert Corporate Name of Church)* , Incorporated, all of whom will serve at the direction and pleasure of the Pastor and Chief Elder;

12. Present the decisions of the Presbytery to the Membership and speak as the voice of authority for the Five-Fold Ministry serving this Church, Presbytery, Deacons, Deaconesses and all boards and committees of this Church;

13. Select a member of the Presbytery to serve as Secretary of the Presbytery (this person may also be the corporate Secretary for this Church). This Secretary will: (i) record the minutes of each meeting of the Presbytery, including a record of who was present at each such meeting (including those persons who were asked to attend and who are not Elders); (ii) create and maintain at all times a current "Roll of Elders and Five-Fold Ministry members serving this Church" which will state the name, address, phone number, date appointed as an Elder/member of Five-Fold Ministry, and date resigned/removed as an Elder/member of the Five-Fold Ministry; and (iii) make, maintain, execute and deliver such documentation as is required by the Pastor and Chief Elder of this Church and by the laws of the State of _____;

14. Direct the Treasurer of this Church, whose responsibility it will be to prepare and maintain adequate and accurate records of the complete finances of this Church. This Treasurer will prepare monthly, quarterly and annual financial reports for the Presbytery, and which reports will contain as much detail as is customary and practical in accordance with generally accepted accounting principles except, however, all such reports that are to be viewed by anyone other than the Presbytery will not show individual compensation for any one person, but rather only in groupings;

15.   Appoint Trustees of this Church for the purpose of holding legal title to the real and personal property owned by this Church. The Pastor and Chief Elder will, on his own authority after consultation with the Presbytery, have the authority to negotiate, make, execute and deliver all documentation needful and necessary for the Church to purchase, contract to purchase, purchase, and take title to real and personal property in the name of the Trustees of this Church; encumber the real and personal property of this Church with notes/mortgages/deeds of trust/guarantees(and otherwise); sell, contract to sell, contract to lease as lessor/lessee, lease, and convey by deed, lease and otherwise as proper and required under the circumstances, real and/or personal property owned/ to be owned/leased/to be leased by this Church, all at and under such terms and conditions as he, in his sole discretion, deems appropriate, and make, execute and deliver on behalf of this Church any and all documentation needful and necessary to fully accomplish any and all of the foregoing;

16.   Except as otherwise specifically limited in these By Laws to the contrary, the Pastor and Chief Elder will have the absolute, unfettered and final authority to make the final decision in all matters and issues that come before this Church for decision at any level of authority. His sole decision in all such cases will be controlling in all respects, regardless of the decisions, thoughts and opinions of all others in this Church to the contrary. This paragraph is to include the authority of the

Pastor and Chief Elder to discipline any person in this Church in any manner he deems best, for what the Pastor and Chief Elder deems to be "just cause."

However, the Pastor and Chief Elder must refrain from making a decision on any issue that concerns his being disciplined or removed from office. The decision of disciplining or removing the Pastor and Chief Elder lies solely with the Five-Fold Ministry, after due consultation with the Presbytery, and the decision of all but one of the Five-Fold Ministry members then serving this Church at the time, will be controlling in all respects on this Church, the Pastor and Chief Elder and the Presbytery;

      17. Be responsible for the adjudication of disputes between Elders, Deacons, Deaconesses, boards, committees and Members of this Church;

      18. Serve as Pastor and Chief Elder to all ministries sent out from this Church, require that all such ministries recognize him as their Pastor and Chief Elder, and delegate to others the authority and responsibilities attendant to the care and support of those ministries;

      19. When the Pastor and Chief Elder deems it proper to do so, delegate some or all his authority and responsibilities to others of his own choosing;

      20. Diligently seek to make and maintain relationships ordained of God with a full compliment of persons who, together, walk in all of the gifts and callings of the Five-Fold Ministry as provided in Ephesians Chapter 4 in order that the people of this Church can continually receive the full God intended benefit of the Five-Fold Ministry to this Church; and

      21. Perform and take such other and further actions, (including rendering such disciplining of an Elder(s)/ Member(s) of this Church as he deems appropriate at the time, after consultation with the Presbytery) as are needful and necessary to fulfill the authority and responsibilities of the Pastor and Chief Elder of this Church as set forth in the Constitution of this Church and these By Laws.

Section 2 - Local Elders (other than The Chief Elder)

A.   Qualification, Selection, Appointment, Term: This Church will have Local Elders, each of whom: (i) must meet the qualifications for an Elder as set forth in I Tim. 3:1-7 and Titus 1:6-9, (ii) will be selected and appointed as a Local Elder by the Pastor and Chief Elder, after consultation with the existing Local Elders and the members of the Five-Fold Ministry serving this Church at the time, and (iii) will serve for such term as the Pastor and Chief Elder will determine from time and as agreed to by such Elder;

B.   Ordination: Newly selected Local Elders will be ordained as such by the Presbytery and the Five-Fold Ministry;

C.   Number: The number of Local Elders will be determined by the Pastor and Chief Elder from time to time;

D.   The Elders as Members of the Presbytery: The Local Elders, together with the Pastor and Chief Elder, will collectively constitute and   function, collectively, as the members of the Presbytery of this Church and, whenever they meet together, they will be meeting as the Presbytery;

E.   The Authority and Responsibility of the Elders: The Local Elders will collectively and individually have such authority and responsibilities as are granted to and required of the Presbytery of this Church as set out in **Section 3** of this **ARTICLE 3**, and as are otherwise required of and granted to them from time to time by the Pastor and Chief Elder of this Church; and

F. Have Direct Access to the Members of the Five-Fold Ministry: The Local Elders will have the privilege of direct access to contact and solicit and receive advice and counsel from the Five-Fold Ministry members serving this Church at the time on any matters which they have diligently and unsuccessfully attempted to resolve with the Pastor and Chief Elder of this Church.

Section 3 - The Presbytery

A. Composition of the Presbytery: The Presbytery of this Church will be composed of the Pastor and Chief Elder and the Local Elders of this Church.

B. Authority and Responsibilities of the Presbytery: The Presbytery will have the Authority and Responsibility, under the authority, supervision and direction of the Pastor and Chief Elder of this Church, to:

1. Show forth a consistent testimony for Christ in keeping with the qualifications for their office as set out in I Tim. 3:1-7 and Titus 1:6-9;

2.   Function in this Church according to the measure of the spiritual gifts given to each of them by Christ, the Head of the Church;

3. Under the authority, supervision and direction of the Pastor and Chief Elder, exercise general superintendence over this Church and the members of this Church, in both temporal and spiritual matters;

4. Serve as counsel to and assist the Pastor and Chief Elder in providing for the pastoral care of the Members of this Church as the Pastor and Chief Elder deems necessary from time to time for the spiritual health and growth of themselves and the Members;

5. Teach the Members of this Church from the Word of God and safeguard them from false doctrine, whatever the source thereof;

6. Recognize, license, and ordain ministers of the Gospel when and as to do so would be proper;

7. Consistently act in accordance with the Laws of the _____ (*Insert Name of State*) _____ and within the charitable, religious and educational purposes stated in Section 501 (c)(3) of the Internal Revenue Code so as to be a valid tax exempt organization at all times; and

8. Perform such other and further acts as are required of the Presbytery by the Pastor and Chief Elder of this Church.

Section 4 - The Five-Fold Ministry

A. **Relationship and Recognition of the Five-Fold Ministry:** The Pastor and Chief Elder, the Local Elders and all others in authority in this Church and the Members of this Church will recognize those members of the Five-Fold Ministry designated as such by the Pastor and Chief Elder, and will submit to their advice, counsel and decisions.

B. **Roll of Recognized Five-Fold Ministry:** The Secretary of the Presbytery will at all times maintain a current "Roll of Recognized Five-Fold Ministry" which will continually identify those in Five-Fold Ministry recognized by the Pastor and Chief Elder of this Church to be the Five-Fold Ministry to this Church. Wherein the term "the Five-Fold Ministry" is used in these By Laws, it will mean all of the members of the Five-Fold Ministry to this Church entered at the time in question on the Roll of Recognized Five-Fold Ministry.

C.   Term of Service: The members of the Five-Fold Ministry of this Church serve this Church in that capacity by virtue of their relationship with the Pastor and Chief Elder of this Church. Accordingly, at such time that a member of the Five-Fold Ministry recognized by this Church deems that the time has come for him to no longer be a part of the Five-Fold Ministry to this Church, it is incumbent upon him to so notify the Pastor and Chief Elder and resign accordingly.

Likewise, in the event that the Pastor and Chief Elder of this Church, after consultation with the other members of the Five-Fold Ministry to this Church and the Local Elders, comes to the decision that, for whatever reason, it is time for a member of the Five-Fold Ministry to this Church to no longer serve this Church in that capacity, then he will (after consultation with the other members of the Five-Fold Ministry then serving this Church) give notice of removal to that Five-Fold Ministry member and such removal will be effected by the giving of such notice; except, however, the Pastor and Chief Elder cannot give any such notice during any period during which the Pastor and Chief Elder is in the process of being investigated, accused and/or disciplined by all of members of the Five-Fold Ministry for any reason.

D.   Responsibility of the Five-Fold Ministry to this Church: It will be the responsibility of the members of the Five-Fold Ministry to this Church to show forth a consistent testimony for Christ in keeping with the qualifications for their office as set out in I Tim. 3:1-7 and Titus 1:6-9, and function in this Church according to the measure of the spiritual gifts given to each of them by Christ, the Head of the Church.

E.   Disciplining/Dismissal of Five-Fold Ministry Member: The members of the Five-Fold Ministry to this Church will at all times be subject to the discipline of the other members of such Five-Fold Ministry and the Pastor and Chief Elder of this Church, even to the point of censure, disciplining and, when required, dismissal from the Five-Fold Ministry of this Church.

Section 5 - Council of Elders

A. Purpose: The purpose of the Council of Elders is to provide an orderly regimen of training for those Members of this Church that the Pastor and Chief Elder, after consultation with the Presbytery, deems have potential to in the future serve as Local Elders of this Church.

B. Qualification, Selection, Appointment, Term, and Number: This Church will have Council of Elders, and each member thereof must: (i) meet the qualifications for a Local Elder as set forth in I Tim. 3:1-7 and Titus 1:6-9; (ii) be selected and appointed by the Pastor and Chief Elder as a member of the Council of Elders; (iii) serve an initial probationary term of one year, and, (iv) thereafter be trained for such term as requested by the Presbytery and agreed upon by the Pastor and Chief Elder . The number of members of the Council of Elders will be as determined by the Pastor and Chief Elder from time to time.

C. Responsibilities: The authority and responsibilities of the members of the Council of Elders will be as determined by the Pastor and Chief Elder, after consultation with the Presbytery, from time to time. However, in any event, it will be the responsibility of the Council of Elders to, upon request of the Presbytery, render advice and counsel of a spiritual and everyday nature to the Presbytery.

Further, given the responsibilities and focus required of the members of the Presbytery in the performance of their duties in that office, the Presbytery has to be careful to continually know and understand the hearts and perceptions of the people in this Church regarding the decisions and actions of the Pastor and Chief Elder and the Presbytery. Therefore, it will also be the responsibility of the Council of Elders to constantly: (i) take upon themselves as a body the affirmative responsibility to continually make the Presbytery aware of what they deem to be the hearts and perceptions of the people concerning the decisions and activities of the Pastor and Chief Elder and the Presbytery; and, (ii) render advice and counsel to the Pastor and Chief Elder and the Presbytery addressing how and when such issues of the hearts and perceptions of the people should be properly addressed by the Pastor and Chief Elder, the Presbytery and otherwise.

ARTICLE 4

THE SERVANTHOOD MINISTRY OF DEACONS, DEACONESSES AND OTHER SERVANTS IN THE CHURCH

Section - 1   Deacons and Deaconesses

Deacons and Deaconesses are those persons spoken of by Peter in Acts Chapter 6. They are the people in the Church who free those in ministry to focus on ministry. Truly, Deacons and Deaconesses were given their calling by God to serve the Church in such a capacity that allows everyone in the Church to maximize their gifts in service to God and the people. Accordingly, Deacons and Deaconesses will:

A.   Be appointed to their positions by, and serve at the discretion of the Pastor and the Chief Elder;

B.   Serve in an advisory capacity to the Pastor and Chief Elder and the Presbytery as requested;

C.   Attend to the temporal needs of this Church as requested and directed by the Pastor and Chief Elder and the Presbytery; and,

D.   Be subject to discipline of the Pastor and Chief Elder after consultation with the Presbytery.

Section 2 - Other Servants in This Church

There are other called servants in the church who do not fit neatly under any particular biblical description yet, their service to the Church is indispensable if the Church is to fulfill its mission in the World. The Presbytery of this Church must be careful to identify, train and encourage these servants and their gifts so as to maximize the effectiveness of these persons in service to the Kingdom of God.

ARTICLE 5

THE MEMBERS OF THIS CHURCH

The entire leadership of this Church is called together by God under the governance of Jesus Christ for one purpose, and that is to at all times serve the Members of this Church as Christ would serve them if He were present in person to do so Himself. The Members of this Church are the purpose for the existence of this Church, and are to be treated as such at all times. The Members are not in this Church for the leaders or for this Church, rather, the leaders are in this Church for the Members. Yet, at the same time, the Presbytery and the Pastor and Chief Elder of this Church will have the authority to render discipline (appropriate as determined by the Pastor and Chief Elder at the time, after consultation with the Presbytery) upon any Member who is conducting him/herself in a manner deemed by the Pastor and Chief Elder to be unworthy of a Member of this Church.

At the same time, the Members of this Church are to accord respect to the leadership of this Church, since the leadership represents the person of Christ, whose mission it is to draw the Members into a closer relationship with God. It is through the leadership and the Members working together as one under the governance of Jesus Christ that the Will of God will be done on earth as it is in Heaven. Members will also agree to submit to the discipline of the Pastor and Chief Elder of this Church if the Member expects to remain a Member of this Church.

It will be the responsibility of the Secretary of this Church to at all times maintain an accurate roll of the Members of this Church. Persons will be added to or removed from the roll of this Church under such criteria as is adopted by the Presbytery from time to time.

ARTICLE 6

FINANCIAL RECORDS

It will be the responsibility of the Presbytery to be careful stewards of the tithes and offerings given to this Church, and at all times use biblical standards to guide their use. Accordingly, the financial records of this Church will be kept at all times in that manner which is in accordance with generally accepted accounting principles in the certified public accounting profession in the United states of America. Annual, and more frequent if necessary or appropriate, independent audits will be conducted by qualified certified public accountants who are not Members of this Church for the purpose of verifying the accuracy of all of the financial accounts of this church.

The Treasurer of this Church will at all times maintain such checking, savings and other accounts with only those persons having the right to withdraw funds therefrom as are authorized in writing to do so as approved by the Presbytery from time to time. The balance of each account will be reconciled within five (5) business days of the receipt of the monthly statement therefor, and any unexplained discrepancies will be immediately reported, in writing, and simultaneously Five-Fold to all members of the Presbytery. Further, the

Treasurer will prepare such financial reports in the form as directed by the Presbytery from time to time.

The financial records of this Church will be open for inspection to any member of this Church, provided that they have exercised their responsibility before God to be obedient in giving tithes and offerings; however, no such records will detail the amount of compensation paid to any particular person but will instead report all salaries in groupings according to occupation, such as Pastors, secretarial, etc.

ARTICLE 7

THE RESOLUTION OF DIFFERENCES BETWEEN THE PEOPLE IN THIS CHURCH

In the event that any persons in this Church should take issue with other persons in this Church, it is the obligation of the person with the issue to first address that issue directly with the one whom he has the issue, and not anyone else. If the addressing of the issue as aforesaid does not resolve the matter, then parties involved are to invoke Matthew 18 and bring the issue to a soon resolution.

ARTICLE 8

INTERPRETATION OF THESE BY LAWS

These By Laws are to be interpreted in the light of The Word of God, and wherever they conflict with God's Word, God's Word will prevail notwithstanding the wording of these By Laws to the contrary. The Pastor and Chief Elder of this Church will have the singular authority to render the final decision on any interpretation of these By Laws, but only after due consultation on the issue at hand with the Presbytery and the members of the Five-Fold Ministry of this Church, and the agreement of all but one of the members of the Five-Fold Ministry on the final resolution of the issue.

ARTICLE 9

AMENDMENTS TO THESE BY LAWS

These By Laws can be amended only by the affirmative agreement of the Pastor and Chief Elder and all but one of the members of the Five-Fold Ministry to this Church. The members of the Five-Fold Ministry and the Pastor and Chief Elder may not take action on any proposed amendment to these By Laws unless and until the proposed amendment has been reduced to writing and discussed by the Pastor and Chief Elder, the Presbytery and the members of the Five-Fold Ministry. Thereafter, the proposed amendment will be deemed adopted when consented to in writing by the signatures of all but one of the members of the Five-Fold Ministry serving this Church.

ARTICLE 10

ADOPTION OF THESE BY LAWS

In the due exercise of the responsibility and authority conferred by the Bible upon the Pastor and Chief Elder of this Church, the Presbytery and the members of the Five-Fold Ministry to this Church, do all hereby execute, and thereby adopt, these By Laws as being the By Laws of _____ (*Insert Corporate Name of Church*)_____ effective this __ day of _____200_.

Members of the Presbytery:	Members of the Five - Fold Ministry:
Pastor & Chief Elder	
Local Elder	Apostle
Local Elder	Prophet
Local Elder	Pastor
Local Elder	Teacher
Local Elder	Evangelist

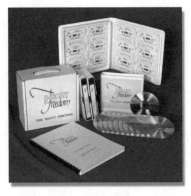

The Insight to Freedom Basic Seminar

A <u>13 hour</u> in-depth study into 12 of the Ways of God learned by John and Donna, while walking out of $6,500,000 indebtedness during a 12 year period.

These ways include: Seeking God, Faith, Chastisement, Authority, Allowing God to Supply Our Needs, Adopting God's Heart and Desire, Obeying God's Word, Wisdom, Forgiveness, Unequally Yoked, Priorities and Giving.

Basic Seminar
Video Cassette Tapes
7 VHS Tapes
$95.00

Basic Seminar
Video DVD's
7 DVD's
$99.00

Basic Seminar
Audio CD's
12 CD's
$59.00

Basic Seminar
Audio Cassette Tapes
12 Cassettes
$49.00

Basic Seminar
Study Guide
1 Study Manual
$17.50

"I have learned more about a proper, Godly life in the 13 hours of your seminar than I did in the first 13 years of my Christian walk." ~ PA

"The principles of and insight into God's word that we have learned throughout your ministry have truly changed our lives forevermore." ~ IN

"I stood on these principle by faith and our once stagnant business nearly doubles each year. I'm not using these tapes to get rich, I'm using them to judge myself." ~ OH

To order materials:
Visit our website at www.InsightToFreedom.com
Call 1.888.667.6581
E-mail us at info@InsightToFreedom.com

Decisions by the Book

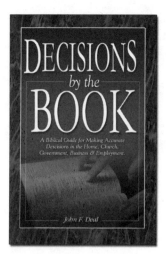

This book contains over 300 topical illustrations including prayer, family, church government, ministry, finances, debt, business matters, marketing, employee relations, ethics, giving, submission, wisdom, fear, depression and many others.

The purpose of this 344 page book, with a 29 page, single spaced cross-index, is to illustrate the wisdom of God found in the Bible for your everyday decision making process.

God did not write the Bible because He had nothing else to do; He wrote it to tell us how to live each day. Use this book to help you learn how to apply His wisdom in your everyday decision making process in your home, church, government, and workplace.

> "Decisions By The Book has brought clarity to my everyday personal and business life. I keep it with me everywhere I go, right next to my Bible."
> ~ DG

> "Decisions By The Book has been an invaluable resource to help me in making decisions regarding most business and personal issues I face. It helps direct me to the Word of God and appropriate scriptures to keep me on course." ~ BR

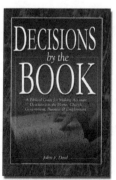

Decisions by the Book
Paperback
$17.50

To order materials:
Visit our website at www.InsightToFreedom.com
Call 1.888.667.6581
E-mail us at info@InsightToFreedom.com

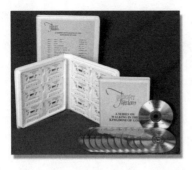

The Insight to Freedom Series on Walking in the Kingdom of God

The purpose of this series is to reinforce and deepen our practical and spiritual insight into the Ways of God as taught in The Insight to Freedom Basic Seminar, The Love Equation Marriage Seminar and *Decisions By The Book*.

The subjects covered thus far in this series are: Rest; Intimacy With God; Intimacy or Delivery; Hope; Hope As Intimacy With God; Allow God to Measure You; What Is Our Place in the Midst of Chaos?; The Five Fold Ministry; Studying the Ways of God; and, The Signet Ring.

The Kingdom of God series is a continuing series. At present, there are <u>15 hours</u> of teaching available for distribution, and other tapes will be made available as they are developed. Follow our website for the availability of these additional tapes in the future.

Walking in the Kingdom of God
Audio Cassette Tapes
12 Cassette Tapes
$49.00

Walking in the Kingdom of God
Audio CD's
12 Audio CD's
$59.00

The Insight to Freedom Love Equation Seminar

This teaching is a <u>6 hour</u> in-depth study into marriage, reconciliation, divorce, and remarriage. John and Donna learned certain principles while counseling hundreds of troubled marriages over a period of many years.

These principles include: The Creation of Marriage, Marriage Belongs to God - Not Man, Marriage Does Not Create Problems, The Key Question In Solving All Husband and Wife Problems, Love Our Mate Where They Are, God's Desire For People In Their Second or Later Marriage, and several other topics.

"As an attorney, I have used the Love Equation tapes in counseling people going through or considering divorce. Every time the parties have listened to and actively applied the life-changing principals taught by John Deal, we have seen reconciliation in the marriage and even termination of divorce proceedings. These rules help troubled couples give God room to work in their marriage, and the results are nothing less than miraculous." ~ Tim Fisher, Tulsa, OK

"For us, Love Equation was the springboard to learning to walk in true covenant relationship." ~ Sam and Ro Ianacone, Rochester, NY

Love Equation
Audio Cassette Tapes
4 - 90 Minute
Cassette Tapes
$36.00

Love Equation
Audio CD's
8 Compact Discs
$45.00

Love Equation
Study Guide
1 Study Manual
$17.50

To order materials:
Visit our website at www.InsightToFreedom.com
Call 1.888.667.6581
E-mail us at info@InsightToFreedom.com